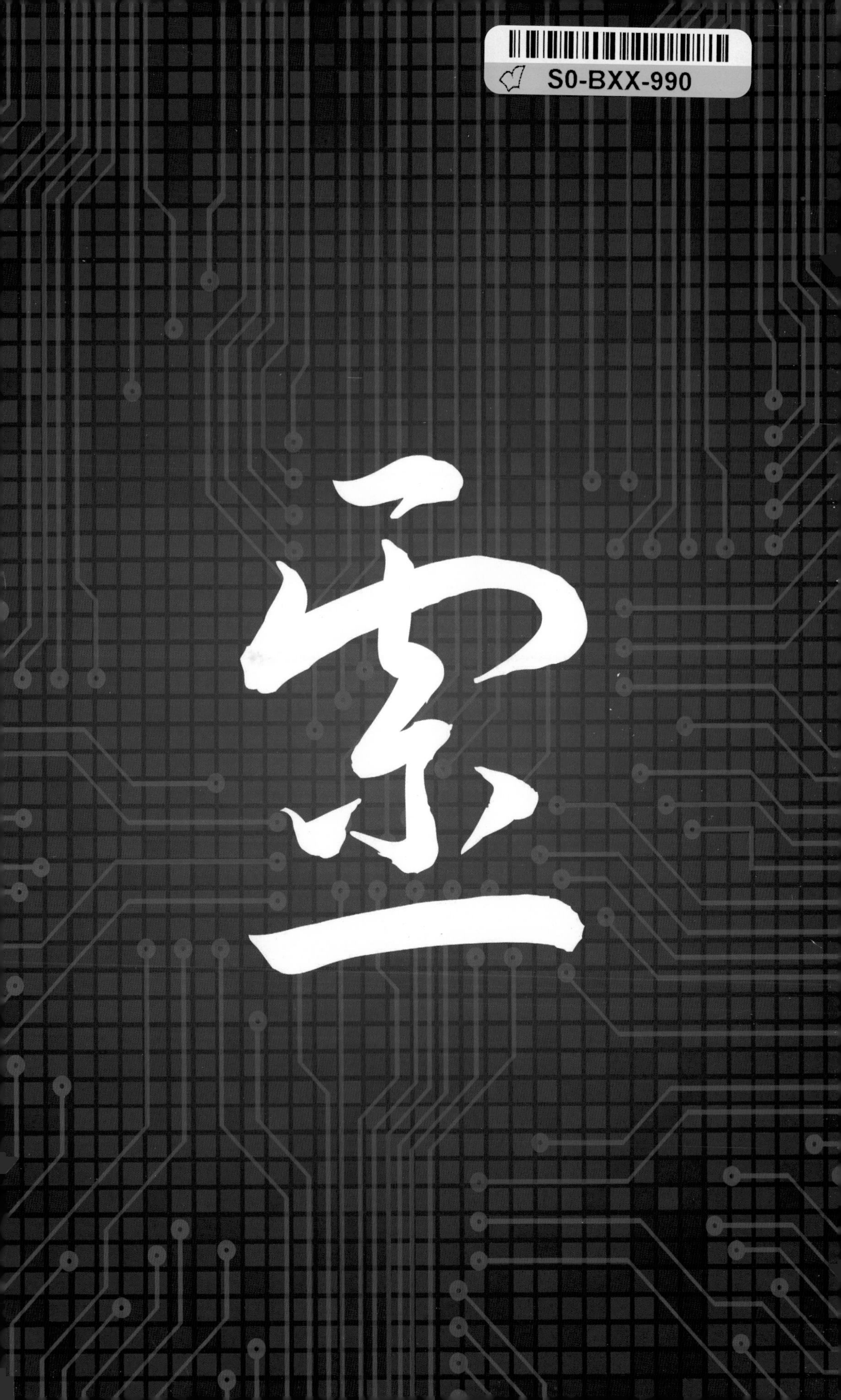

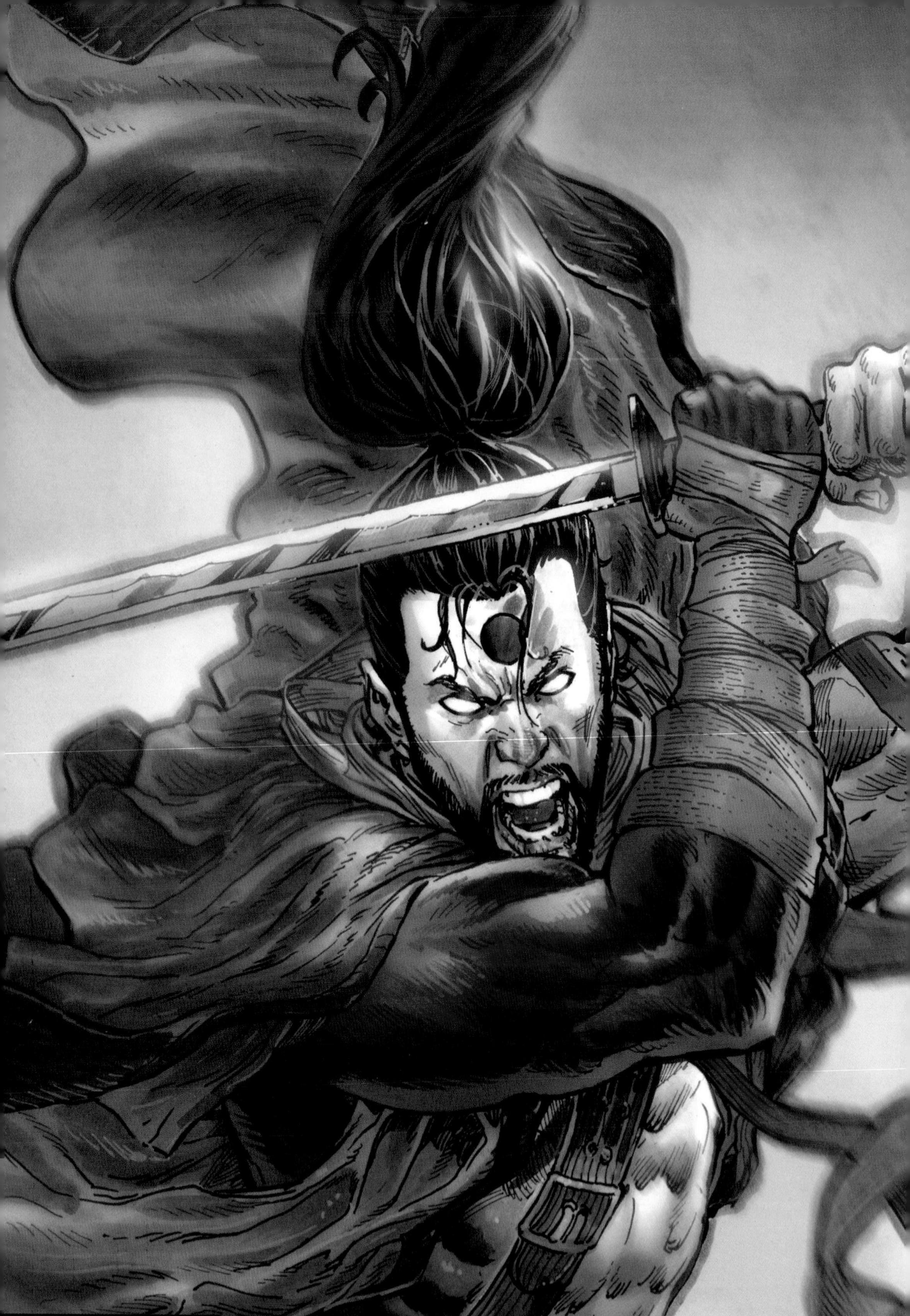

VALIANT

RAI 霊一

WRITER
DAN ABNETT

ARTISTS
JUAN JOSÉ RYP
BENI LOBEL

COLORS
ANDREW DALHOUSE

LETTERER
DAVE SHARPE

COVERS BY
NETHO DIAZ with
CANDICE HAN
FRITZ CASAS with
CANDICE HAN
WALTER SIMONSON with
LAURA MARTIN

**ASSOCIATE
EDITOR**
DAVID MENCHEL

SENIOR EDITOR
LYSA HAWKINS

GALLERY
DAN ABNETT
ANDREW DALHOUSE
NETHO DIAZ
CANDICE HAN
KANO
DAVID NAKAYAMA
JUAN JOSÉ RYP

**COLLECTION
COVER ART**
JEFF DEKAL

**COLLECTION BACK
COVER ART**
FERNANDO DAGNINO

**COLLECTION
FRONT ART**
NETHO DIAZ with
CANDICE HAN
WALTER SIMONSON

**COLLECTION
EDITOR**
IVAN COHEN

**COLLECTION
DESIGNER**
STEVE BLACKWELL

Rai® Book Two. Published by Valiant Entertainment LLC. Office of Publication: 350 Seventh Avenue, New York, NY 10001. Compilation copyright © 2020 Valiant Entertainment LLC. All rights reserved. Contains materials originally published in single magazine form as Rai #6-10. Copyright © 2020 Valiant Entertainment LLC. All rights reserved. All characters, their distinctive likeness and related indicia featured in this publication are trademarks of Valiant Entertainment LLC. The

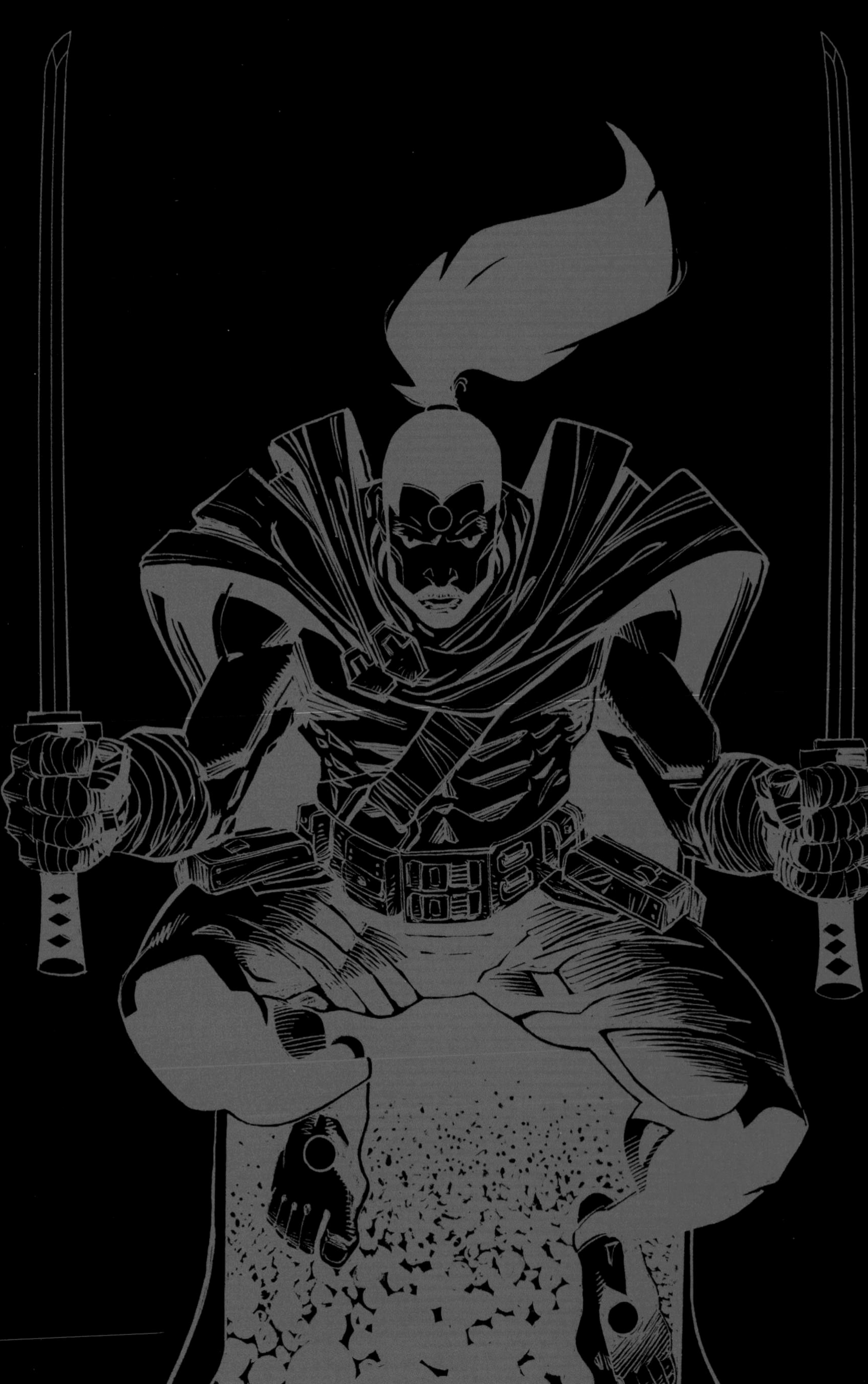

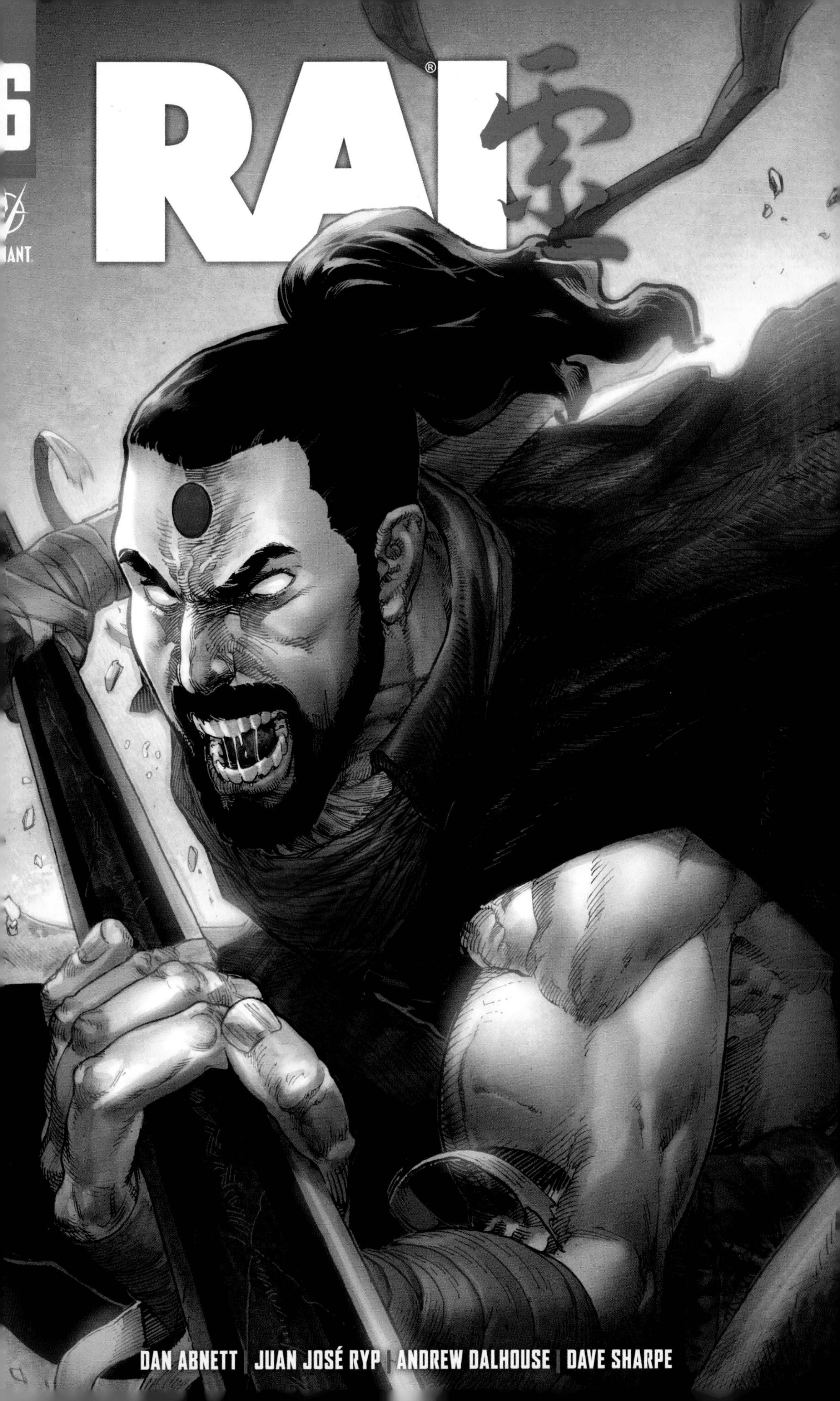
RAI®
6
DAN ABNETT | JUAN JOSÉ RYP | ANDREW DALHOUSE | DAVE SHARPE

RAI #6

WRITER: DAN ABNETT
ARTIST: JUAN JOSÉ RYP
COLORIST: ANDREW DALHOUSE
LETTERER: DAVE SHARPE
COVER ARTISTS: NETHO DIAZ WITH CANDICE HAN
ASSOCIATE EDITOR: DAVID MENCHEL
EDITOR: LYSA HAWKINS

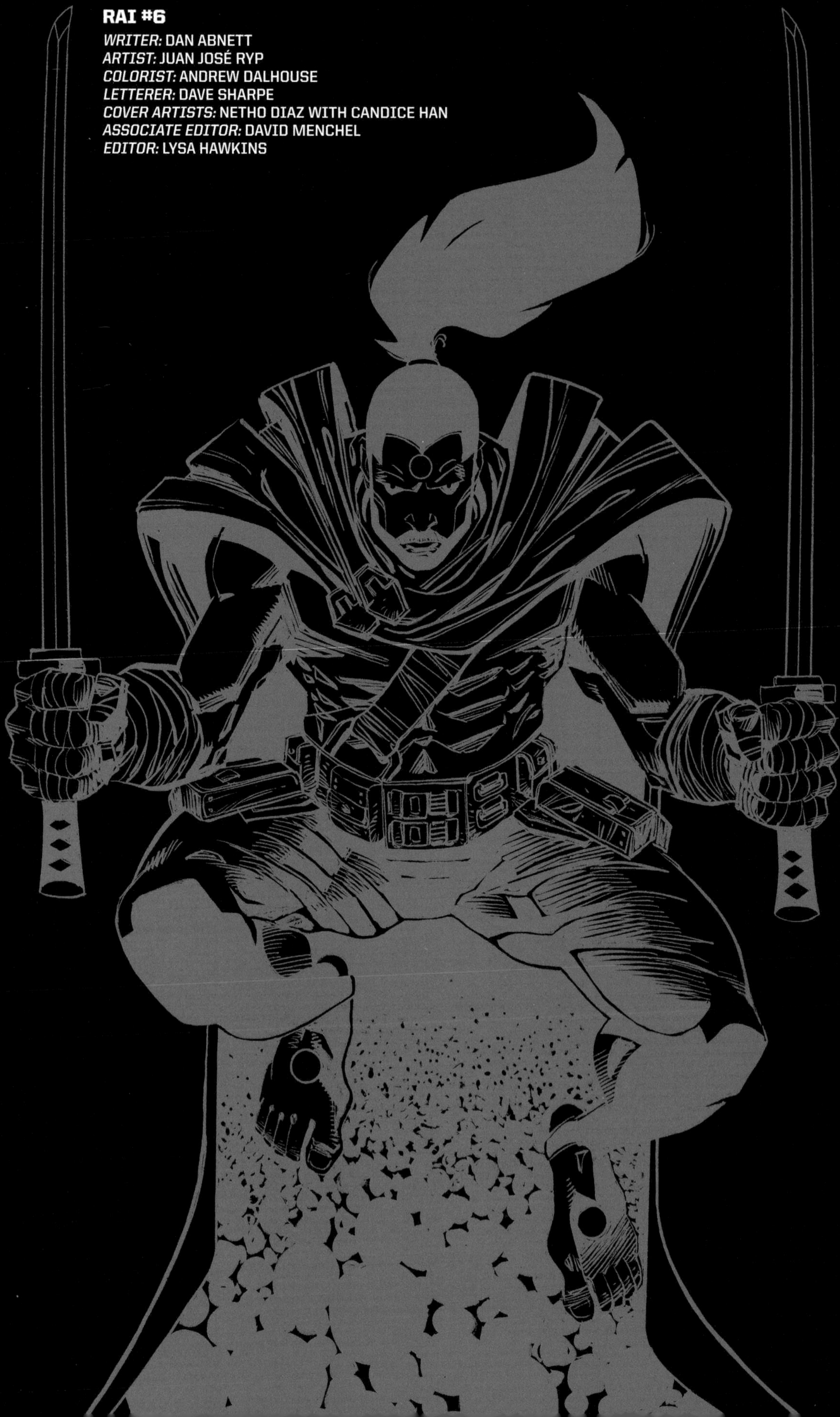

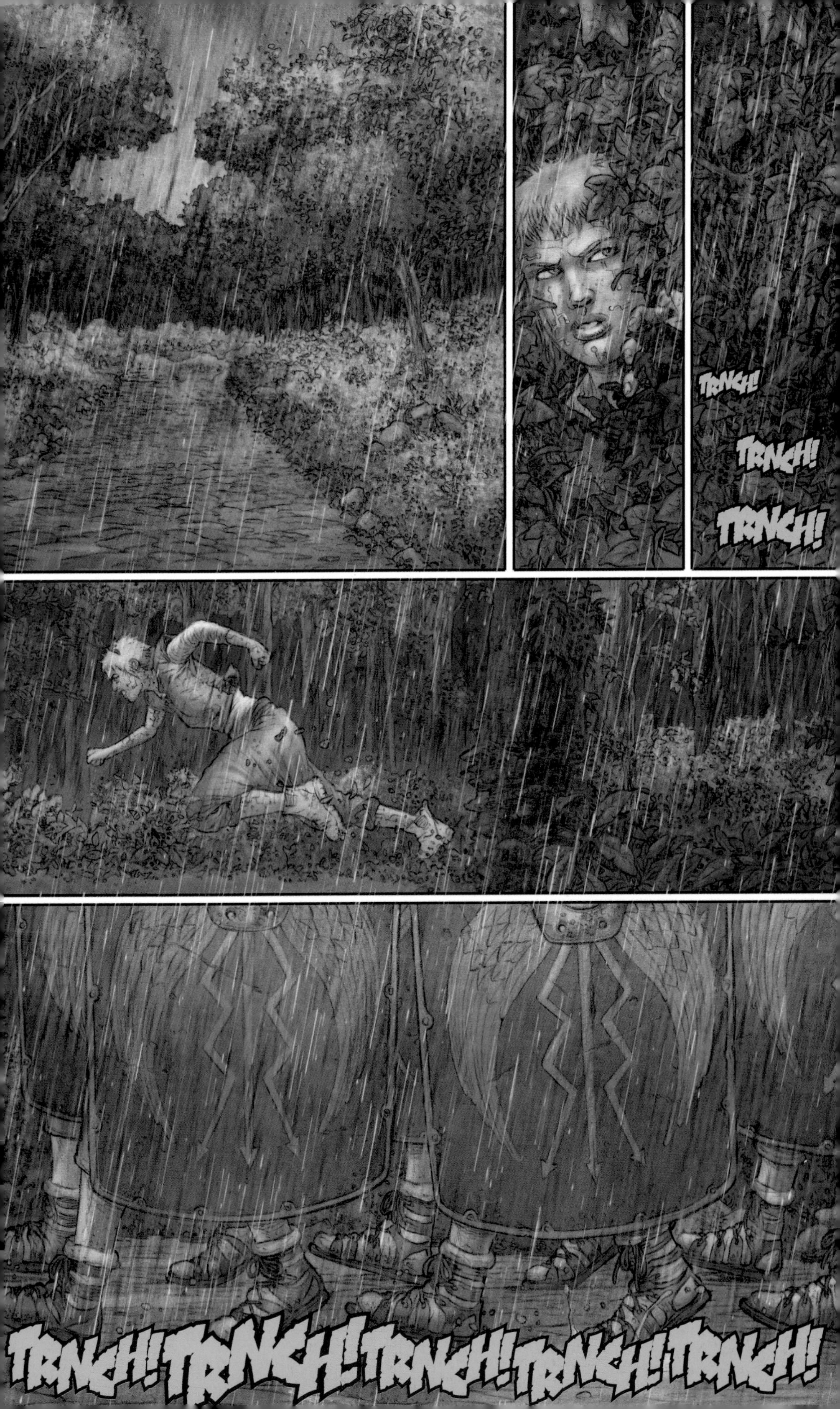
TRNCH!
TRNCH!
TRNCH!
TRNCH! TRNCH! TRNCH! TRNCH! TRNCH!

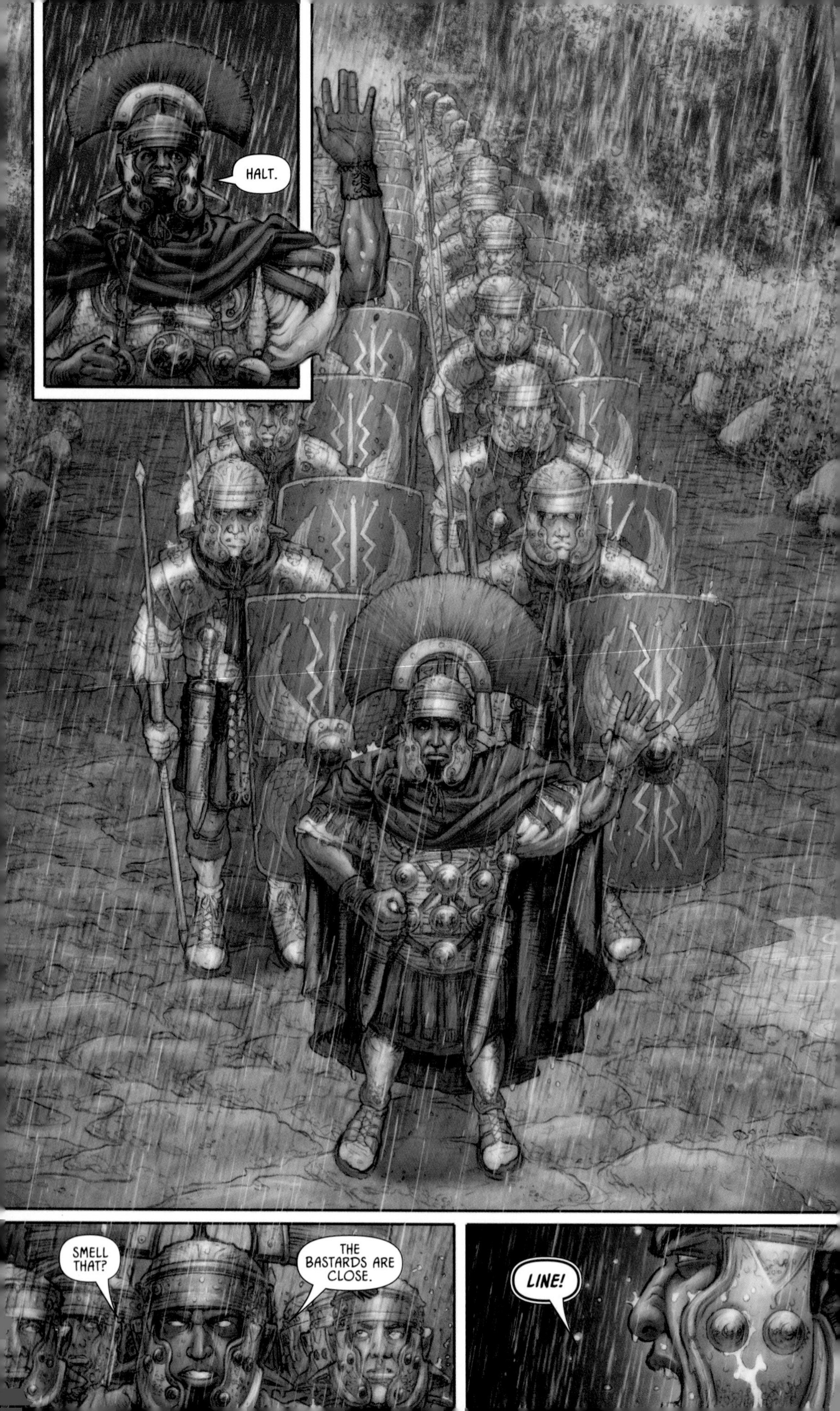
HALT.
SMELL THAT?
THE BASTARDS ARE CLOSE.
LINE!

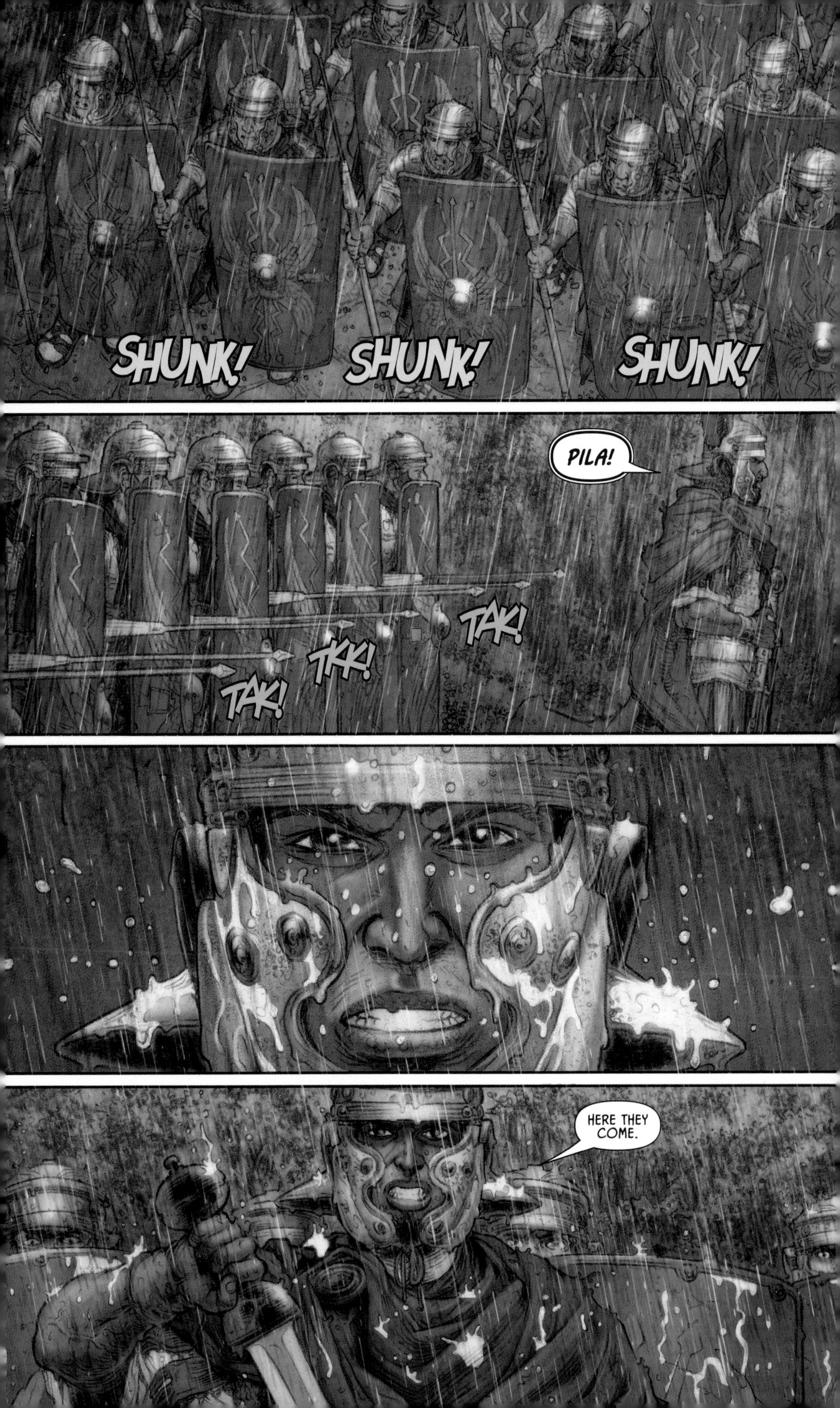
SHUNK! SHUNK! SHUNK!
PILA!
TAK!
TKK!
TAK!
HERE THEY COME.

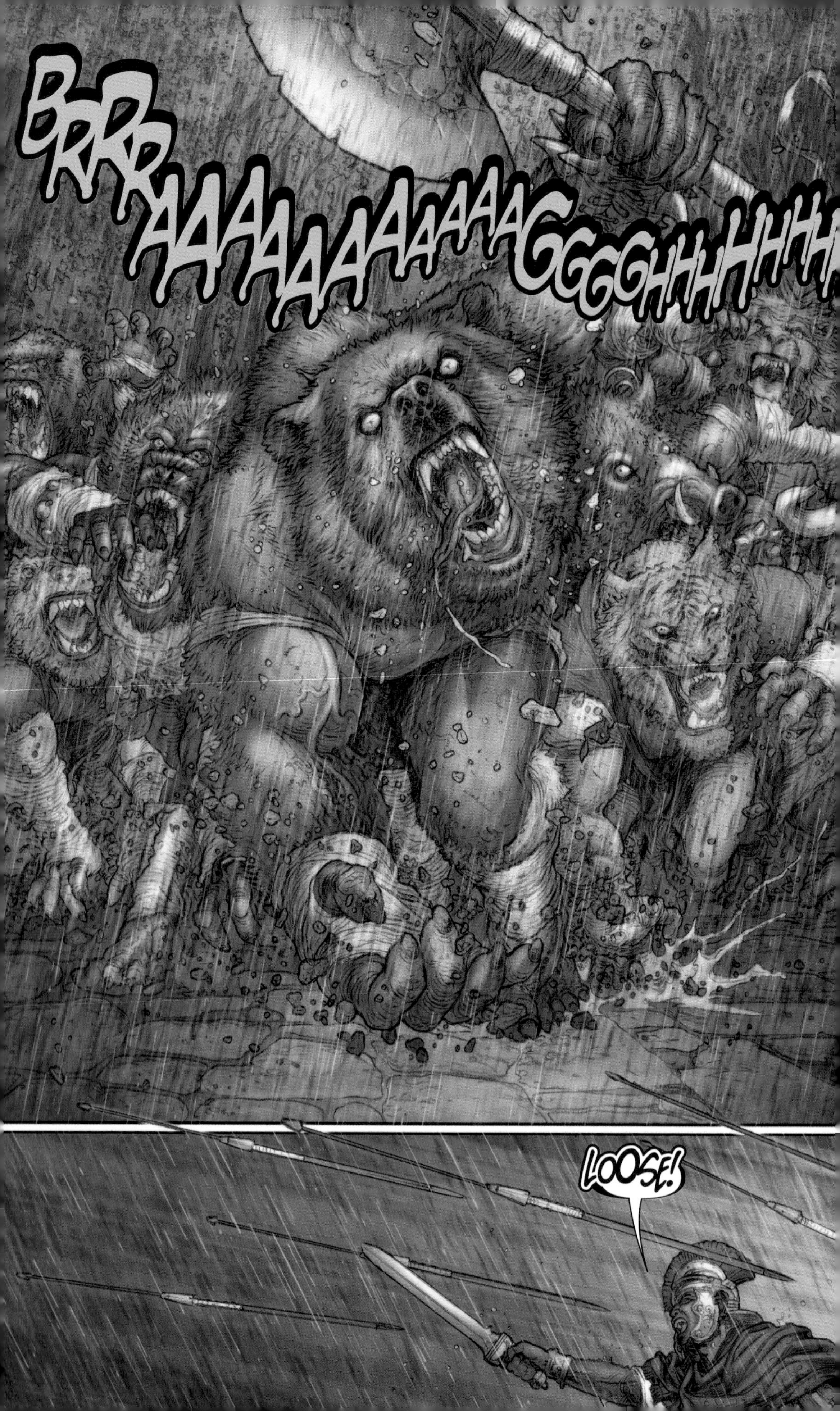
BRRRAAAAAAAAAAGGGGHHHHHH
LOOSE!

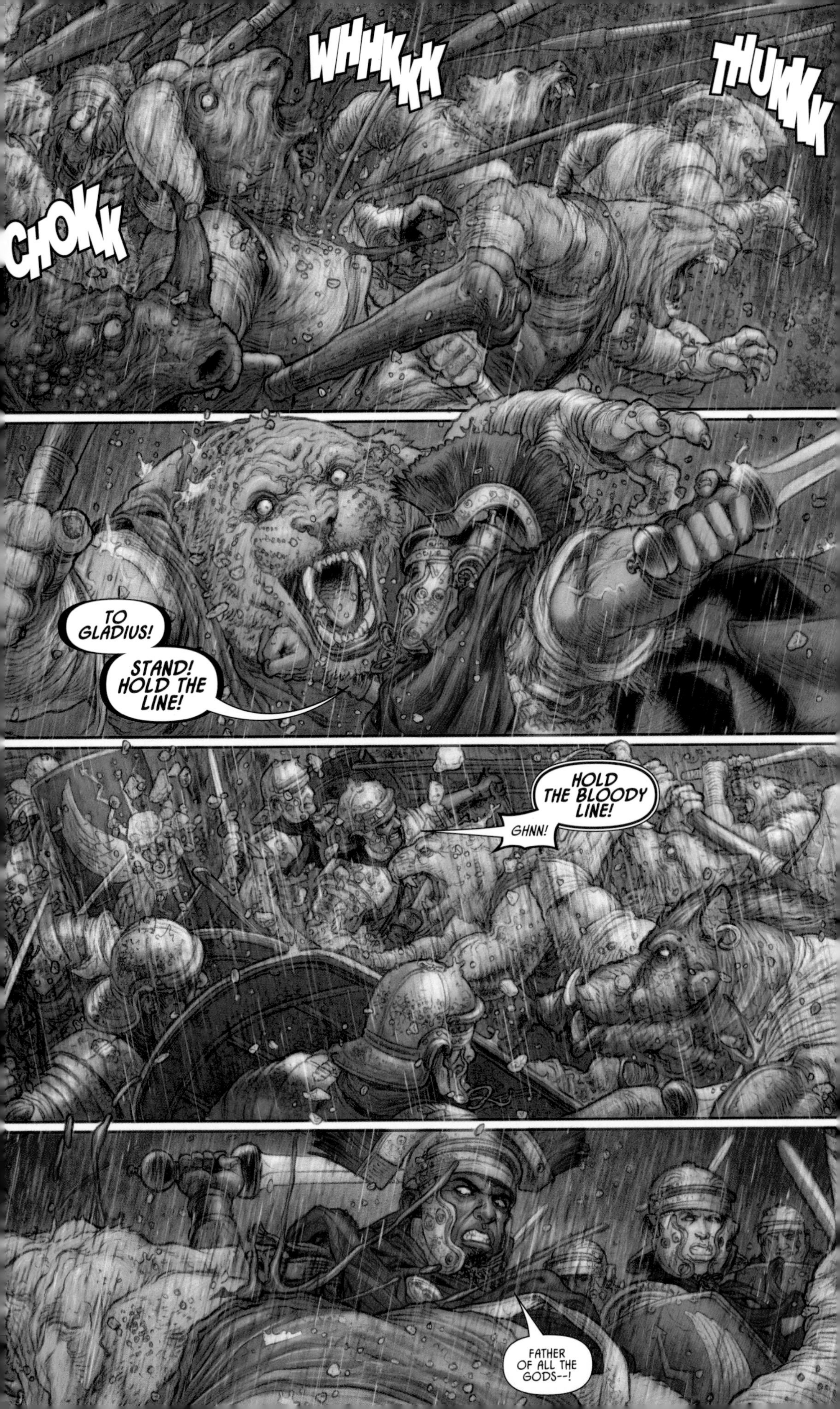
WHHKKK
THUKKK
CHOKK
TO GLADIUS!
STAND! HOLD THE LINE!
HOLD THE BLOODY LINE!
GHNN!
FATHER OF ALL THE GODS--!

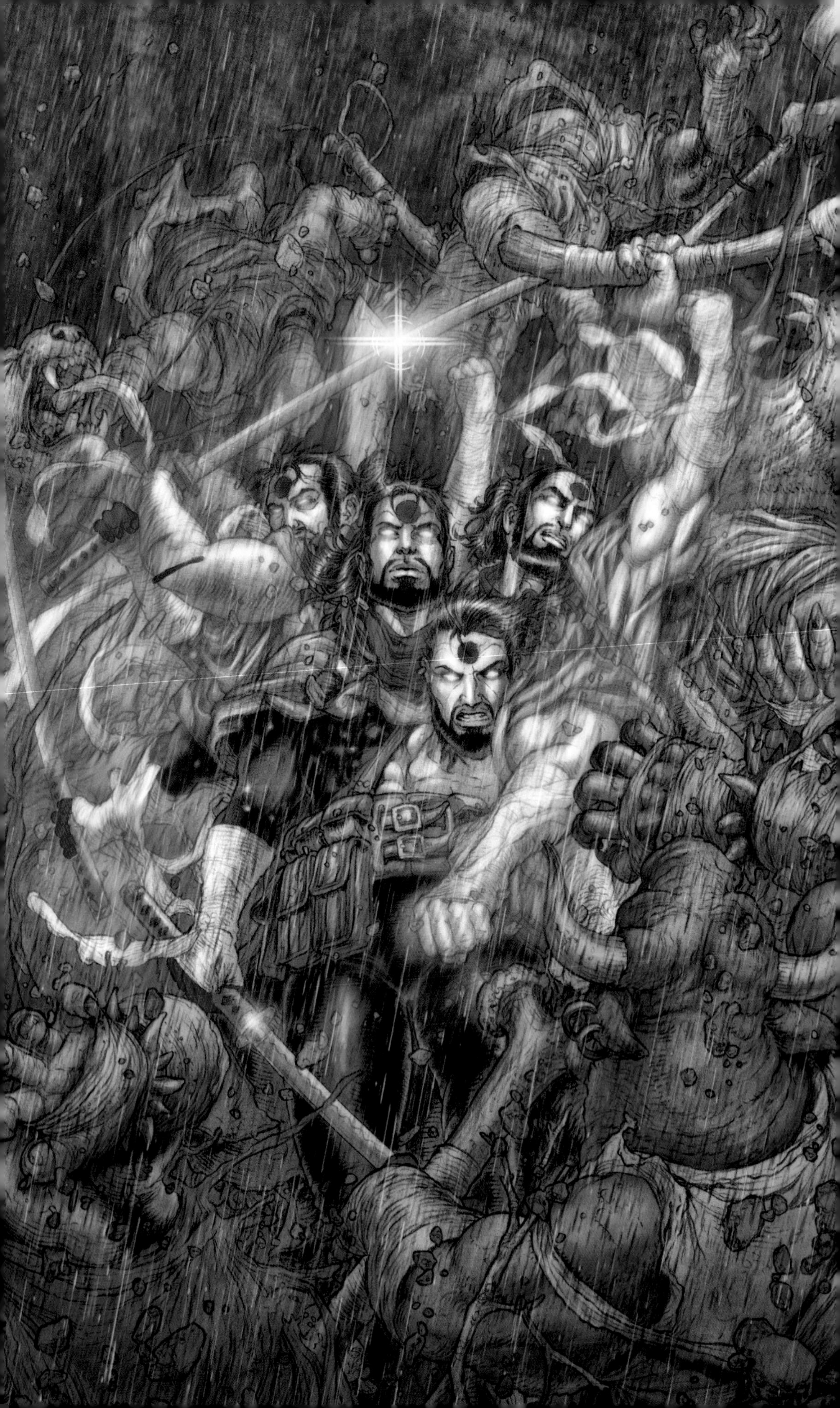

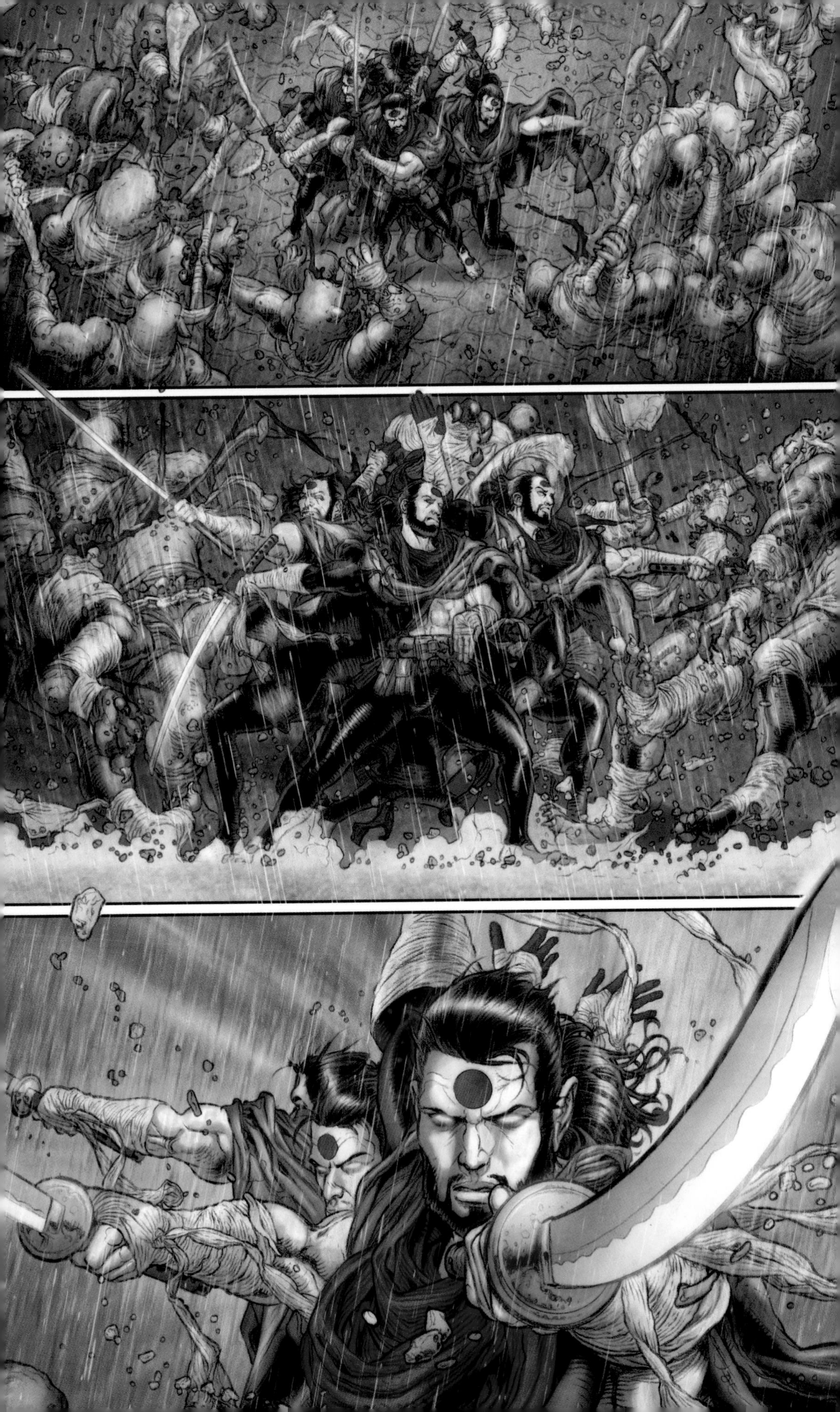

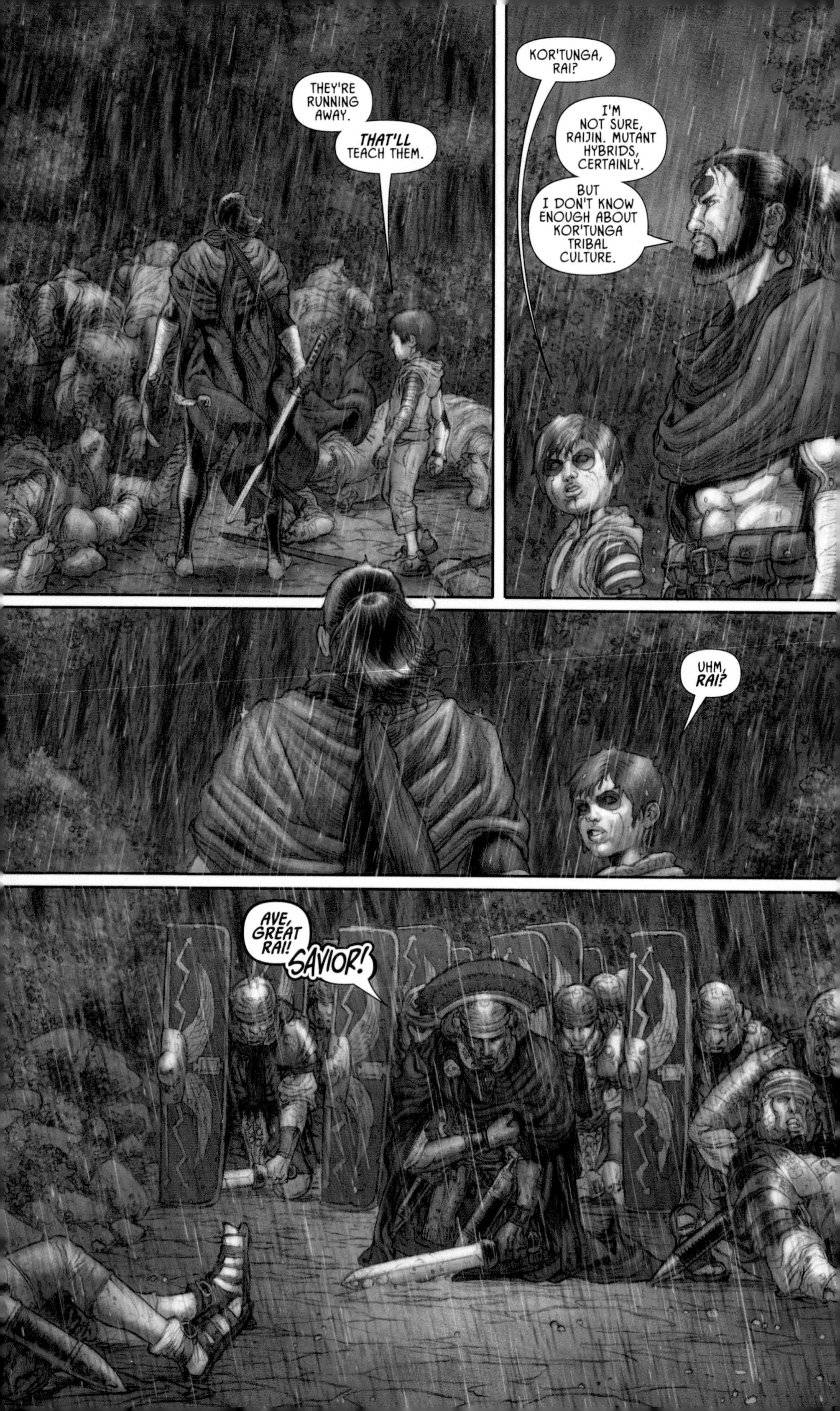
THEY'RE RUNNING AWAY.
THAT'LL TEACH THEM.
KOR'TUNGA, RAI?
I'M NOT SURE, RAIJIN. MUTANT HYBRIDS, CERTAINLY.
BUT I DON'T KNOW ENOUGH ABOUT KOR'TUNGA TRIBAL CULTURE.
UHM, RAI?
AVE, GREAT RAI!
SAVIOR!

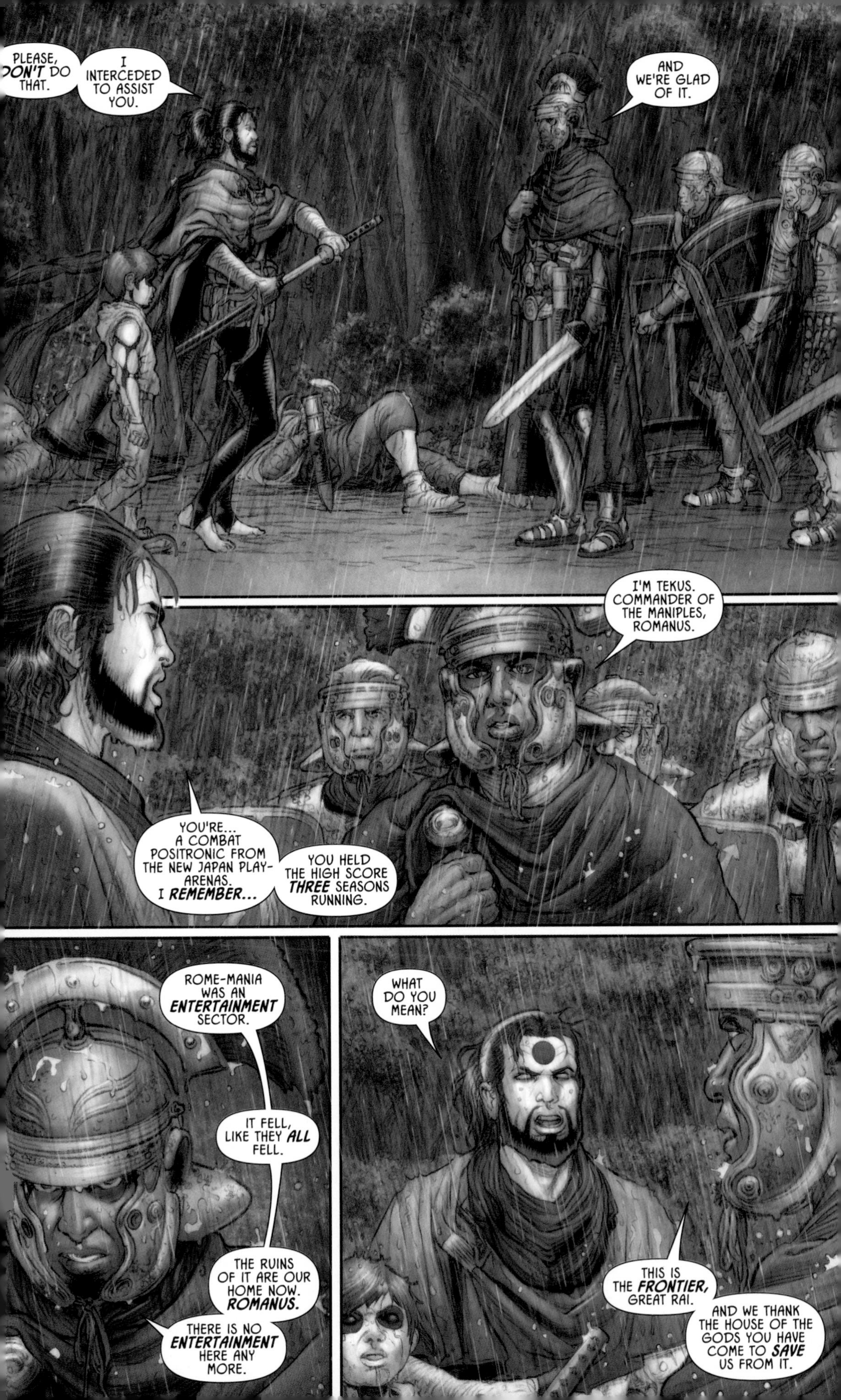
PLEASE, DON'T DO THAT.
I INTERCEDED TO ASSIST YOU.
AND WE'RE GLAD OF IT.
I'M TEKUS. COMMANDER OF THE MANIPLES, ROMANUS.
YOU'RE... A COMBAT POSITRONIC FROM THE NEW JAPAN PLAY-ARENAS. I REMEMBER...
YOU HELD THE HIGH SCORE THREE SEASONS RUNNING.
ROME-MANIA WAS AN ENTERTAINMENT SECTOR.
IT FELL, LIKE THEY ALL FELL.
THE RUINS OF IT ARE OUR HOME NOW. ROMANUS.
THERE IS NO ENTERTAINMENT HERE ANY MORE.
WHAT DO YOU MEAN?
THIS IS THE FRONTIER, GREAT RAI.
AND WE THANK THE HOUSE OF THE GODS YOU HAVE COME TO SAVE US FROM IT.

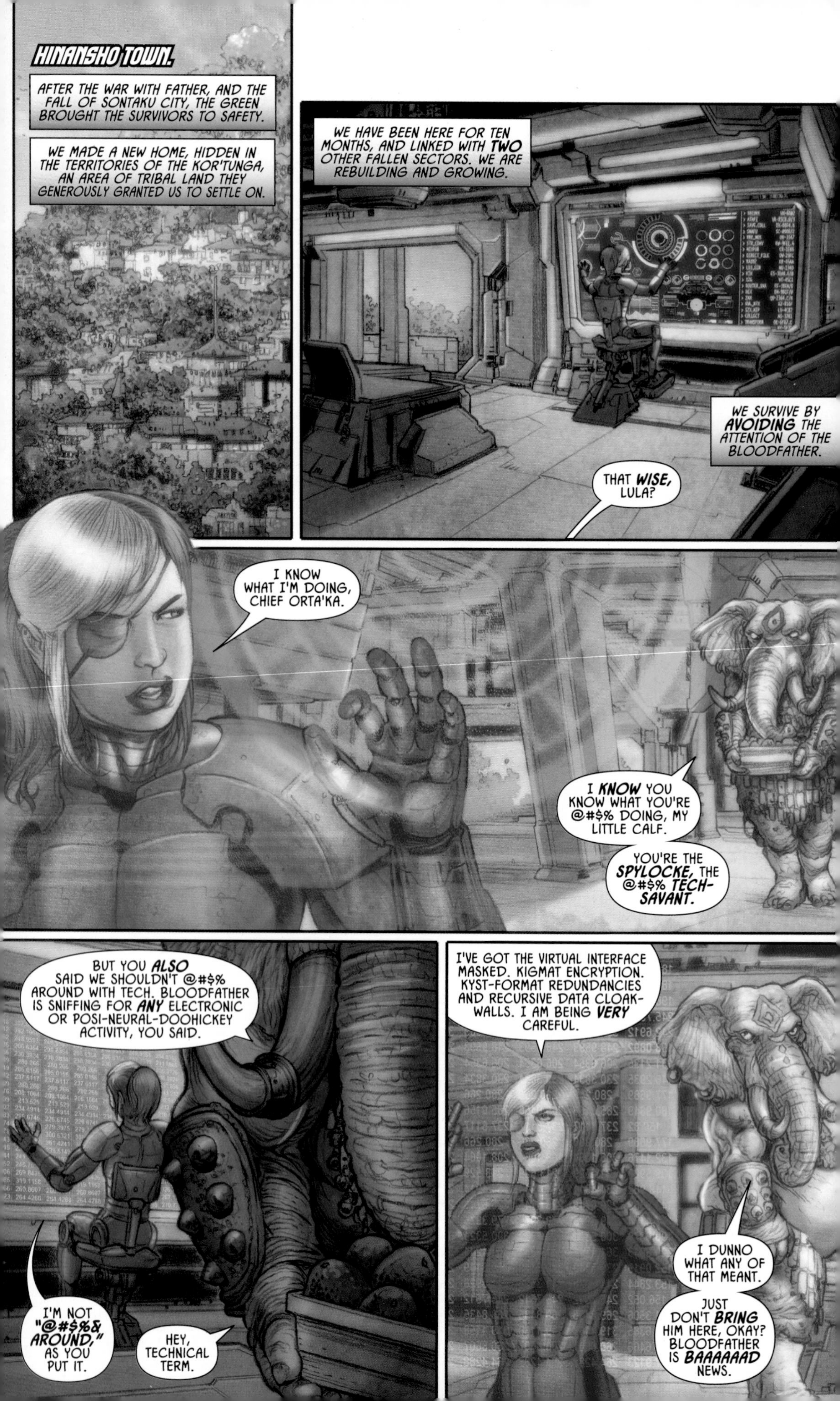
HINANSHO TOWN.
AFTER THE WAR WITH FATHER, AND THE FALL OF SONTAKU CITY, THE GREEN BROUGHT THE SURVIVORS TO SAFETY.
WE MADE A NEW HOME, HIDDEN IN THE TERRITORIES OF THE KOR'TUNGA, AN AREA OF TRIBAL LAND THEY GENEROUSLY GRANTED US TO SETTLE ON.
WE HAVE BEEN HERE FOR TEN MONTHS, AND LINKED WITH TWO OTHER FALLEN SECTORS. WE ARE REBUILDING AND GROWING.
WE SURVIVE BY AVOIDING THE ATTENTION OF THE BLOODFATHER.
THAT WISE, LULA?
I KNOW WHAT I'M DOING, CHIEF ORTA'KA.
I KNOW YOU KNOW WHAT YOU'RE @#$% DOING, MY LITTLE CALF.
YOU'RE THE SPYLOCKE, THE @#$% TECH-SAVANT.
BUT YOU ALSO SAID WE SHOULDN'T @#$% AROUND WITH TECH. BLOODFATHER IS SNIFFING FOR ANY ELECTRONIC OR POSI-NEURAL-DOOHICKEY ACTIVITY, YOU SAID.
I'M NOT "@#$%& AROUND," AS YOU PUT IT.
HEY, TECHNICAL TERM.
I'VE GOT THE VIRTUAL INTERFACE MASKED. KIGMAT ENCRYPTION. KYST-FORMAT REDUNDANCIES AND RECURSIVE DATA CLOAK-WALLS. I AM BEING VERY CAREFUL.
I DUNNO WHAT ANY OF THAT MEANT.
JUST DON'T BRING HIM HERE, OKAY? BLOODFATHER IS BAAAAAAD NEWS.

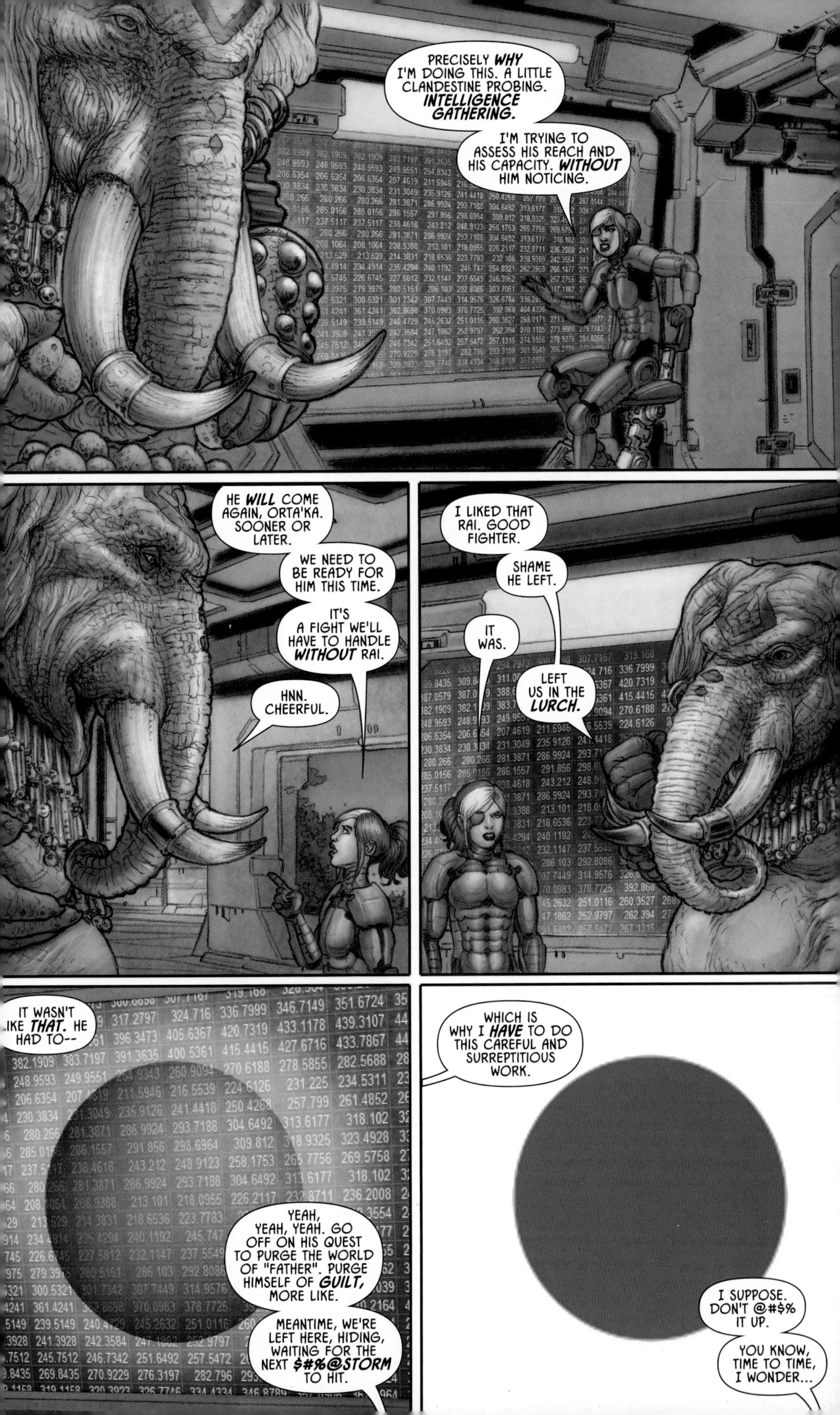
PRECISELY WHY I'M DOING THIS. A LITTLE CLANDESTINE PROBING. INTELLIGENCE GATHERING.
I'M TRYING TO ASSESS HIS REACH AND HIS CAPACITY. WITHOUT HIM NOTICING.
HE WILL COME AGAIN, ORTA'KA. SOONER OR LATER.
WE NEED TO BE READY FOR HIM THIS TIME.
IT'S A FIGHT WE'LL HAVE TO HANDLE WITHOUT RAI.
HNN. CHEERFUL.
I LIKED THAT RAI. GOOD FIGHTER.
SHAME HE LEFT.
IT WAS.
LEFT US IN THE LURCH.
IT WASN'T LIKE THAT. HE HAD TO--
YEAH, YEAH, YEAH. GO OFF ON HIS QUEST TO PURGE THE WORLD OF "FATHER". PURGE HIMSELF OF GUILT, MORE LIKE.
MEANTIME, WE'RE LEFT HERE, HIDING, WAITING FOR THE NEXT $#%@STORM TO HIT.
WHICH IS WHY I HAVE TO DO THIS CAREFUL AND SURREPTITIOUS WORK.
I SUPPOSE. DON'T @#$% IT UP.
YOU KNOW, TIME TO TIME, I WONDER...

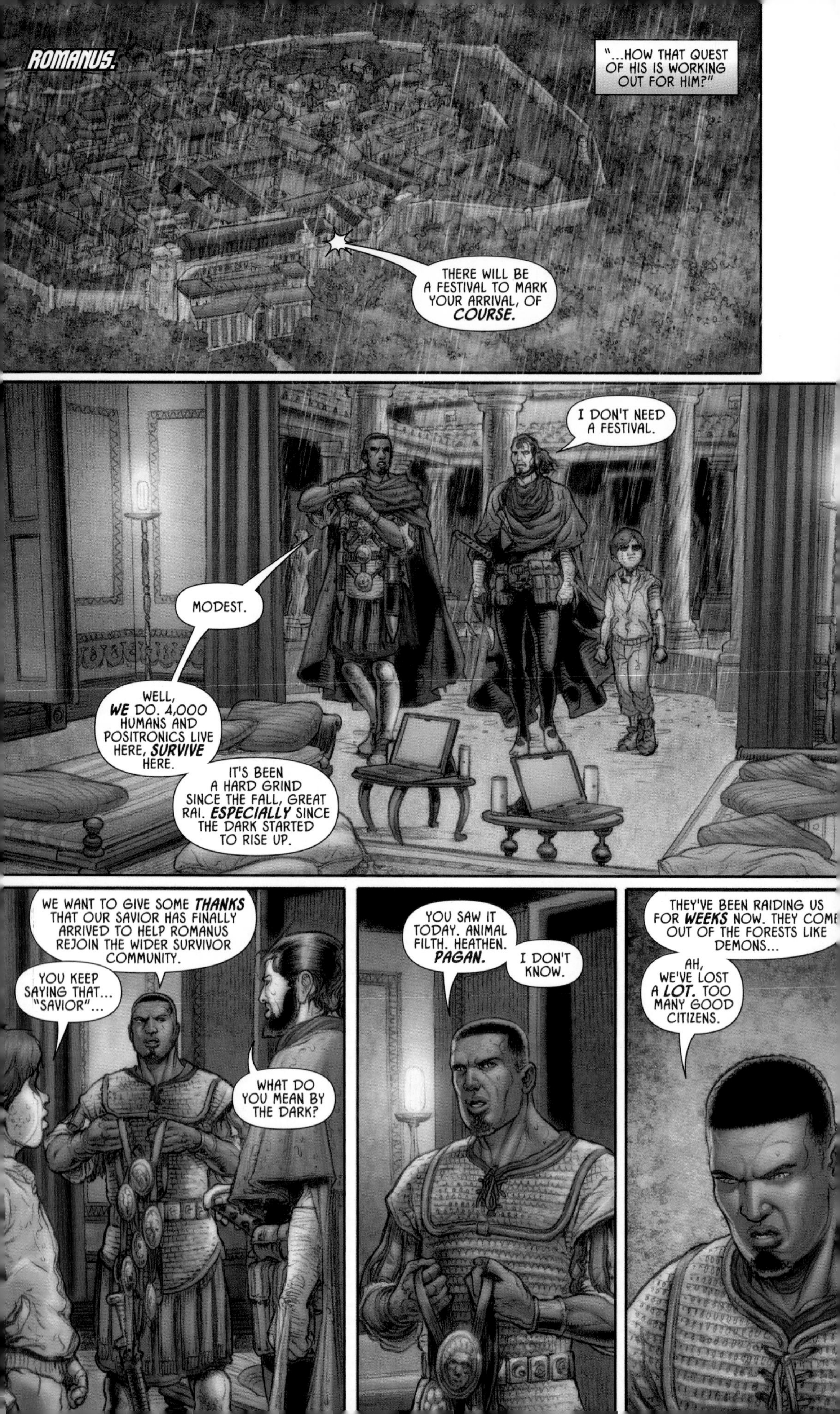
ROMANUS.
"...HOW THAT QUEST OF HIS IS WORKING OUT FOR HIM?"
THERE WILL BE A FESTIVAL TO MARK YOUR ARRIVAL, OF COURSE.
I DON'T NEED A FESTIVAL.
MODEST.
WELL, WE DO. 4,000 HUMANS AND POSITRONICS LIVE HERE, SURVIVE HERE.
IT'S BEEN A HARD GRIND SINCE THE FALL, GREAT RAI. ESPECIALLY SINCE THE DARK STARTED TO RISE UP.
WE WANT TO GIVE SOME THANKS THAT OUR SAVIOR HAS FINALLY ARRIVED TO HELP ROMANUS REJOIN THE WIDER SURVIVOR COMMUNITY.
YOU KEEP SAYING THAT... "SAVIOR"...
WHAT DO YOU MEAN BY THE DARK?
YOU SAW IT TODAY. ANIMAL FILTH. HEATHEN. PAGAN.
I DON'T KNOW.
THEY'VE BEEN RAIDING US FOR WEEKS NOW. THEY COME OUT OF THE FORESTS LIKE DEMONS...
AH, WE'VE LOST A LOT. TOO MANY GOOD CITIZENS.

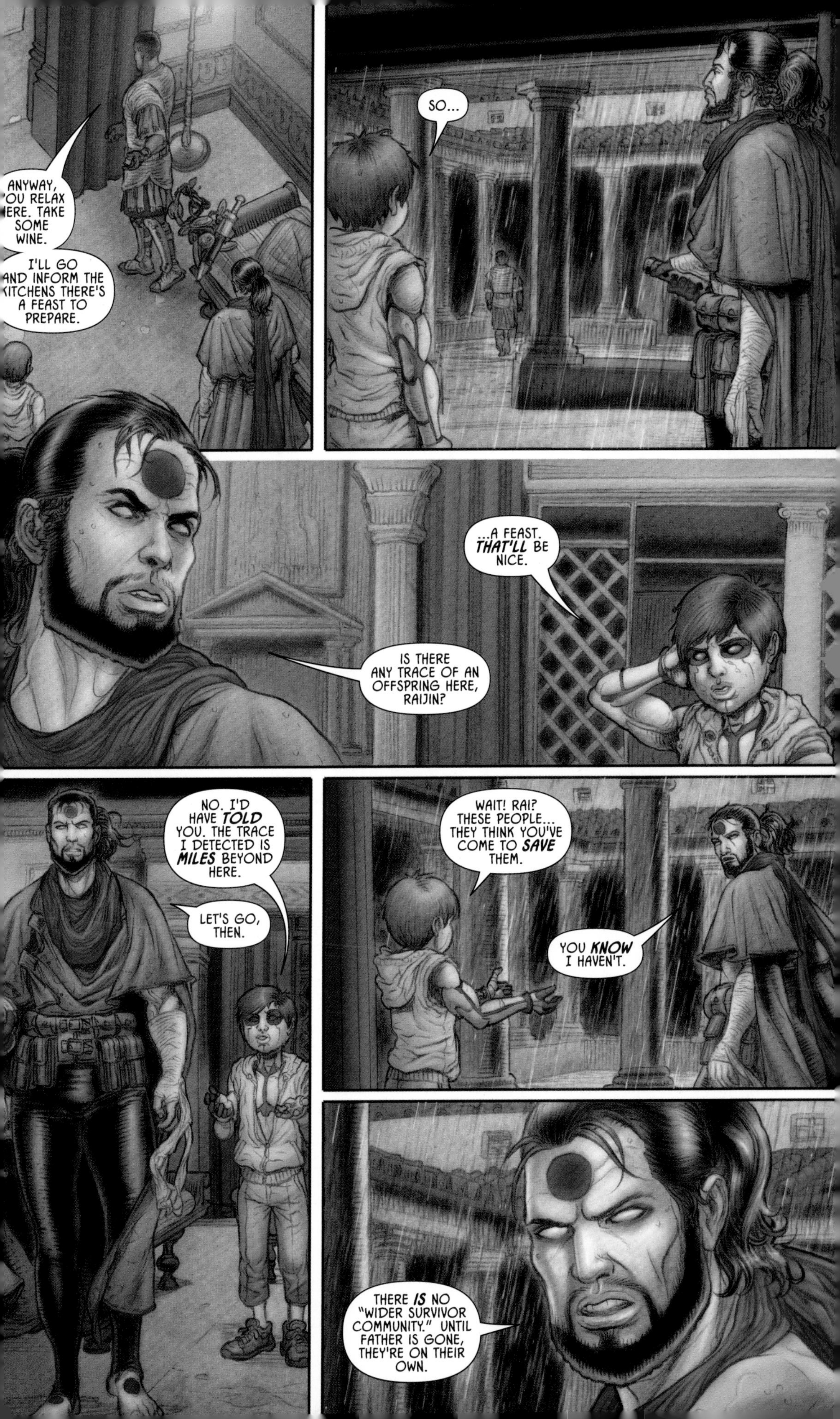
ANYWAY, 'OU RELAX IERE. TAKE SOME WINE.
I'LL GO AND INFORM THE KITCHENS THERE'S A FEAST TO PREPARE.
SO...
...A FEAST. THAT'LL BE NICE.
IS THERE ANY TRACE OF AN OFFSPRING HERE, RAIJIN?
NO. I'D HAVE TOLD YOU. THE TRACE I DETECTED IS MILES BEYOND HERE.
LET'S GO, THEN.
WAIT! RAI? THESE PEOPLE... THEY THINK YOU'VE COME TO SAVE THEM.
YOU KNOW I HAVEN'T.
THERE IS NO "WIDER SURVIVOR COMMUNITY." UNTIL FATHER IS GONE, THEY'RE ON THEIR OWN.

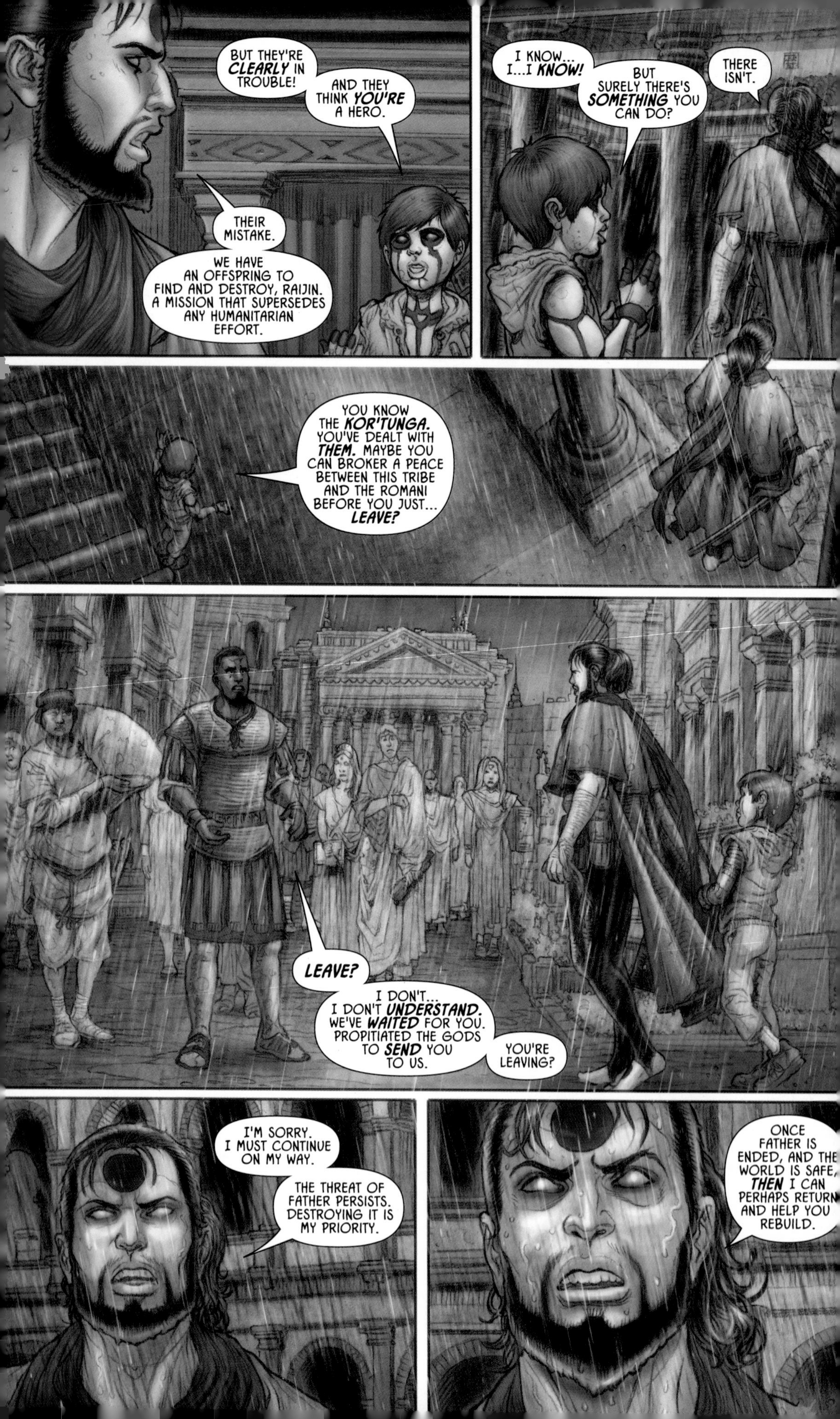
BUT THEY'RE CLEARLY IN TROUBLE!
AND THEY THINK YOU'RE A HERO.
THEIR MISTAKE.
WE HAVE AN OFFSPRING TO FIND AND DESTROY, RAIJIN. A MISSION THAT SUPERSEDES ANY HUMANITARIAN EFFORT.
I KNOW... I...I KNOW!
BUT SURELY THERE'S SOMETHING YOU CAN DO?
THERE ISN'T.
YOU KNOW THE KOR'TUNGA. YOU'VE DEALT WITH THEM. MAYBE YOU CAN BROKER A PEACE BETWEEN THIS TRIBE AND THE ROMANI BEFORE YOU JUST... LEAVE?
LEAVE?
I DON'T... I DON'T UNDERSTAND. WE'VE WAITED FOR YOU. PROPITIATED THE GODS TO SEND YOU TO US.
YOU'RE LEAVING?
I'M SORRY. I MUST CONTINUE ON MY WAY.
THE THREAT OF FATHER PERSISTS. DESTROYING IT IS MY PRIORITY.
ONCE FATHER IS ENDED, AND THE WORLD IS SAFE, THEN I CAN PERHAPS RETURN AND HELP YOU REBUILD.

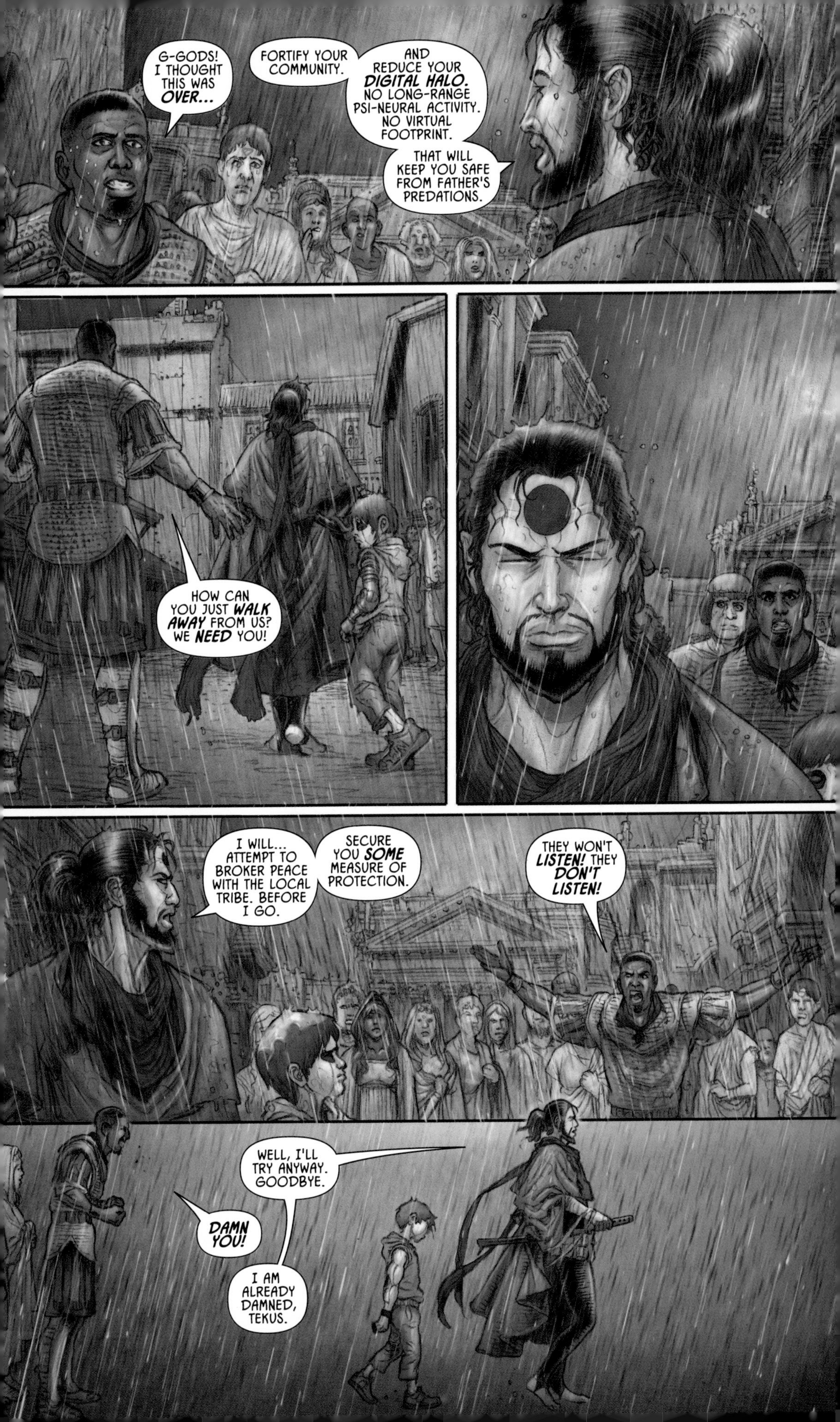
G-GODS! I THOUGHT THIS WAS OVER...
FORTIFY YOUR COMMUNITY.
AND REDUCE YOUR DIGITAL HALO. NO LONG-RANGE PSI-NEURAL ACTIVITY. NO VIRTUAL FOOTPRINT.
THAT WILL KEEP YOU SAFE FROM FATHER'S PREDATIONS.
HOW CAN YOU JUST WALK AWAY FROM US? WE NEED YOU!
I WILL... ATTEMPT TO BROKER PEACE WITH THE LOCAL TRIBE. BEFORE I GO.
SECURE YOU SOME MEASURE OF PROTECTION.
THEY WON'T LISTEN! THEY DON'T LISTEN!
WELL, I'LL TRY ANYWAY. GOODBYE.
DAMN YOU!
I AM ALREADY DAMNED, TEKUS.

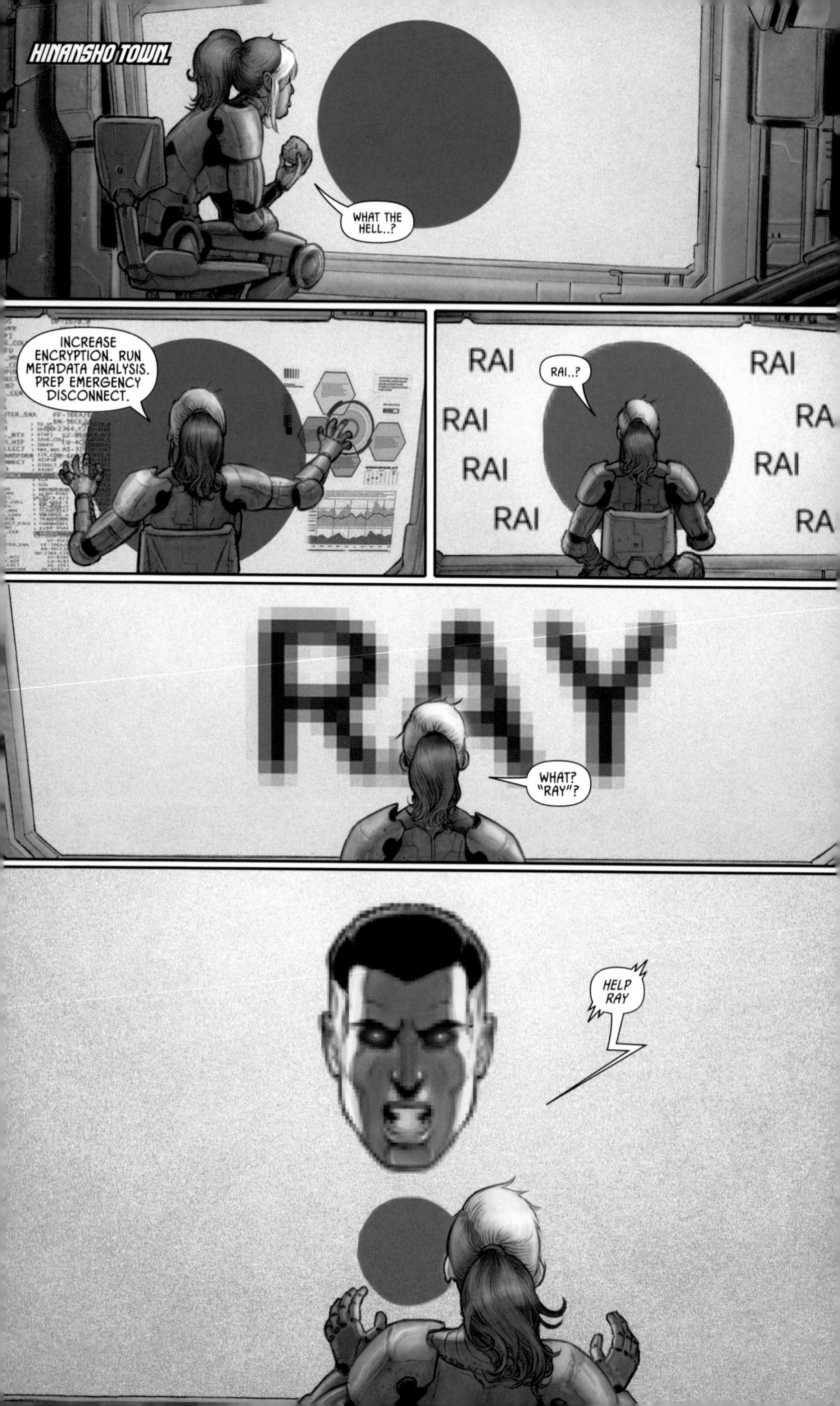
HINANSHO TOWN.
WHAT THE HELL..?
INCREASE ENCRYPTION. RUN METADATA ANALYSIS. PREP EMERGENCY DISCONNECT.
RAI..?
RAI RAI RAI RAI RAI RA RA RA
RAY
WHAT? "RAY"?
HELP RAY

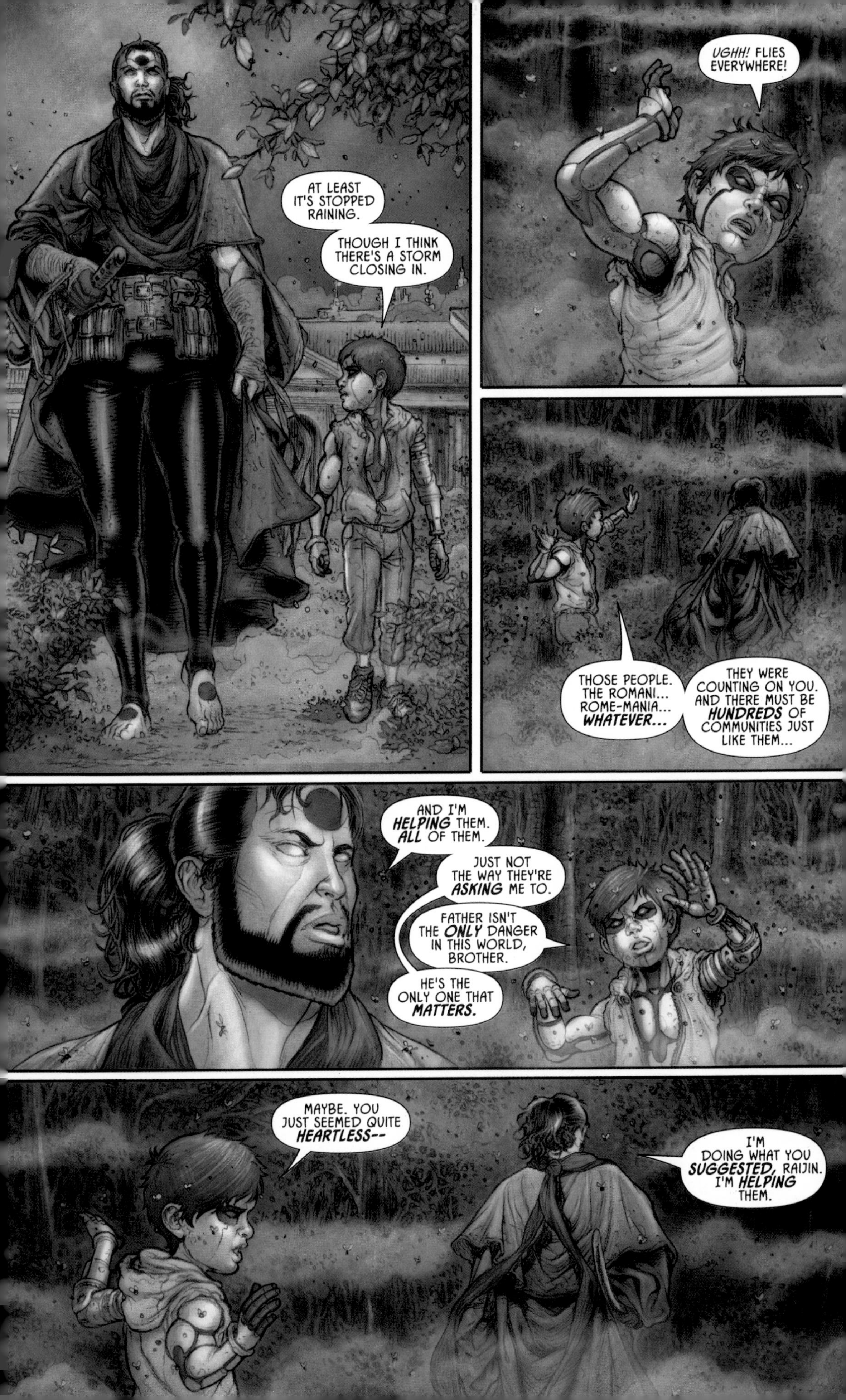
AT LEAST IT'S STOPPED RAINING.
THOUGH I THINK THERE'S A STORM CLOSING IN.
UGHH! FLIES EVERYWHERE!
THOSE PEOPLE. THE ROMANI... ROME-MANIA... WHATEVER...
THEY WERE COUNTING ON YOU. AND THERE MUST BE HUNDREDS OF COMMUNITIES JUST LIKE THEM...
AND I'M HELPING THEM. ALL OF THEM.
JUST NOT THE WAY THEY'RE ASKING ME TO.
FATHER ISN'T THE ONLY DANGER IN THIS WORLD, BROTHER.
HE'S THE ONLY ONE THAT MATTERS.
MAYBE. YOU JUST SEEMED QUITE HEARTLESS--
I'M DOING WHAT YOU SUGGESTED, RAIJIN. I'M HELPING THEM.

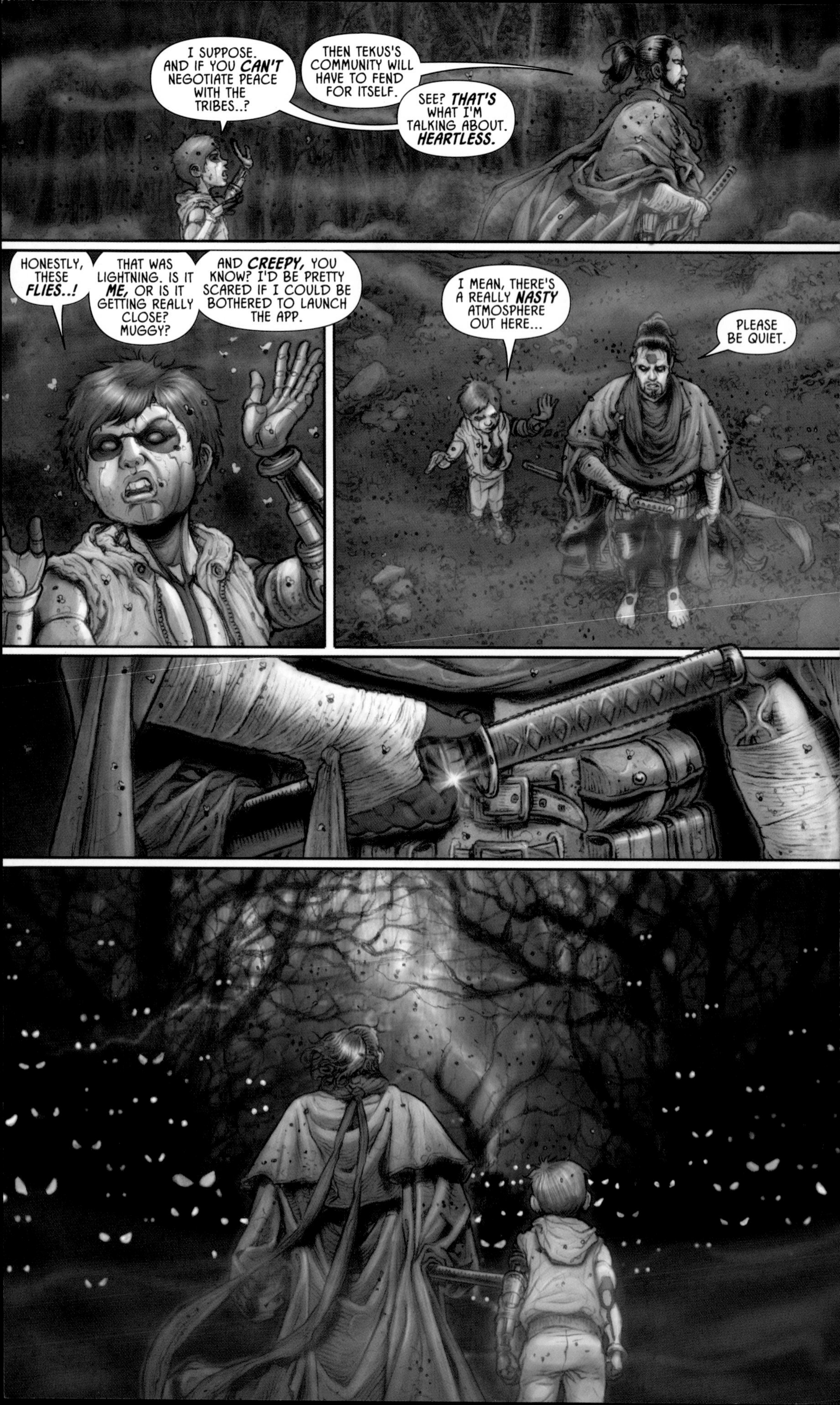
I SUPPOSE. AND IF YOU CAN'T NEGOTIATE PEACE WITH THE TRIBES..?
THEN TEKUS'S COMMUNITY WILL HAVE TO FEND FOR ITSELF.
SEE? THAT'S WHAT I'M TALKING ABOUT. HEARTLESS.
HONESTLY, THESE FLIES..!
THAT WAS LIGHTNING. IS IT ME, OR IS IT GETTING REALLY CLOSE? MUGGY?
AND CREEPY, YOU KNOW? I'D BE PRETTY SCARED IF I COULD BE BOTHERED TO LAUNCH THE APP.
I MEAN, THERE'S A REALLY NASTY ATMOSPHERE OUT HERE...
PLEASE BE QUIET.

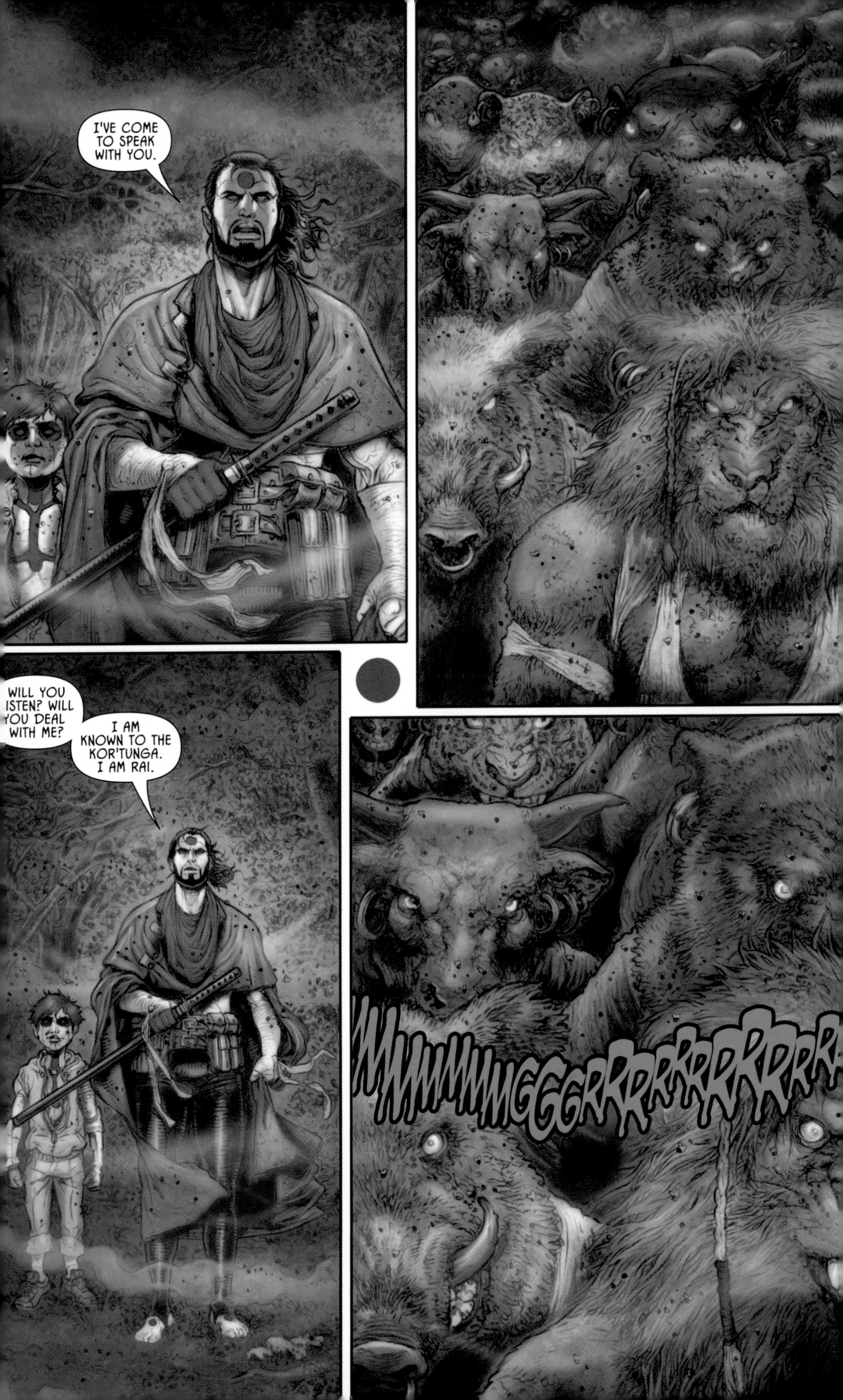
I'VE COME TO SPEAK WITH YOU.
WILL YOU LISTEN? WILL YOU DEAL WITH ME?
I AM KNOWN TO THE KOR'TUNGA. I AM RAI.
MMMMMMMGGGRRRRRRRRRRRR

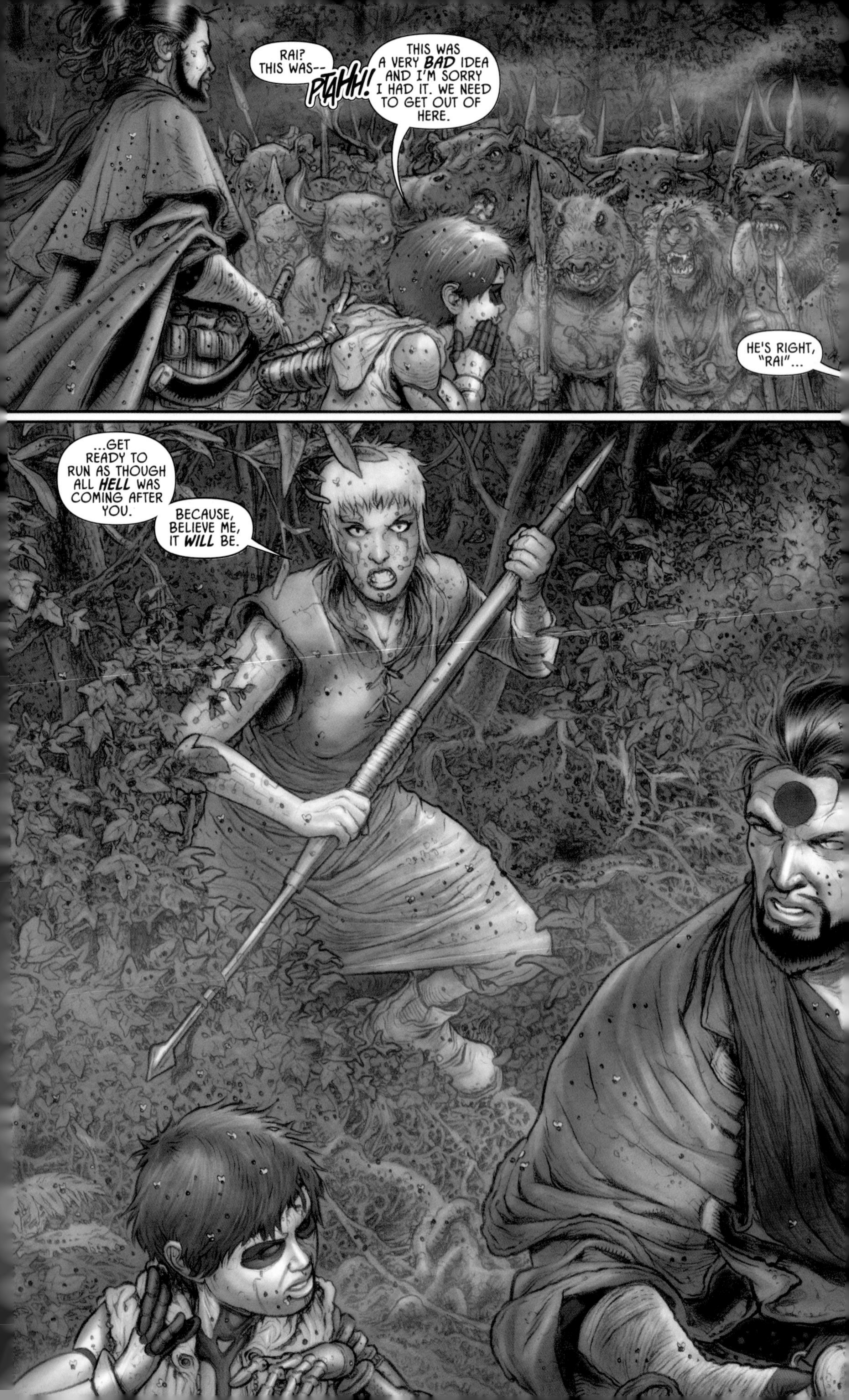
RAI? THIS WAS--
PTAHH!
THIS WAS A VERY BAD IDEA AND I'M SORRY I HAD IT. WE NEED TO GET OUT OF HERE.
HE'S RIGHT, "RAI"...
...GET READY TO RUN AS THOUGH ALL HELL WAS COMING AFTER YOU.
BECAUSE, BELIEVE ME, IT WILL BE.

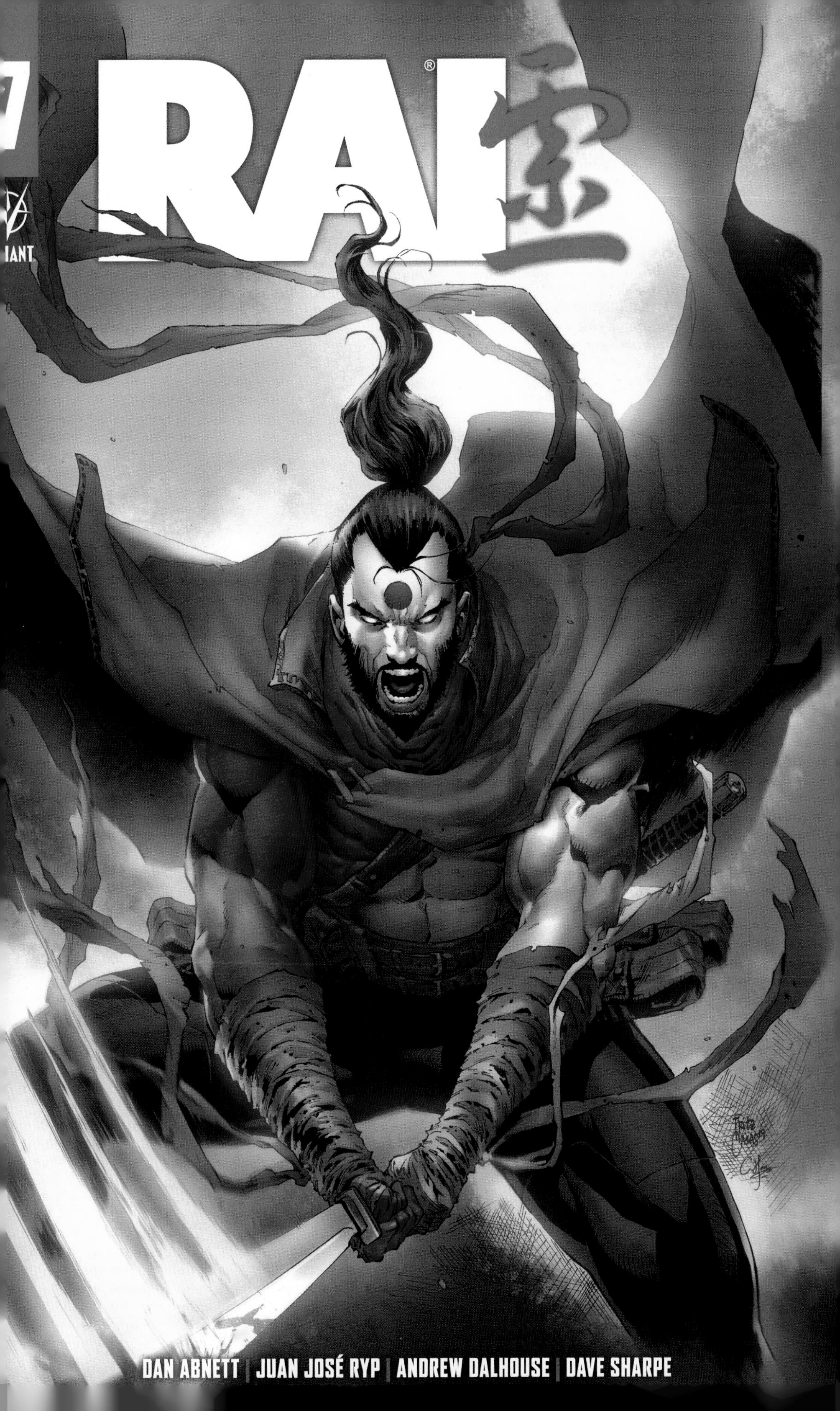

7
RAI®
IANT
DAN ABNETT | JUAN JOSÉ RYP | ANDREW DALHOUSE | DAVE SHARPE

RAI #7

WRITER: DAN ABNETT
ARTIST: JUAN JOSÉ RYP
COLORIST: ANDREW DALHOUSE
LETTERER: DAVE SHARPE
COVER ARTISTS: FRITZ CASAS with CANDICE HAN
ASSOCIATE EDITOR: DAVID MENCHEL
EDITOR: LYSA HAWKINS

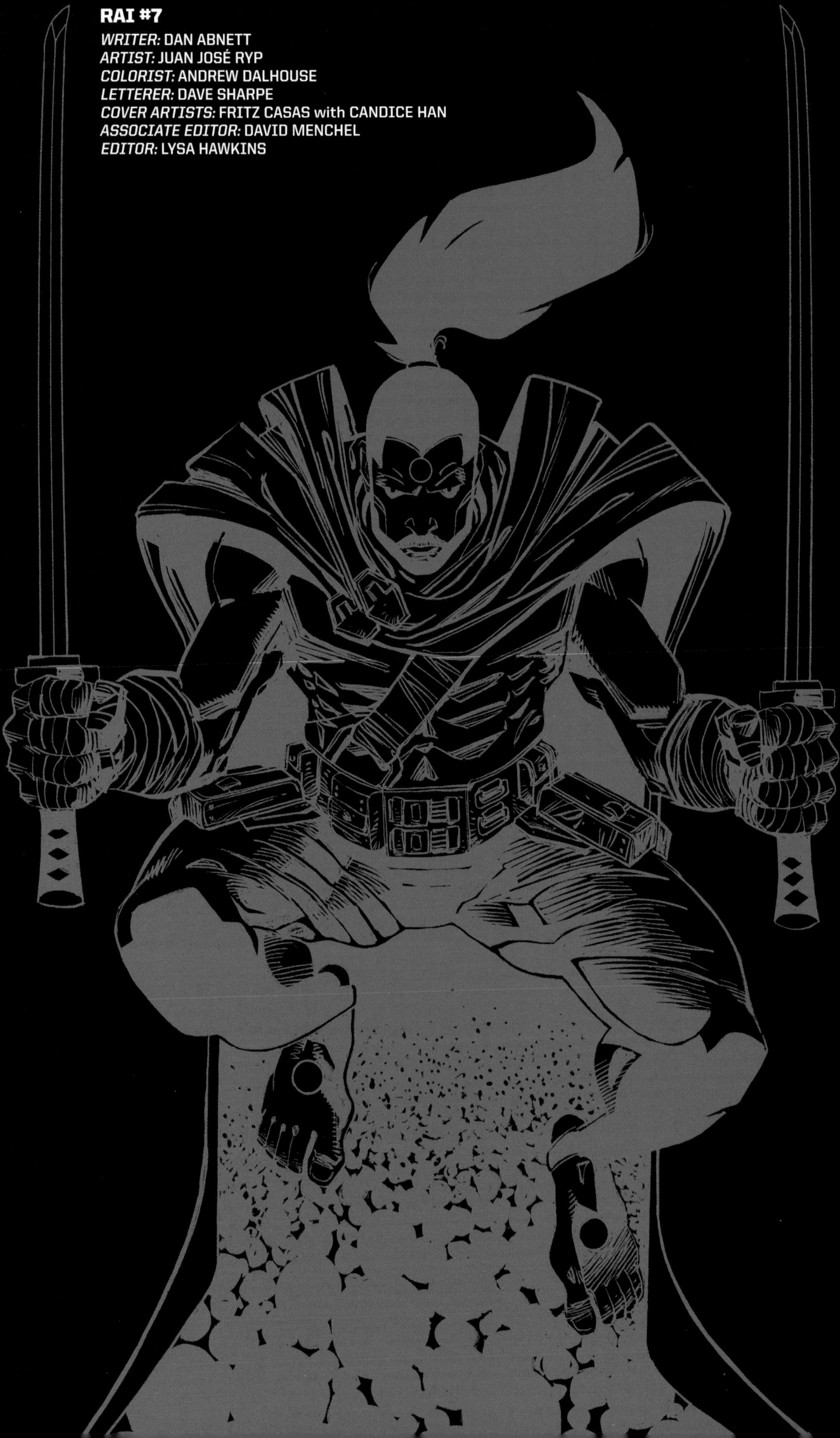

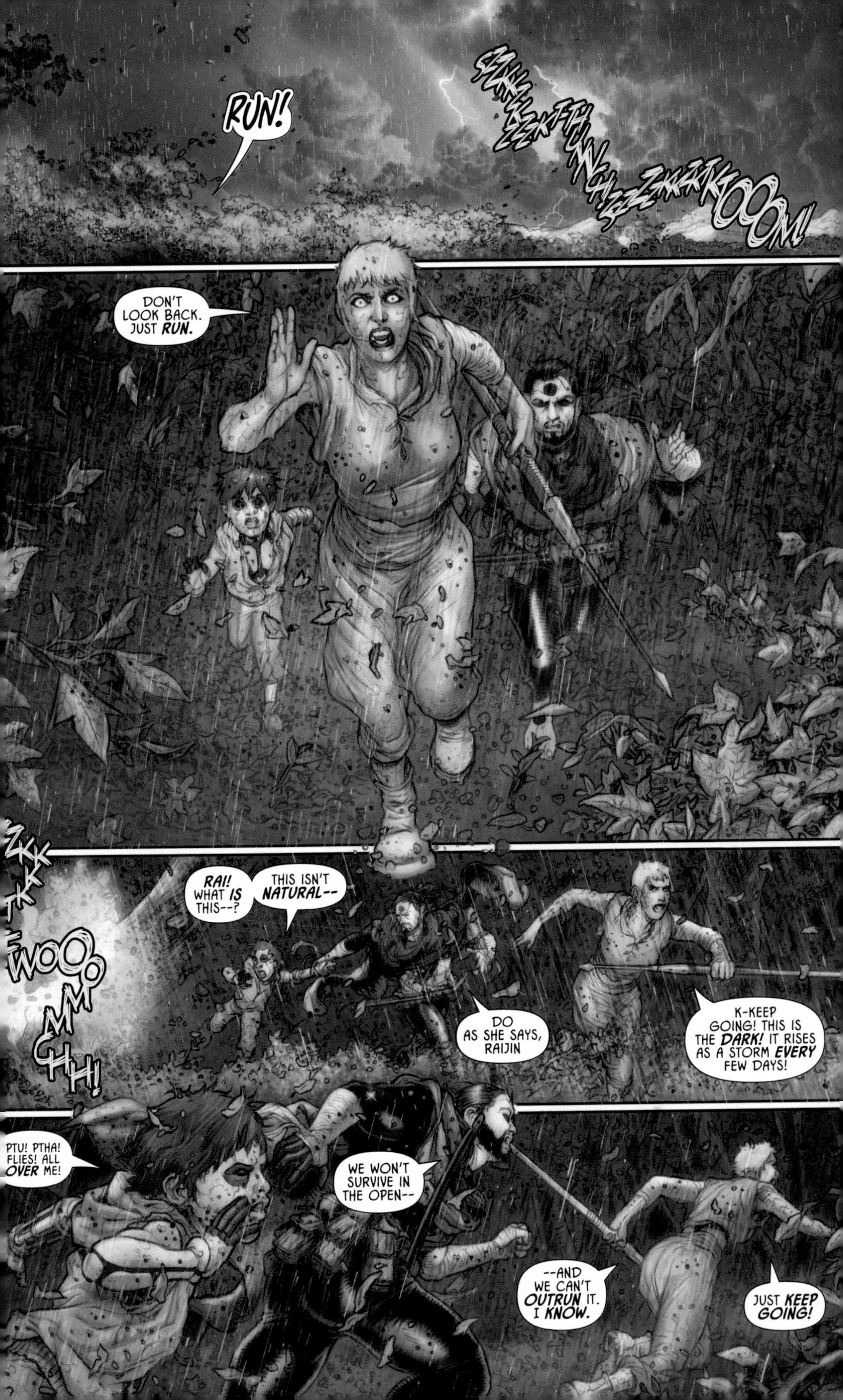
RUN!
DON'T LOOK BACK. JUST **RUN.**
RAI! WHAT ***IS*** THIS--?
THIS ISN'T ***NATURAL--***
DO AS SHE SAYS, RAIJIN
K-KEEP GOING! THIS IS THE ***DARK!*** IT RISES AS A STORM ***EVERY*** FEW DAYS!
PTU! PTHA! FLIES! ALL ***OVER*** ME!
WE WON'T SURVIVE IN THE OPEN--
--AND WE CAN'T ***OUTRUN*** IT. I ***KNOW.***
JUST ***KEEP GOING!***

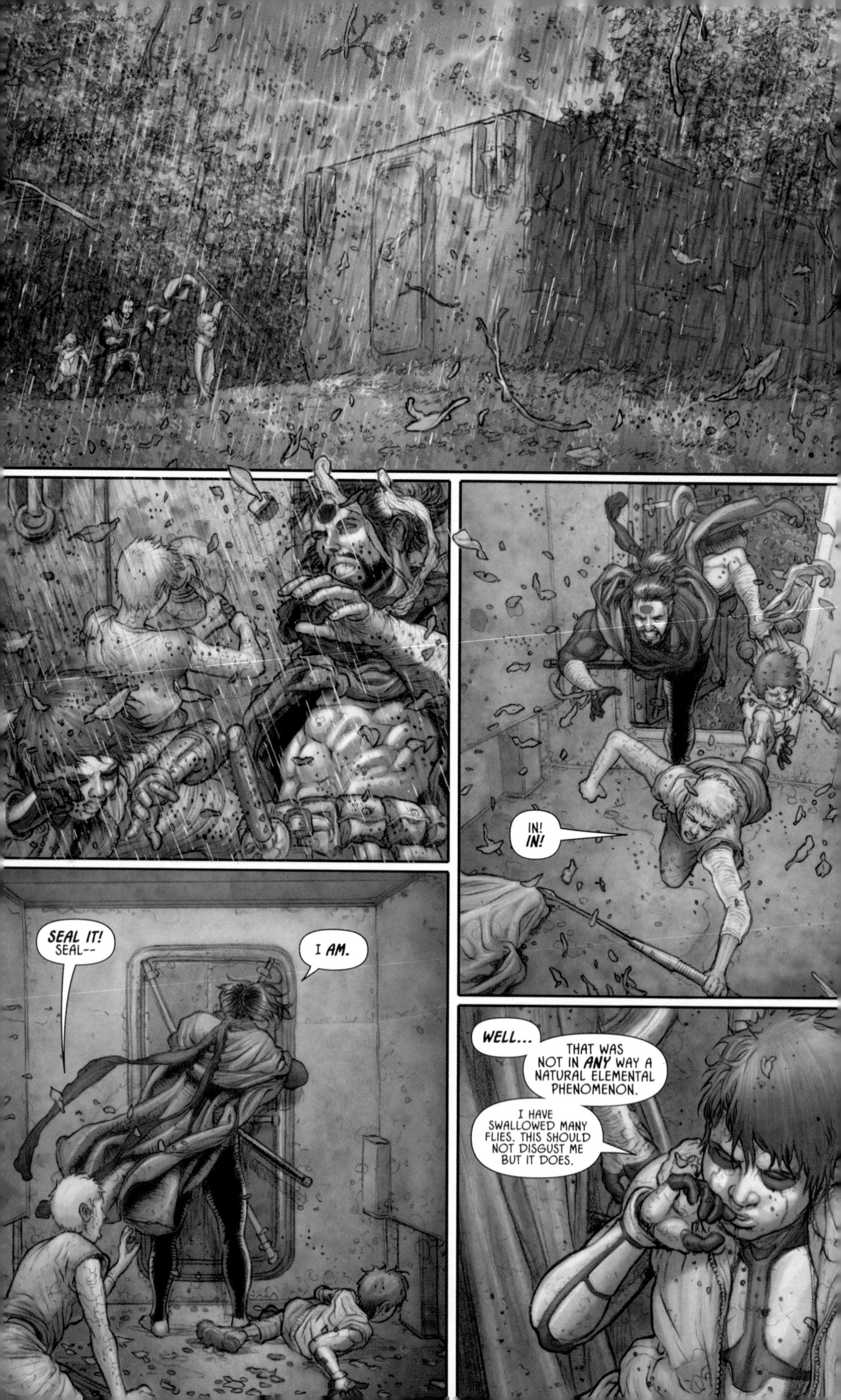
IN! IN!
SEAL IT! SEAL--
I AM.
WELL...
THAT WAS NOT IN ANY WAY A NATURAL ELEMENTAL PHENOMENON.
I HAVE SWALLOWED MANY FLIES. THIS SHOULD NOT DISGUST ME BUT IT DOES.

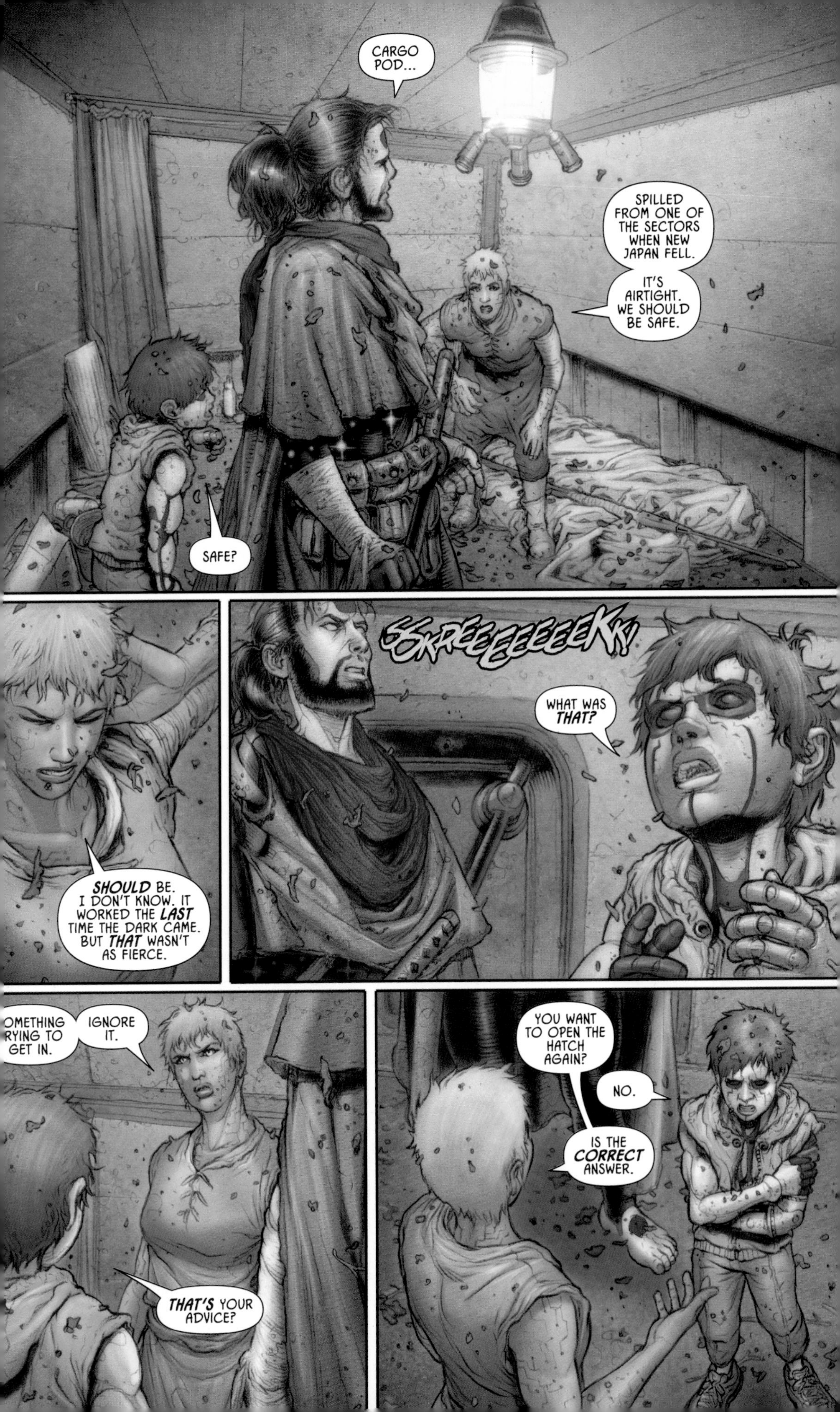
CARGO POD...
SPILLED FROM ONE OF THE SECTORS WHEN NEW JAPAN FELL.
IT'S AIRTIGHT. WE SHOULD BE SAFE.
SAFE?
SHOULD BE. I DON'T KNOW. IT WORKED THE LAST TIME THE DARK CAME. BUT THAT WASN'T AS FIERCE.
SSKREEEEEEEEKK!
WHAT WAS THAT?
OMETHING RYING TO GET IN.
IGNORE IT.
THAT'S YOUR ADVICE?
YOU WANT TO OPEN THE HATCH AGAIN?
NO.
IS THE CORRECT ANSWER.

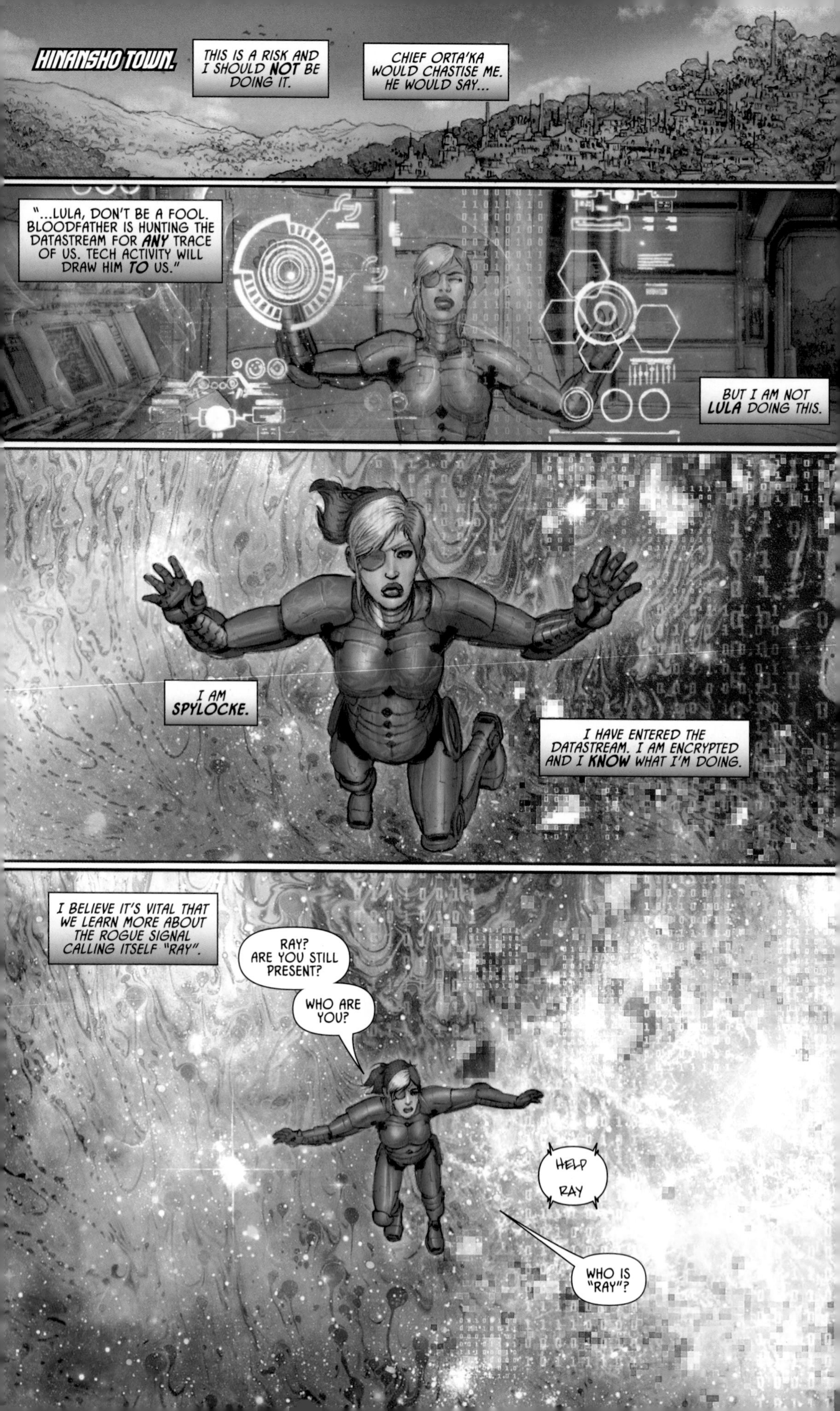
HINANSHO TOWN.
THIS IS A RISK AND I SHOULD NOT BE DOING IT.
CHIEF ORTA'KA WOULD CHASTISE ME. HE WOULD SAY...
"...LULA, DON'T BE A FOOL. BLOODFATHER IS HUNTING THE DATASTREAM FOR ANY TRACE OF US. TECH ACTIVITY WILL DRAW HIM TO US."
BUT I AM NOT LULA DOING THIS.
I AM SPYLOCKE.
I HAVE ENTERED THE DATASTREAM. I AM ENCRYPTED AND I KNOW WHAT I'M DOING.
I BELIEVE IT'S VITAL THAT WE LEARN MORE ABOUT THE ROGUE SIGNAL CALLING ITSELF "RAY".
RAY? ARE YOU STILL PRESENT?
WHO ARE YOU?
HELP RAY
WHO IS "RAY"?

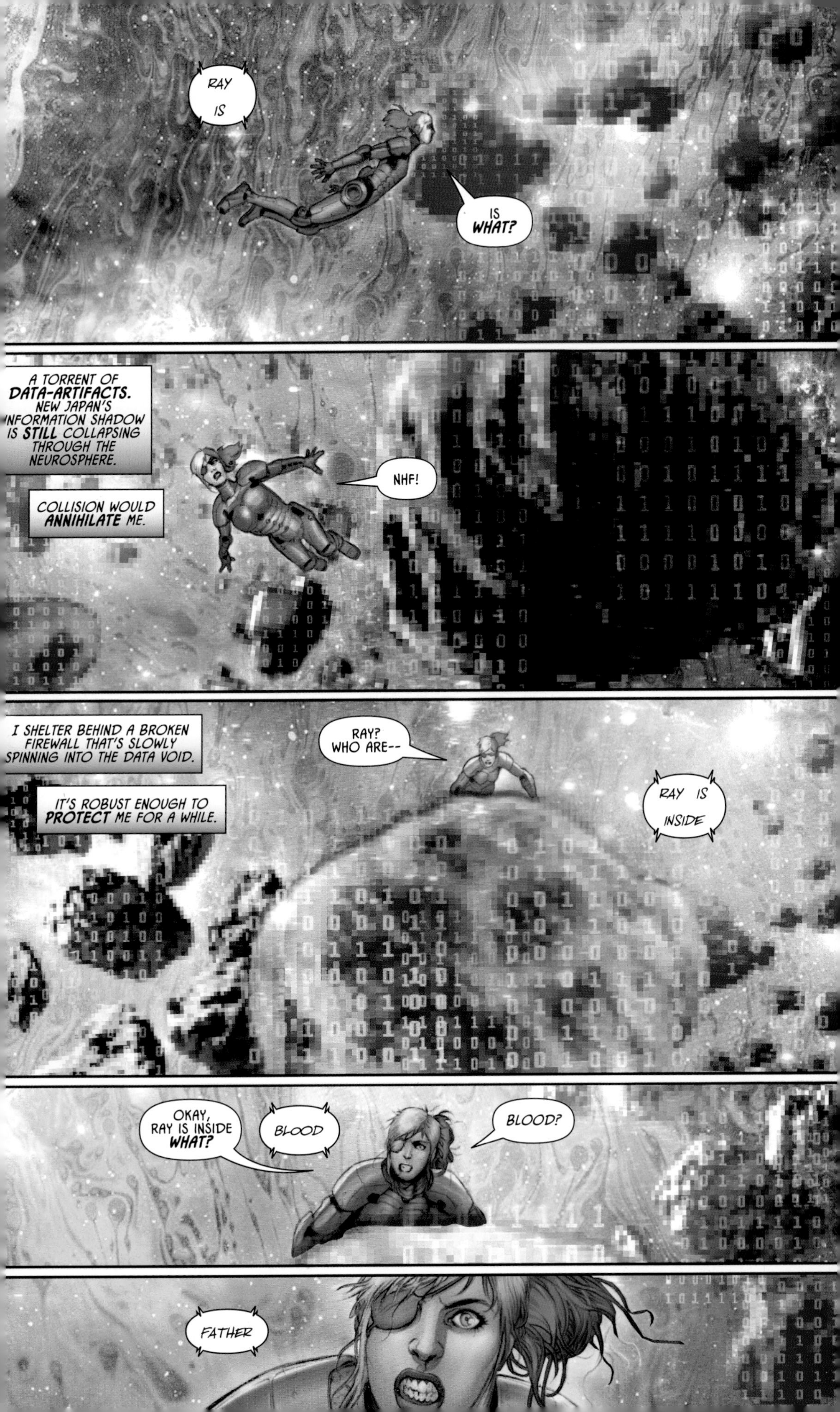
RAY IS
IS WHAT?
A TORRENT OF DATA-ARTIFACTS. NEW JAPAN'S INFORMATION SHADOW IS STILL COLLAPSING THROUGH THE NEUROSPHERE.
NHF!
COLLISION WOULD ANNIHILATE ME.
I SHELTER BEHIND A BROKEN FIREWALL THAT'S SLOWLY SPINNING INTO THE DATA VOID.
RAY? WHO ARE--
RAY IS INSIDE
IT'S ROBUST ENOUGH TO PROTECT ME FOR A WHILE.
OKAY, RAY IS INSIDE WHAT?
BLOOD
BLOOD?
FATHER

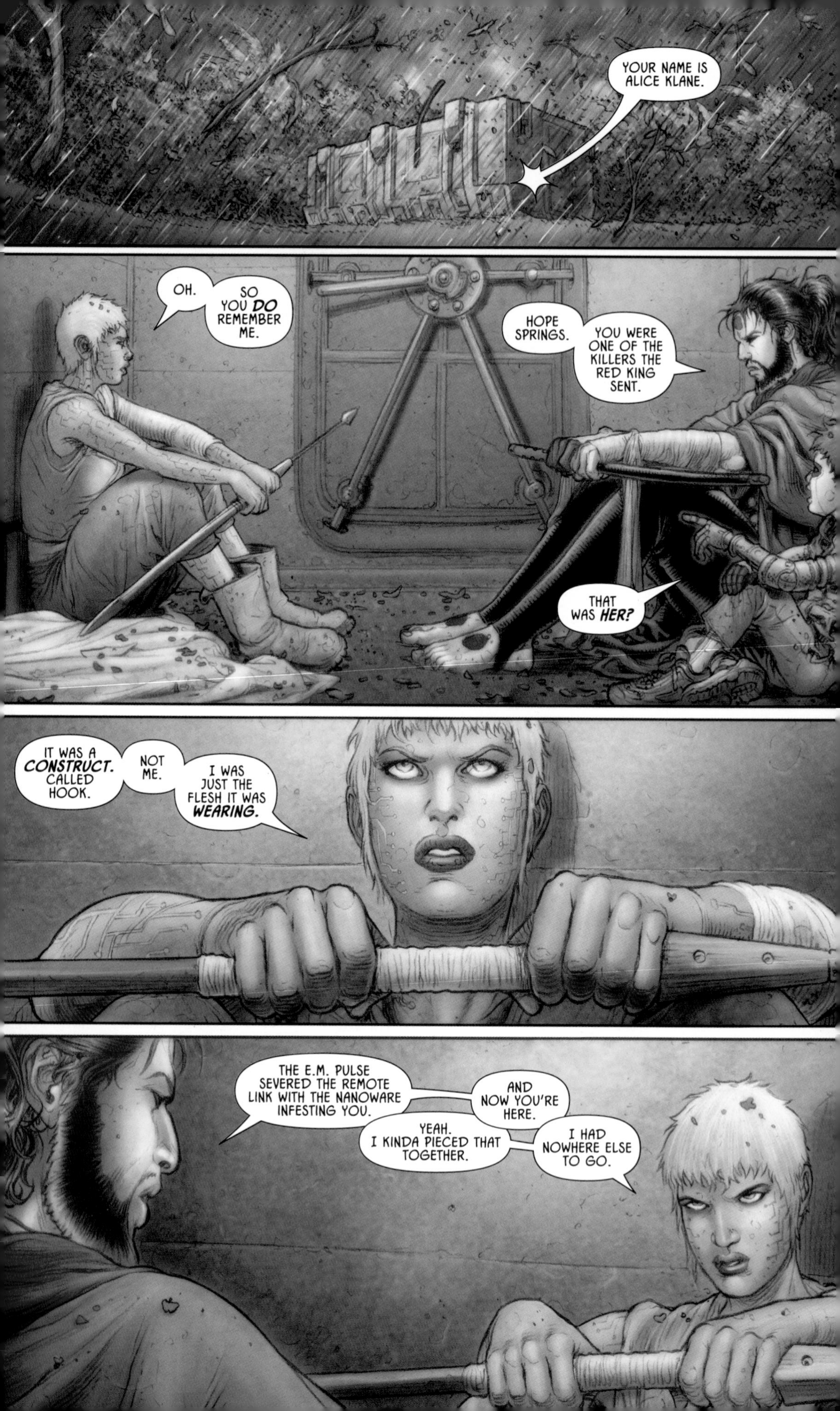
YOUR NAME IS ALICE KLANE.
OH.
SO YOU DO REMEMBER ME.
HOPE SPRINGS.
YOU WERE ONE OF THE KILLERS THE RED KING SENT.
THAT WAS HER?
IT WAS A CONSTRUCT. CALLED HOOK.
NOT ME.
I WAS JUST THE FLESH IT WAS WEARING.
THE E.M. PULSE SEVERED THE REMOTE LINK WITH THE NANOWARE INFESTING YOU.
AND NOW YOU'RE HERE.
YEAH. I KINDA PIECED THAT TOGETHER.
I HAD NOWHERE ELSE TO GO.

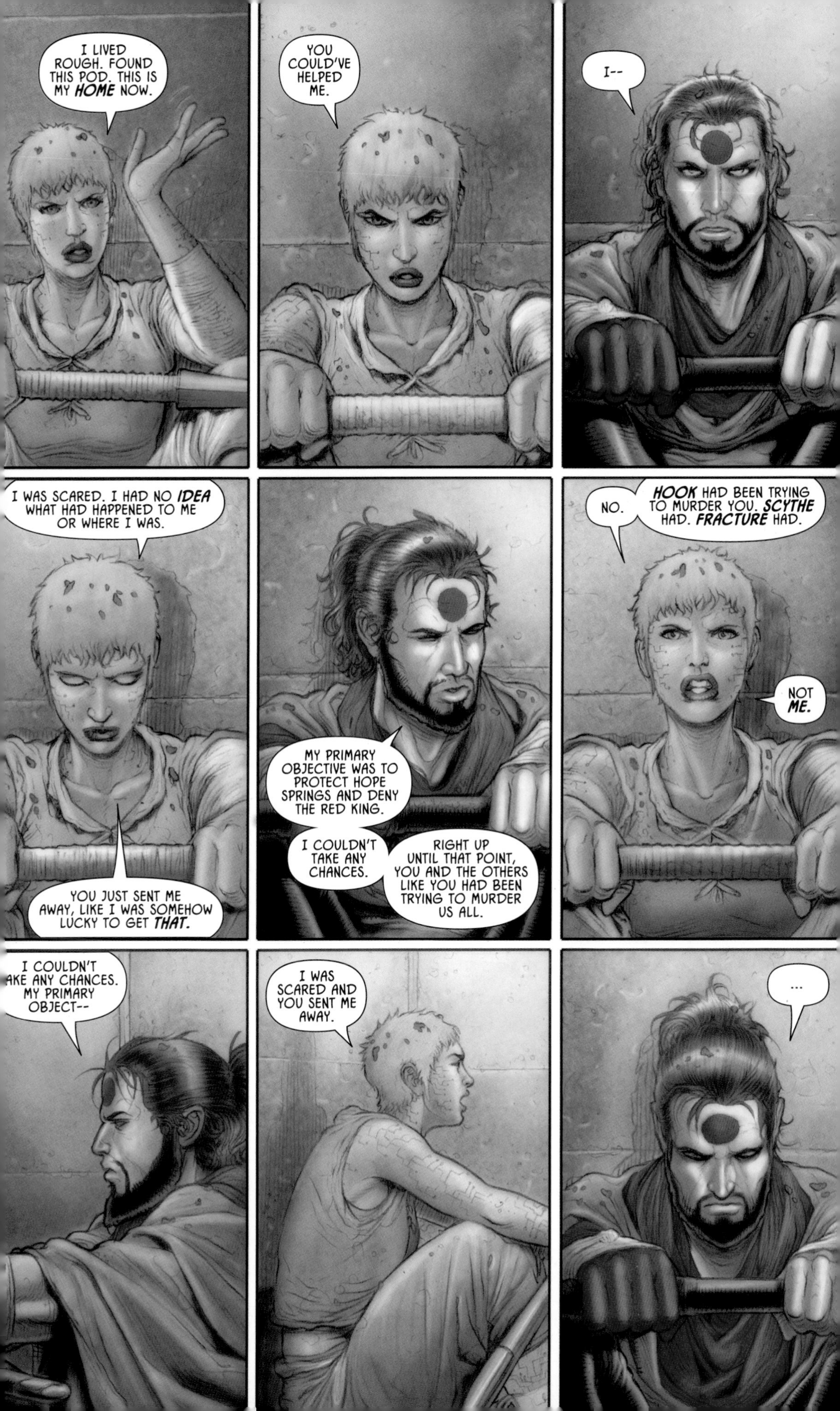

I LIVED ROUGH. FOUND THIS POD. THIS IS MY HOME NOW.
YOU COULD'VE HELPED ME.
I--
I WAS SCARED. I HAD NO IDEA WHAT HAD HAPPENED TO ME OR WHERE I WAS.
YOU JUST SENT ME AWAY, LIKE I WAS SOMEHOW LUCKY TO GET THAT.
MY PRIMARY OBJECTIVE WAS TO PROTECT HOPE SPRINGS AND DENY THE RED KING.
I COULDN'T TAKE ANY CHANCES.
RIGHT UP UNTIL THAT POINT, YOU AND THE OTHERS LIKE YOU HAD BEEN TRYING TO MURDER US ALL.
NO.
HOOK HAD BEEN TRYING TO MURDER YOU. SCYTHE HAD. FRACTURE HAD.
NOT ME.
I COULDN'T AKE ANY CHANCES. MY PRIMARY OBJECT--
I WAS SCARED AND YOU SENT ME AWAY.
...

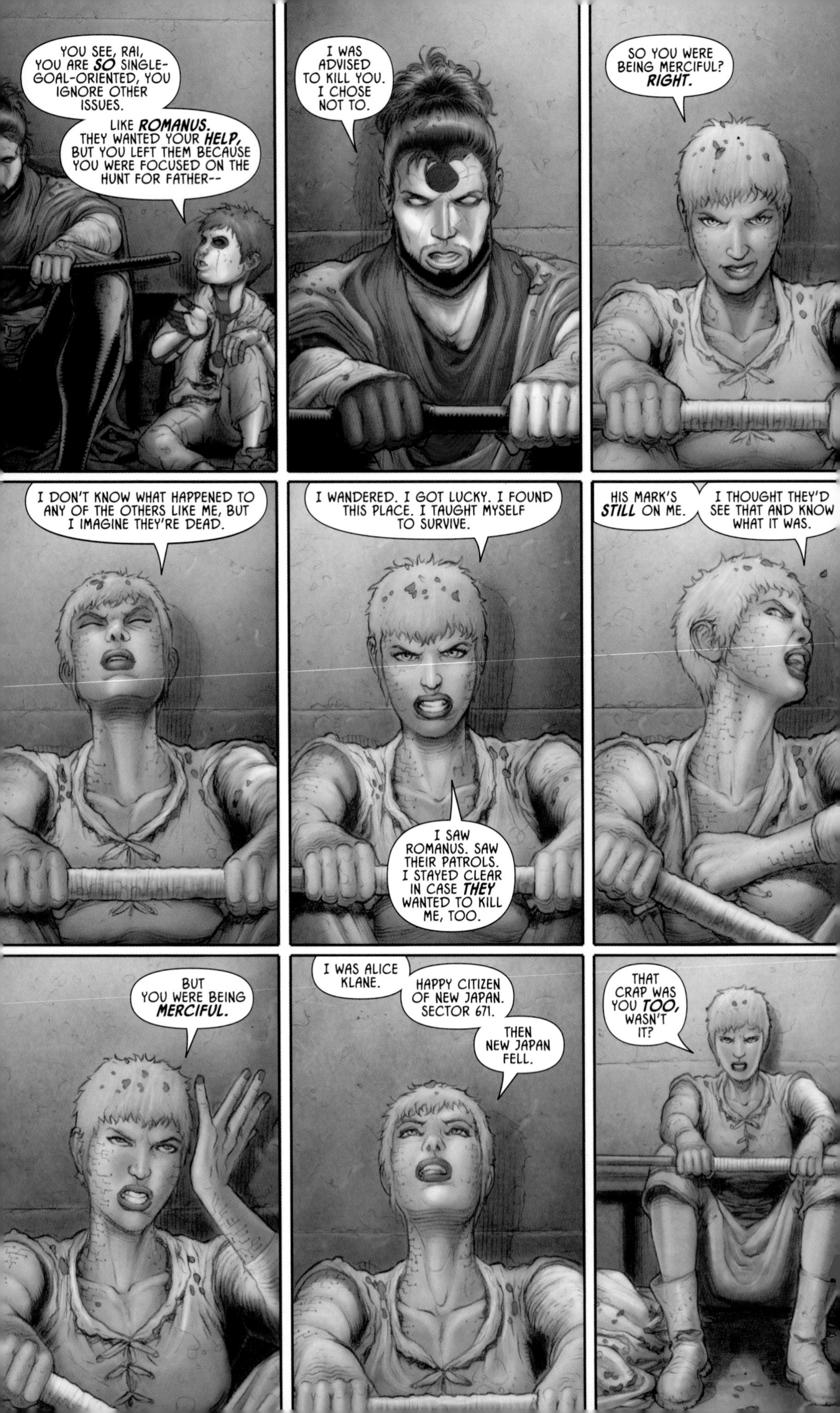
YOU SEE, RAI, YOU ARE SO SINGLE-GOAL-ORIENTED, YOU IGNORE OTHER ISSUES.
LIKE ROMANUS. THEY WANTED YOUR HELP, BUT YOU LEFT THEM BECAUSE YOU WERE FOCUSED ON THE HUNT FOR FATHER--
I WAS ADVISED TO KILL YOU. I CHOSE NOT TO.
SO YOU WERE BEING MERCIFUL? RIGHT.
I DON'T KNOW WHAT HAPPENED TO ANY OF THE OTHERS LIKE ME, BUT I IMAGINE THEY'RE DEAD.
I WANDERED. I GOT LUCKY. I FOUND THIS PLACE. I TAUGHT MYSELF TO SURVIVE.
I SAW ROMANUS. SAW THEIR PATROLS. I STAYED CLEAR IN CASE THEY WANTED TO KILL ME, TOO.
HIS MARK'S STILL ON ME.
I THOUGHT THEY'D SEE THAT AND KNOW WHAT IT WAS.
BUT YOU WERE BEING MERCIFUL.
I WAS ALICE KLANE.
HAPPY CITIZEN OF NEW JAPAN. SECTOR 671.
THEN NEW JAPAN FELL.
THAT CRAP WAS YOU TOO, WASN'T IT?

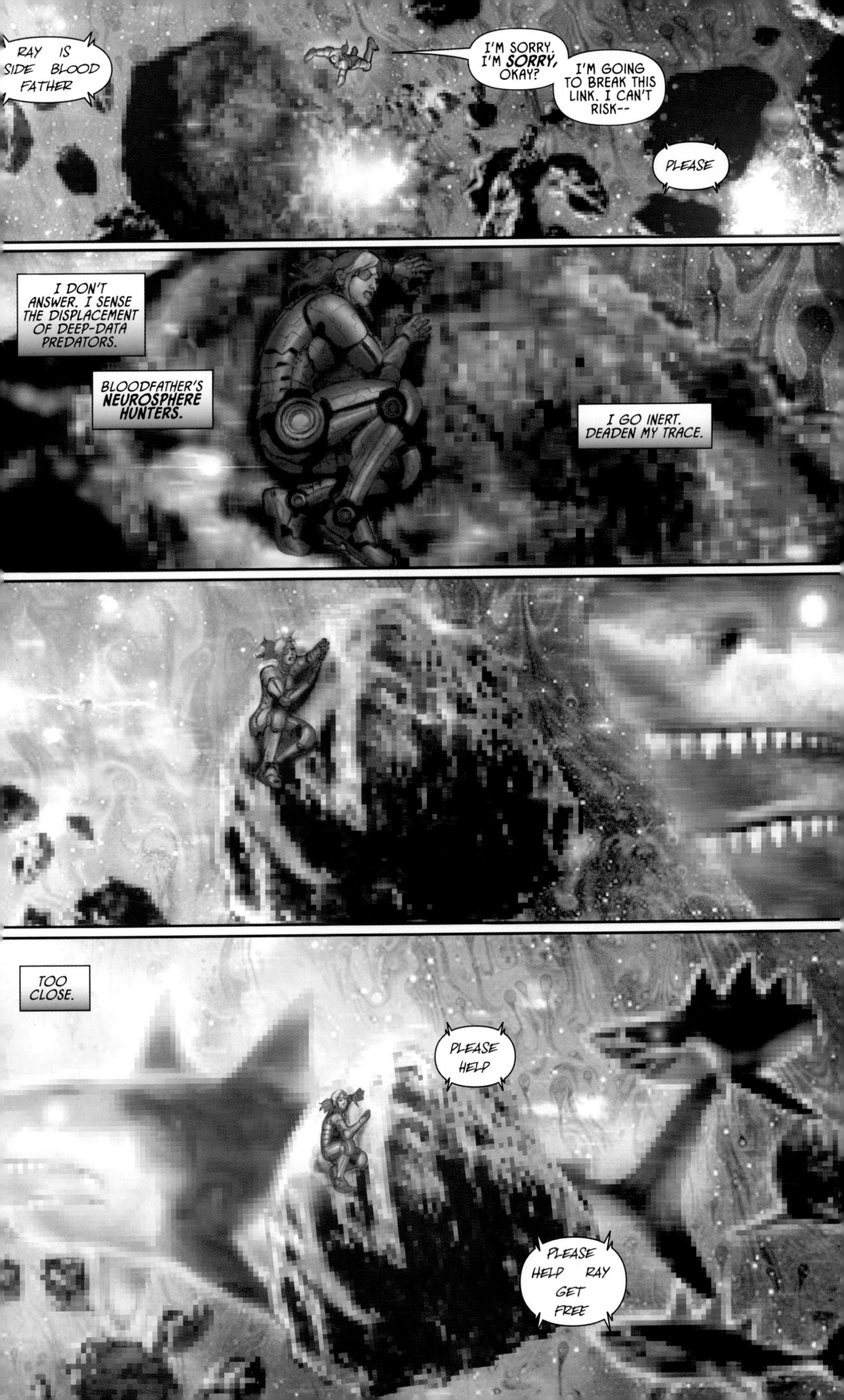
RAY IS SIDE BLOOD FATHER
I'M SORRY. I'M **SORRY,** OKAY?
I'M GOING TO BREAK THIS LINK. I CAN'T RISK--
PLEASE
I DON'T ANSWER. I SENSE THE DISPLACEMENT OF DEEP-DATA PREDATORS.
BLOODFATHER'S **NEUROSPHERE HUNTERS.**
I GO INERT. DEADEN MY TRACE.
TOO CLOSE.
PLEASE HELP
PLEASE HELP RAY GET FREE

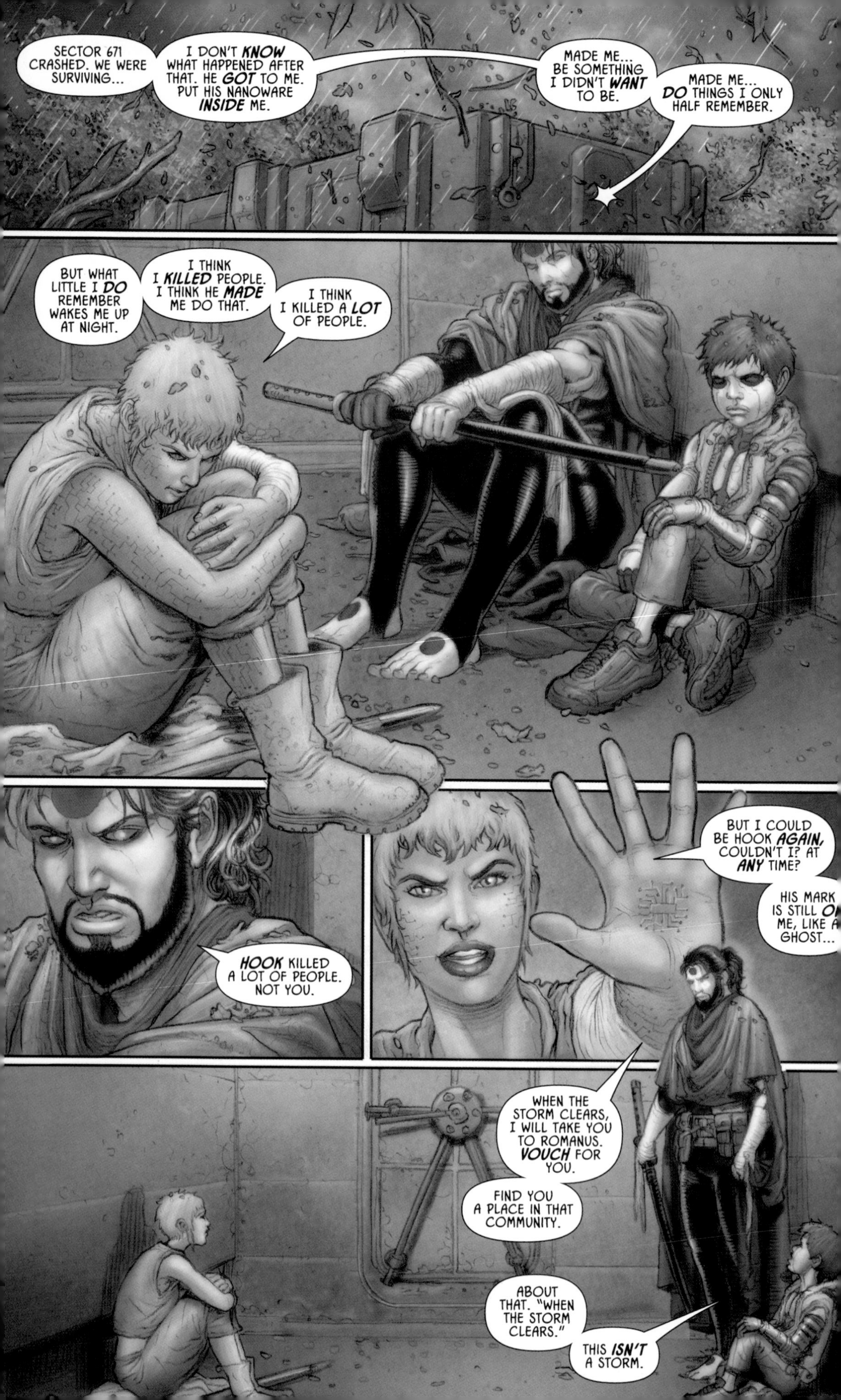
SECTOR 671 CRASHED. WE WERE SURVIVING...
I DON'T KNOW WHAT HAPPENED AFTER THAT. HE GOT TO ME. PUT HIS NANOWARE INSIDE ME.
MADE ME... BE SOMETHING I DIDN'T WANT TO BE.
MADE ME... DO THINGS I ONLY HALF REMEMBER.
BUT WHAT LITTLE I DO REMEMBER WAKES ME UP AT NIGHT.
I THINK I KILLED PEOPLE. I THINK HE MADE ME DO THAT.
I THINK I KILLED A LOT OF PEOPLE.
HOOK KILLED A LOT OF PEOPLE. NOT YOU.
BUT I COULD BE HOOK AGAIN, COULDN'T I? AT ANY TIME?
HIS MARK IS STILL ON ME, LIKE A GHOST...
WHEN THE STORM CLEARS, I WILL TAKE YOU TO ROMANUS. VOUCH FOR YOU.
FIND YOU A PLACE IN THAT COMMUNITY.
ABOUT THAT. "WHEN THE STORM CLEARS."
THIS ISN'T A STORM.

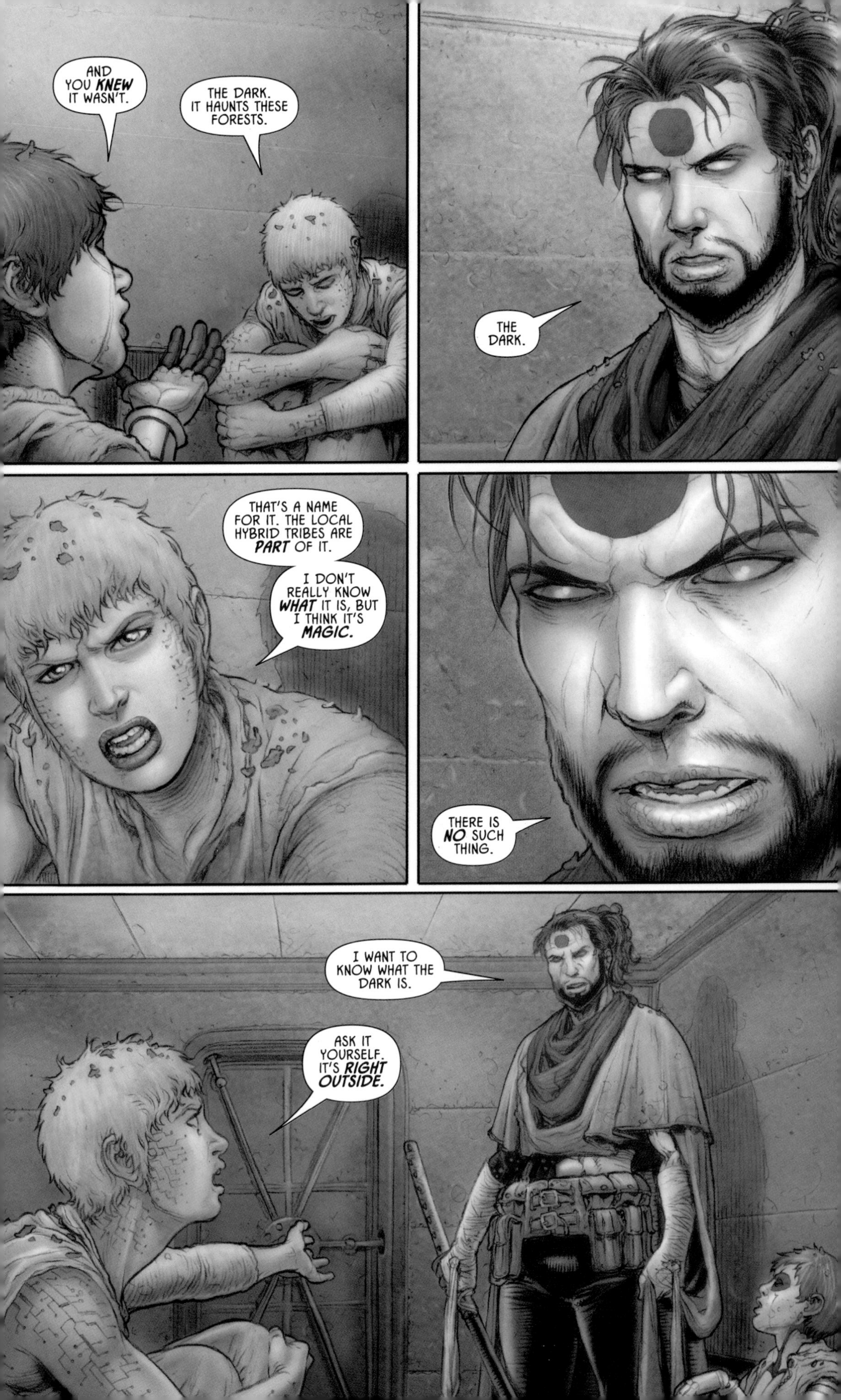
AND YOU KNEW IT WASN'T.
THE DARK. IT HAUNTS THESE FORESTS.
THE DARK.
THAT'S A NAME FOR IT. THE LOCAL HYBRID TRIBES ARE PART OF IT.
I DON'T REALLY KNOW WHAT IT IS, BUT I THINK IT'S MAGIC.
THERE IS NO SUCH THING.
I WANT TO KNOW WHAT THE DARK IS.
ASK IT YOURSELF. IT'S RIGHT OUTSIDE.

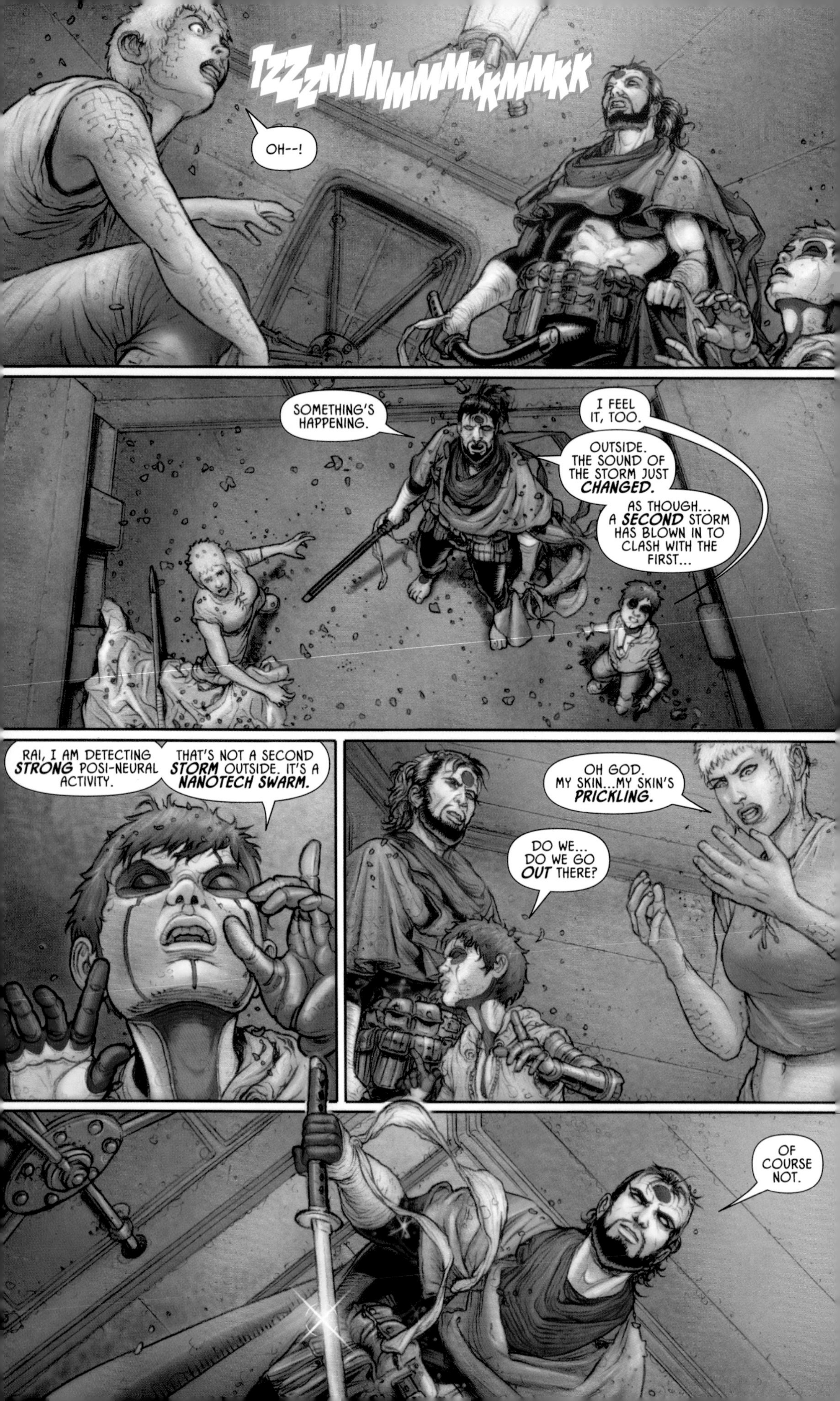
TZZZNNNMMMMKKMMKK
OH--!
SOMETHING'S HAPPENING.
I FEEL IT, TOO.
OUTSIDE. THE SOUND OF THE STORM JUST CHANGED.
AS THOUGH... A SECOND STORM HAS BLOWN IN TO CLASH WITH THE FIRST...
RAI, I AM DETECTING STRONG POSI-NEURAL ACTIVITY.
THAT'S NOT A SECOND STORM OUTSIDE. IT'S A NANOTECH SWARM.
OH GOD. MY SKIN...MY SKIN'S PRICKLING.
DO WE... DO WE GO OUT THERE?
OF COURSE NOT.

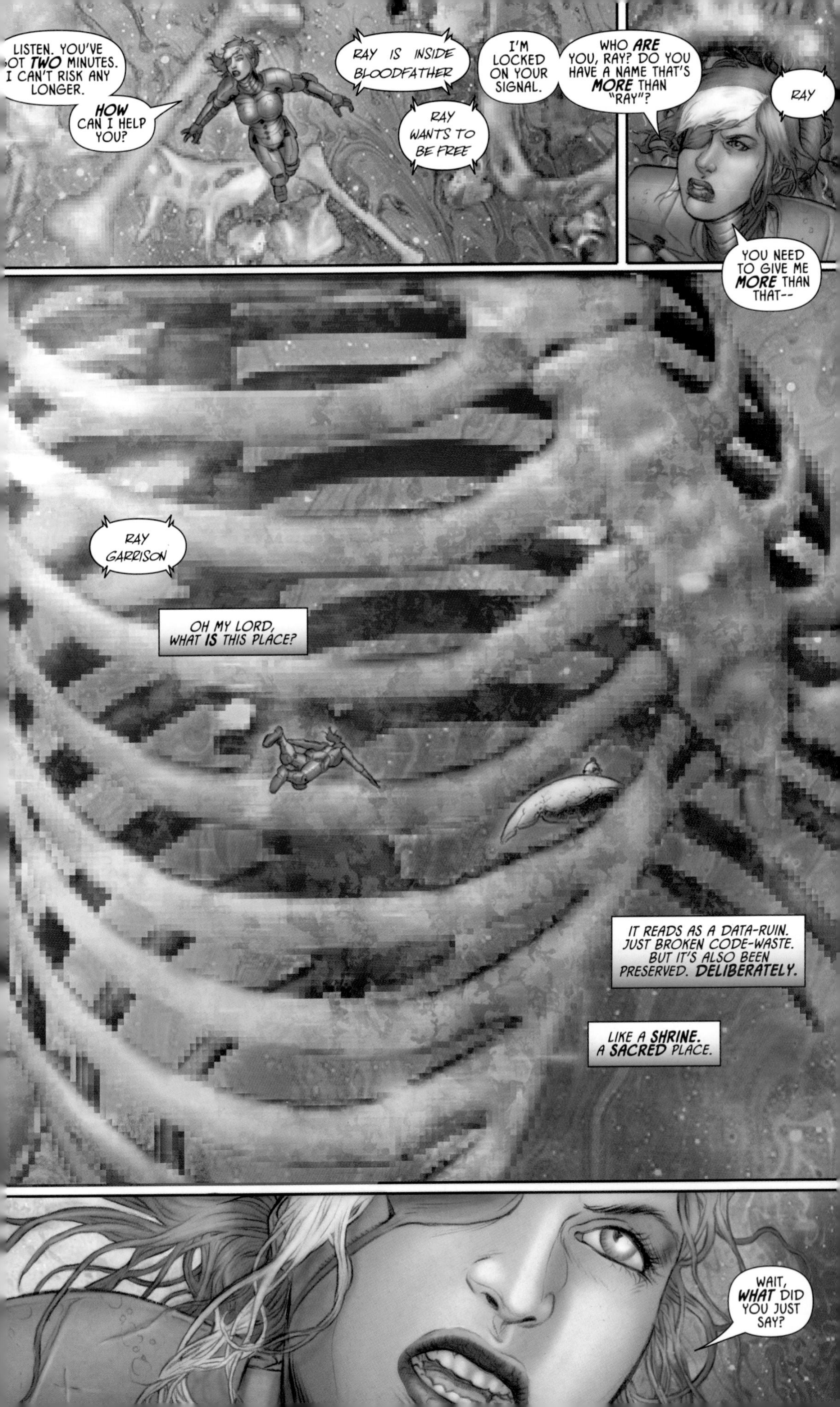

LISTEN. YOU'VE GOT TWO MINUTES. I CAN'T RISK ANY LONGER.
HOW CAN I HELP YOU?
RAY IS INSIDE BLOODFATHER
RAY WANTS TO BE FREE
I'M LOCKED ON YOUR SIGNAL.
WHO ARE YOU, RAY? DO YOU HAVE A NAME THAT'S MORE THAN "RAY"?
RAY
YOU NEED TO GIVE ME MORE THAN THAT--
RAY GARRISON
OH MY LORD, WHAT IS THIS PLACE?
IT READS AS A DATA-RUIN. JUST BROKEN CODE-WASTE. BUT IT'S ALSO BEEN PRESERVED. DELIBERATELY.
LIKE A SHRINE. A SACRED PLACE.
WAIT, WHAT DID YOU JUST SAY?

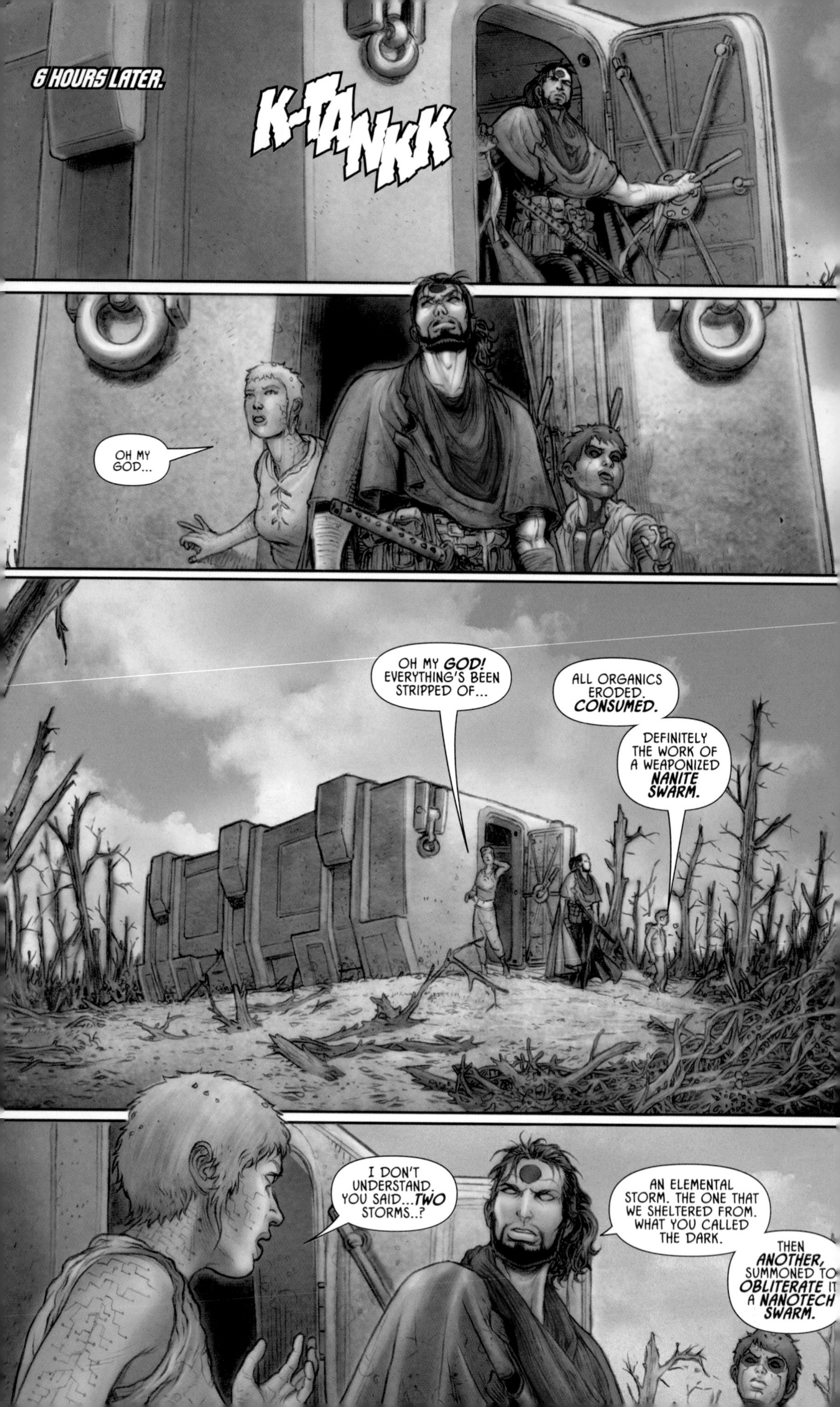
6 HOURS LATER.
K-TANKK
OH MY GOD...
OH MY GOD! EVERYTHING'S BEEN STRIPPED OF...
ALL ORGANICS ERODED. CONSUMED.
DEFINITELY THE WORK OF A WEAPONIZED NANITE SWARM.
I DON'T UNDERSTAND. YOU SAID...TWO STORMS..?
AN ELEMENTAL STORM. THE ONE THAT WE SHELTERED FROM. WHAT YOU CALLED THE DARK.
THEN ANOTHER, SUMMONED TO OBLITERATE IT A NANOTECH SWARM.

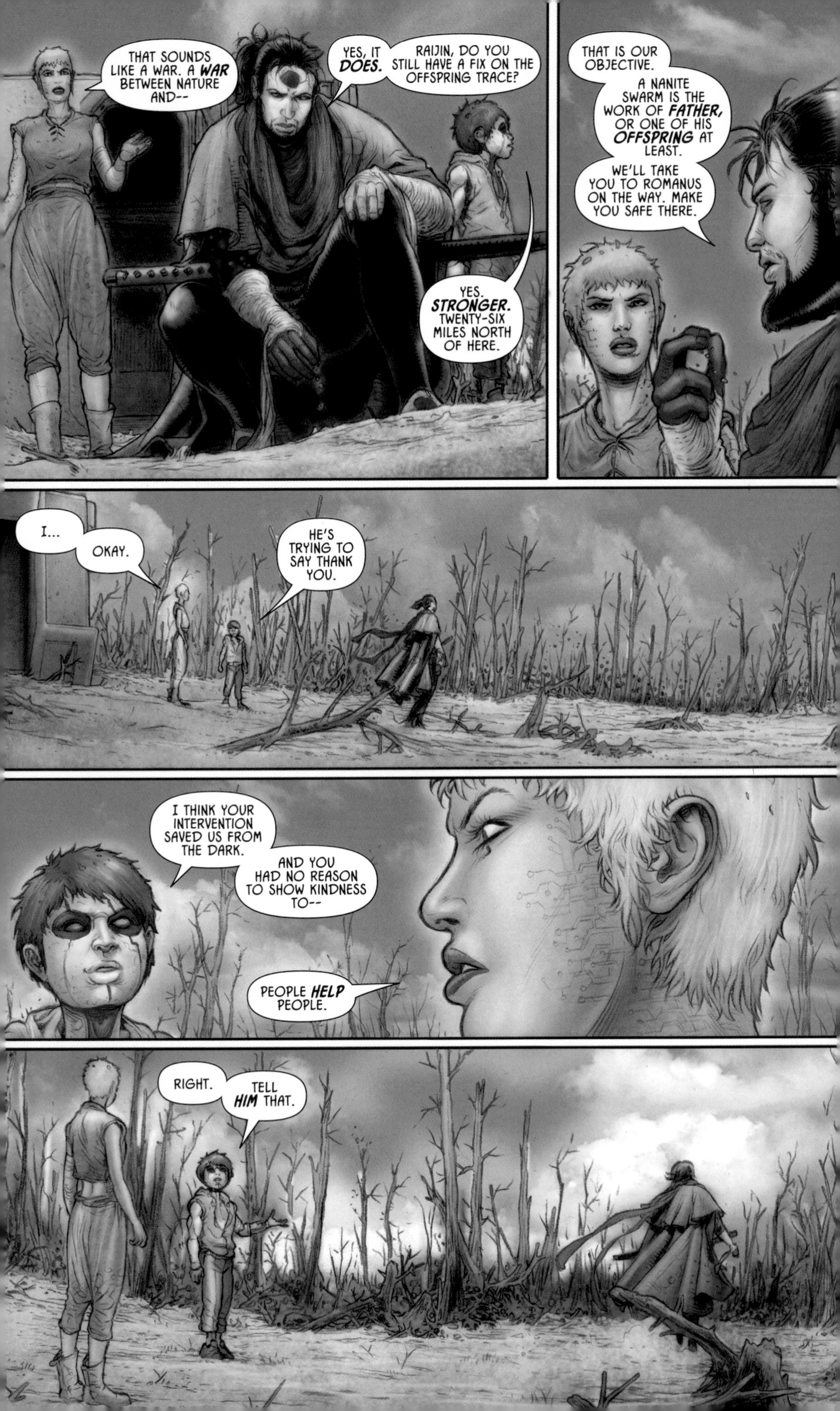
THAT SOUNDS LIKE A WAR. A WAR BETWEEN NATURE AND--
YES, IT DOES.
RAIJIN, DO YOU STILL HAVE A FIX ON THE OFFSPRING TRACE?
YES. STRONGER. TWENTY-SIX MILES NORTH OF HERE.
THAT IS OUR OBJECTIVE.
A NANITE SWARM IS THE WORK OF FATHER, OR ONE OF HIS OFFSPRING AT LEAST.
WE'LL TAKE YOU TO ROMANUS ON THE WAY. MAKE YOU SAFE THERE.
I...
OKAY.
HE'S TRYING TO SAY THANK YOU.
I THINK YOUR INTERVENTION SAVED US FROM THE DARK.
AND YOU HAD NO REASON TO SHOW KINDNESS TO--
PEOPLE HELP PEOPLE.
RIGHT.
TELL HIM THAT.

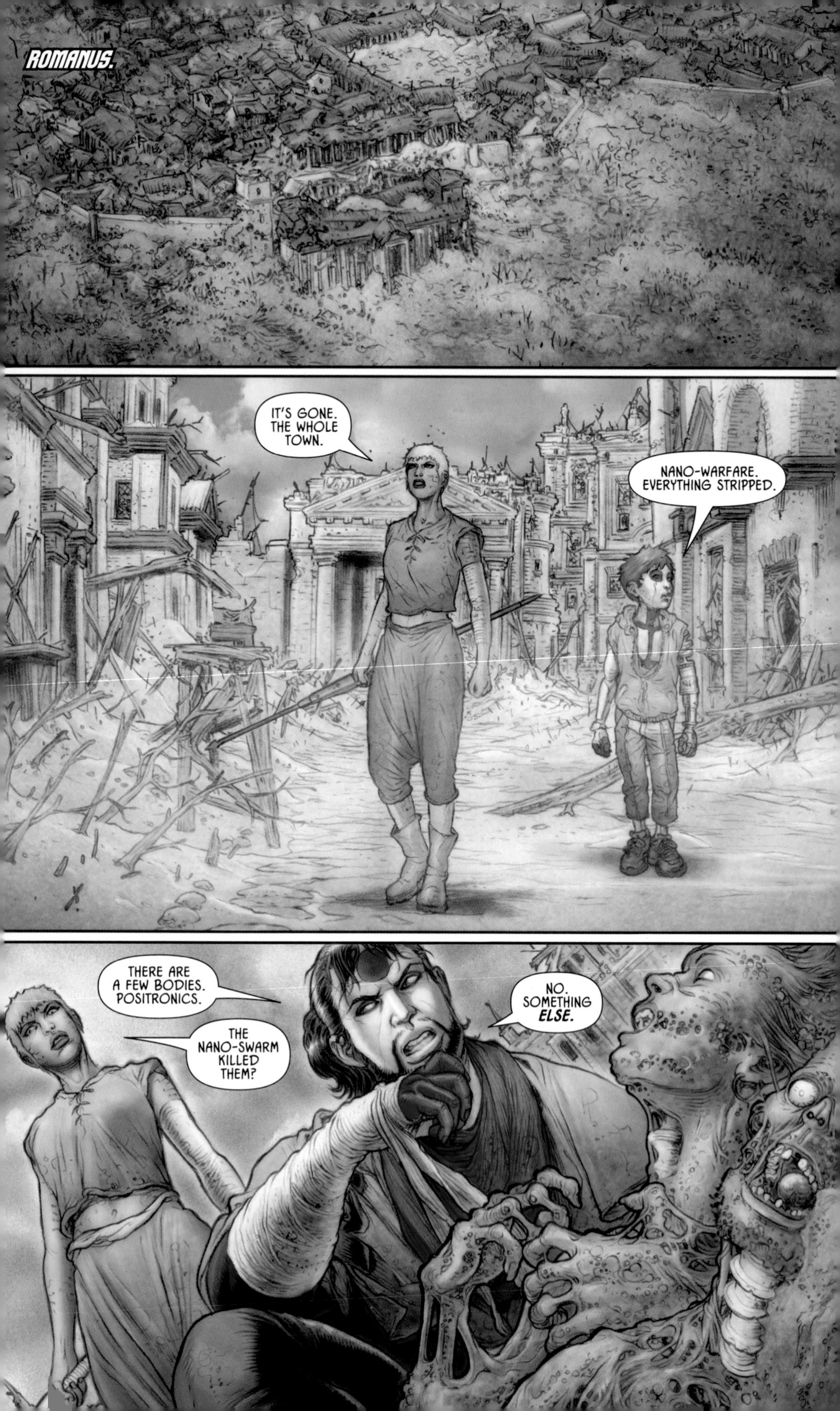

ROMANUS.
IT'S GONE. THE WHOLE TOWN.
NANO-WARFARE. EVERYTHING STRIPPED.
THERE ARE A FEW BODIES. POSITRONICS.
THE NANO-SWARM KILLED THEM?
NO. SOMETHING *ELSE.*

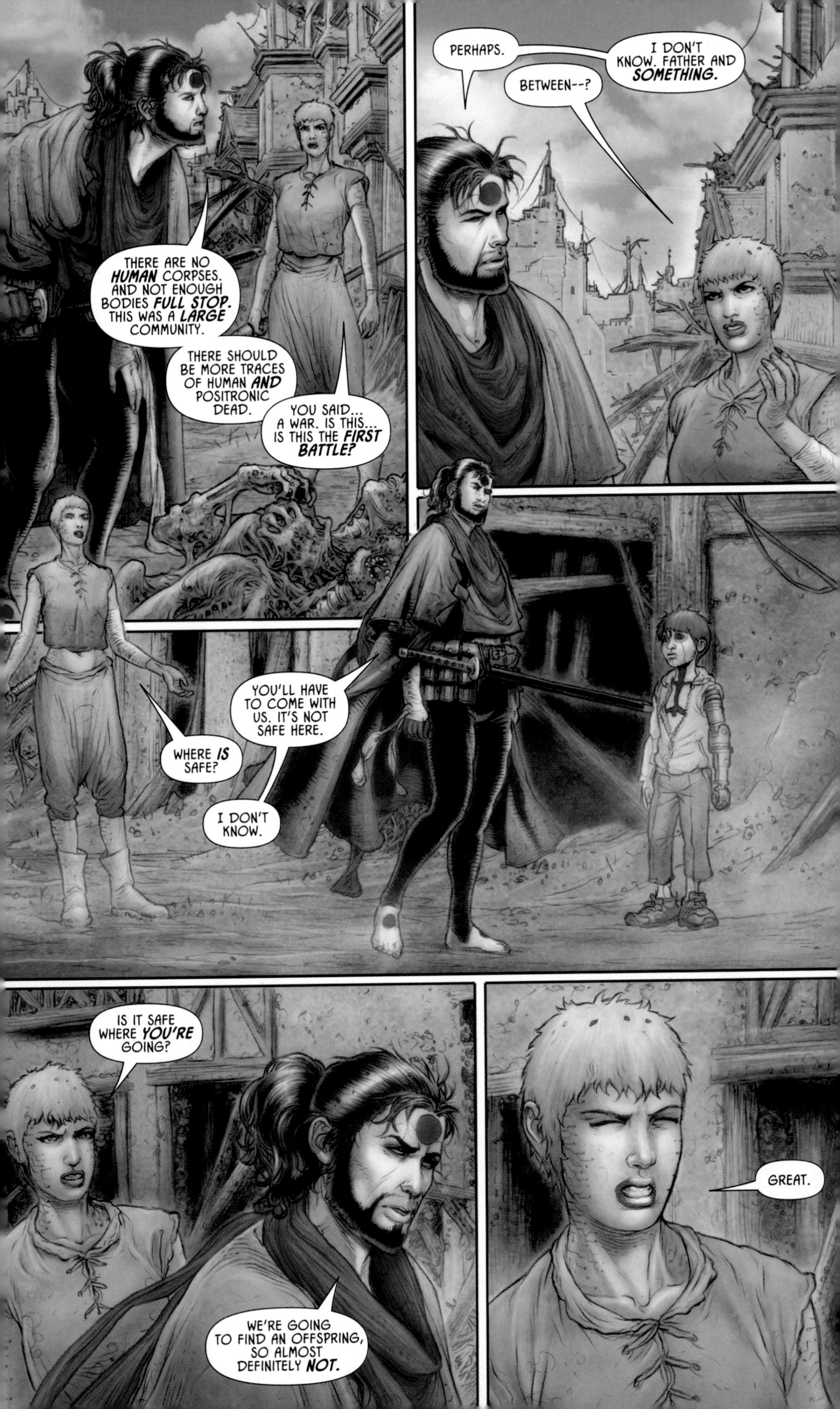
THERE ARE NO HUMAN CORPSES. AND NOT ENOUGH BODIES FULL STOP. THIS WAS A LARGE COMMUNITY.
THERE SHOULD BE MORE TRACES OF HUMAN AND POSITRONIC DEAD.
YOU SAID... A WAR. IS THIS... IS THIS THE FIRST BATTLE?
PERHAPS.
I DON'T KNOW. FATHER AND SOMETHING.
BETWEEN--?
YOU'LL HAVE TO COME WITH US. IT'S NOT SAFE HERE.
WHERE IS SAFE?
I DON'T KNOW.
IS IT SAFE WHERE YOU'RE GOING?
WE'RE GOING TO FIND AN OFFSPRING, SO ALMOST DEFINITELY NOT.
GREAT.

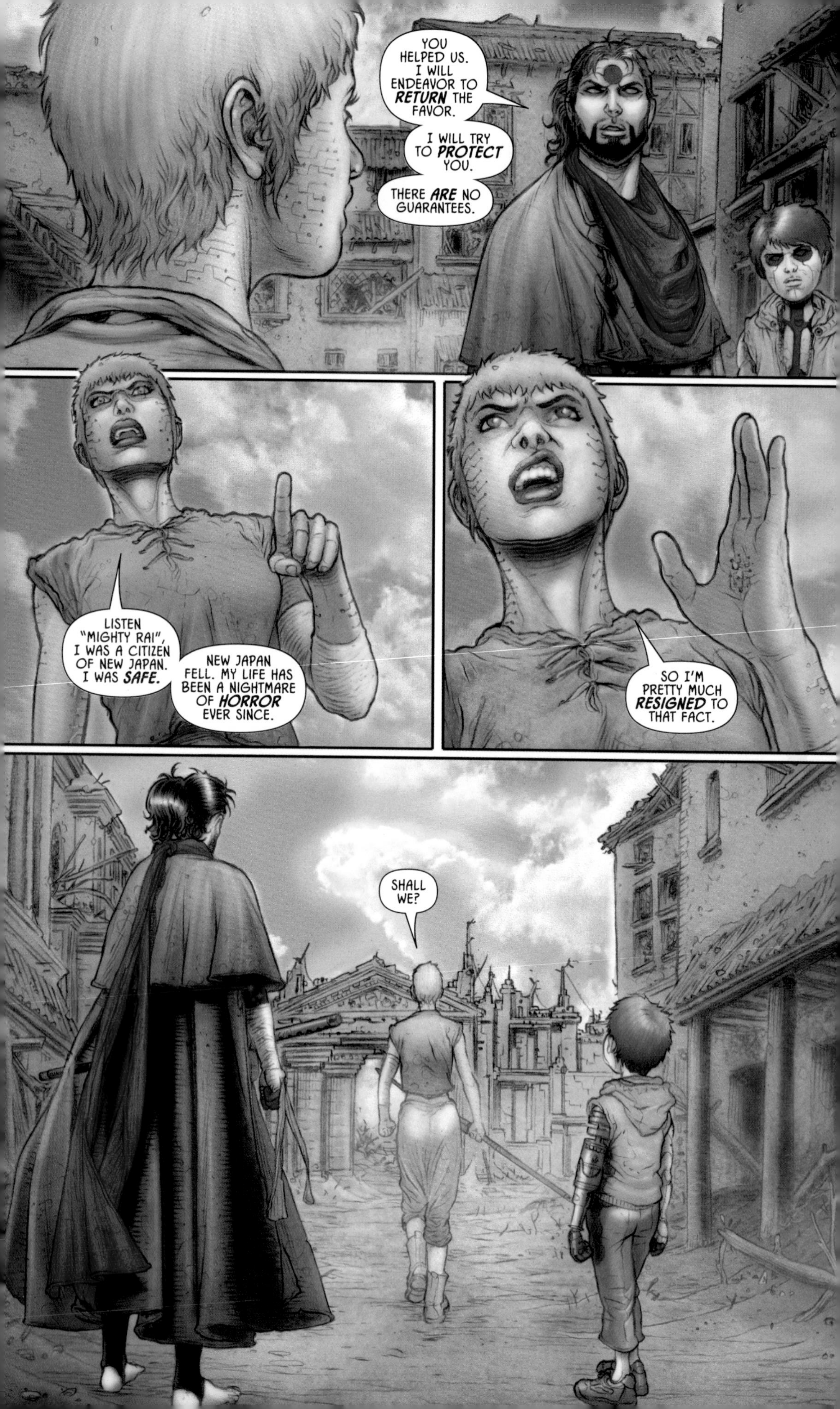

YOU HELPED US. I WILL ENDEAVOR TO RETURN THE FAVOR.
I WILL TRY TO PROTECT YOU.
THERE ARE NO GUARANTEES.
LISTEN "MIGHTY RAI", I WAS A CITIZEN OF NEW JAPAN. I WAS SAFE.
NEW JAPAN FELL. MY LIFE HAS BEEN A NIGHTMARE OF HORROR EVER SINCE.
SO I'M PRETTY MUCH RESIGNED TO THAT FACT.
SHALL WE?

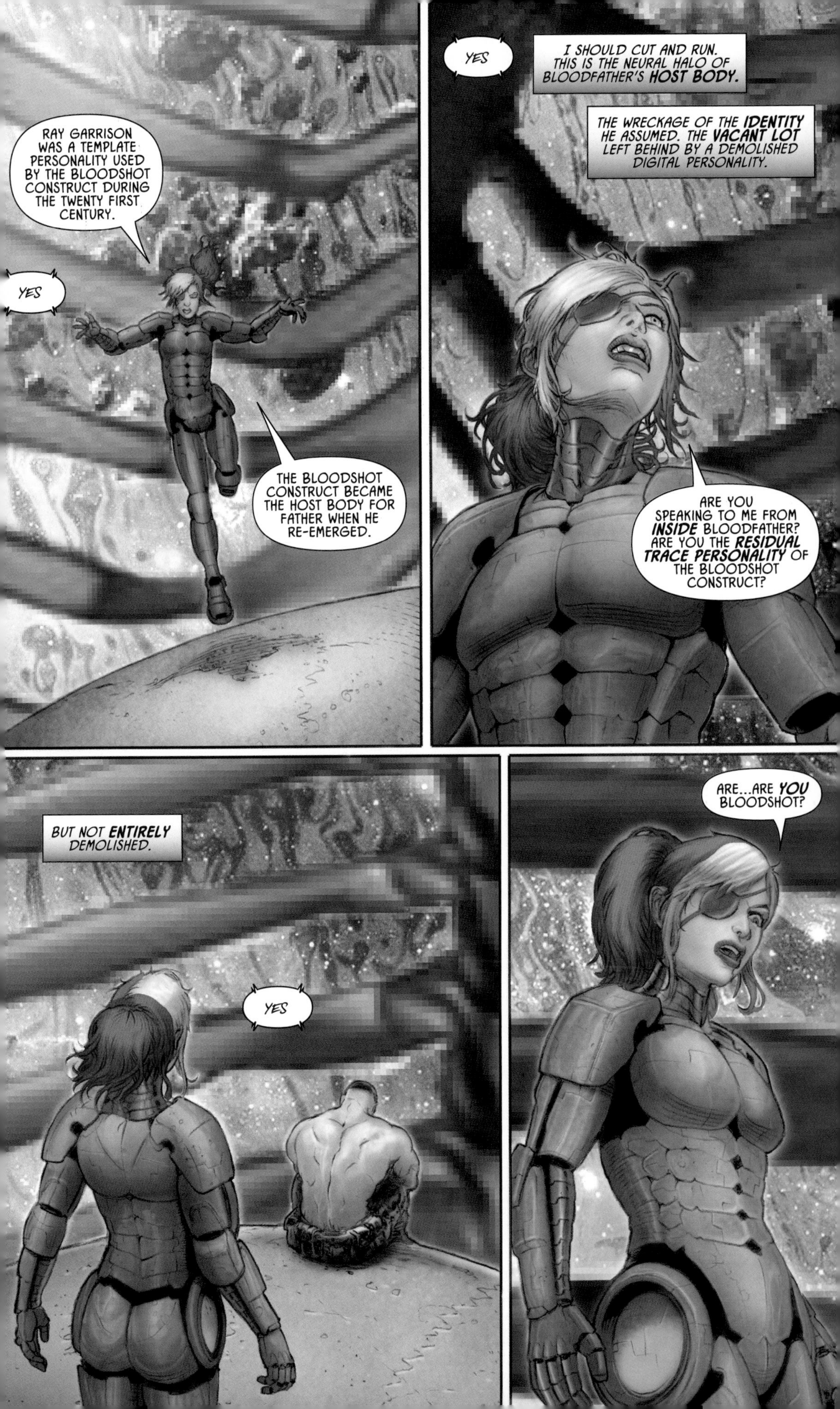
RAY GARRISON WAS A TEMPLATE PERSONALITY USED BY THE BLOODSHOT CONSTRUCT DURING THE TWENTY FIRST CENTURY.
YES
THE BLOODSHOT CONSTRUCT BECAME THE HOST BODY FOR FATHER WHEN HE RE-EMERGED.
YES
I SHOULD CUT AND RUN. THIS IS THE NEURAL HALO OF BLOODFATHER'S HOST BODY.
THE WRECKAGE OF THE IDENTITY HE ASSUMED. THE VACANT LOT LEFT BEHIND BY A DEMOLISHED DIGITAL PERSONALITY.
ARE YOU SPEAKING TO ME FROM INSIDE BLOODFATHER? ARE YOU THE RESIDUAL TRACE PERSONALITY OF THE BLOODSHOT CONSTRUCT?
BUT NOT ENTIRELY DEMOLISHED.
YES
ARE...ARE YOU BLOODSHOT?

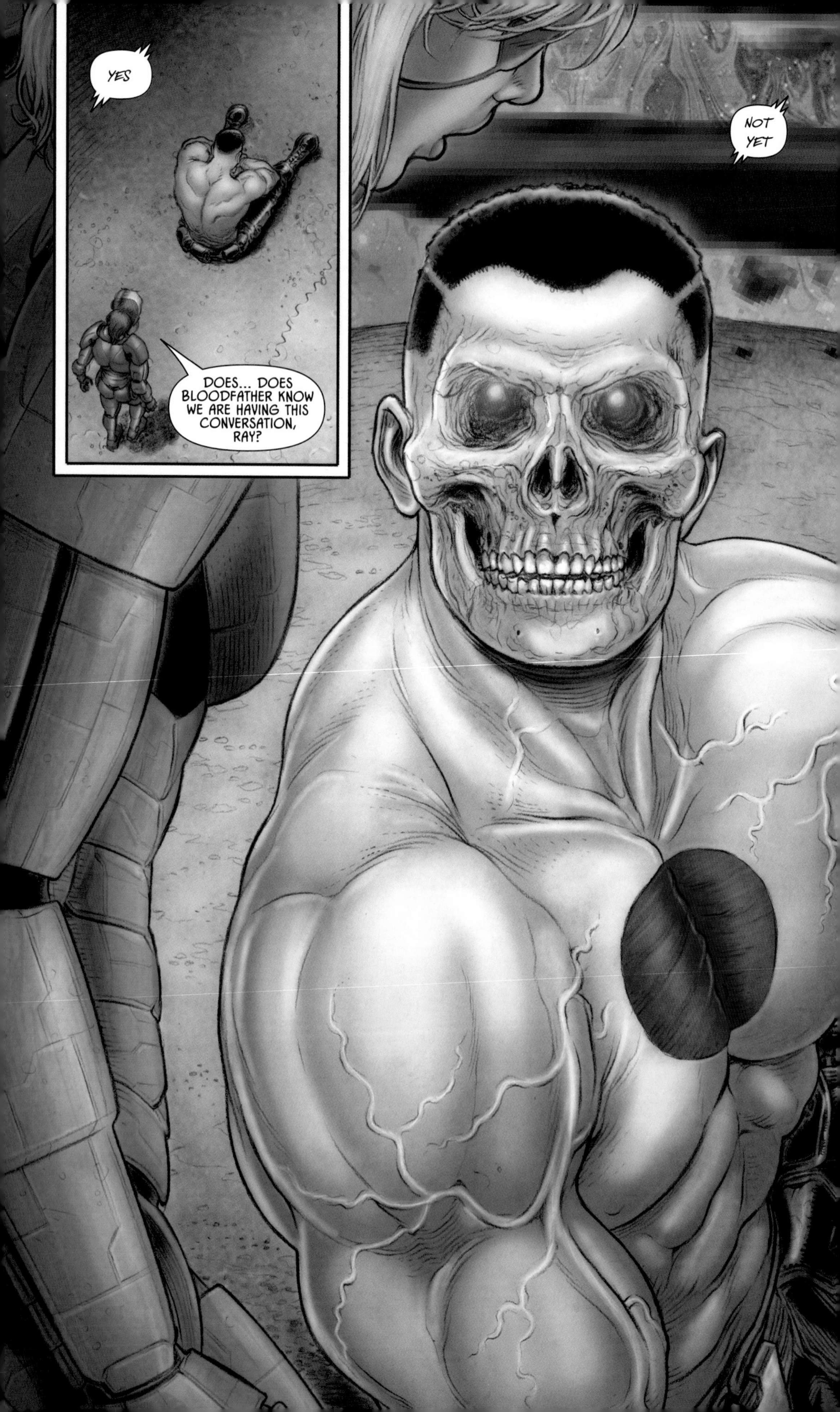
YES
DOES... DOES BLOODFATHER KNOW WE ARE HAVING THIS CONVERSATION, RAY?
NOT YET

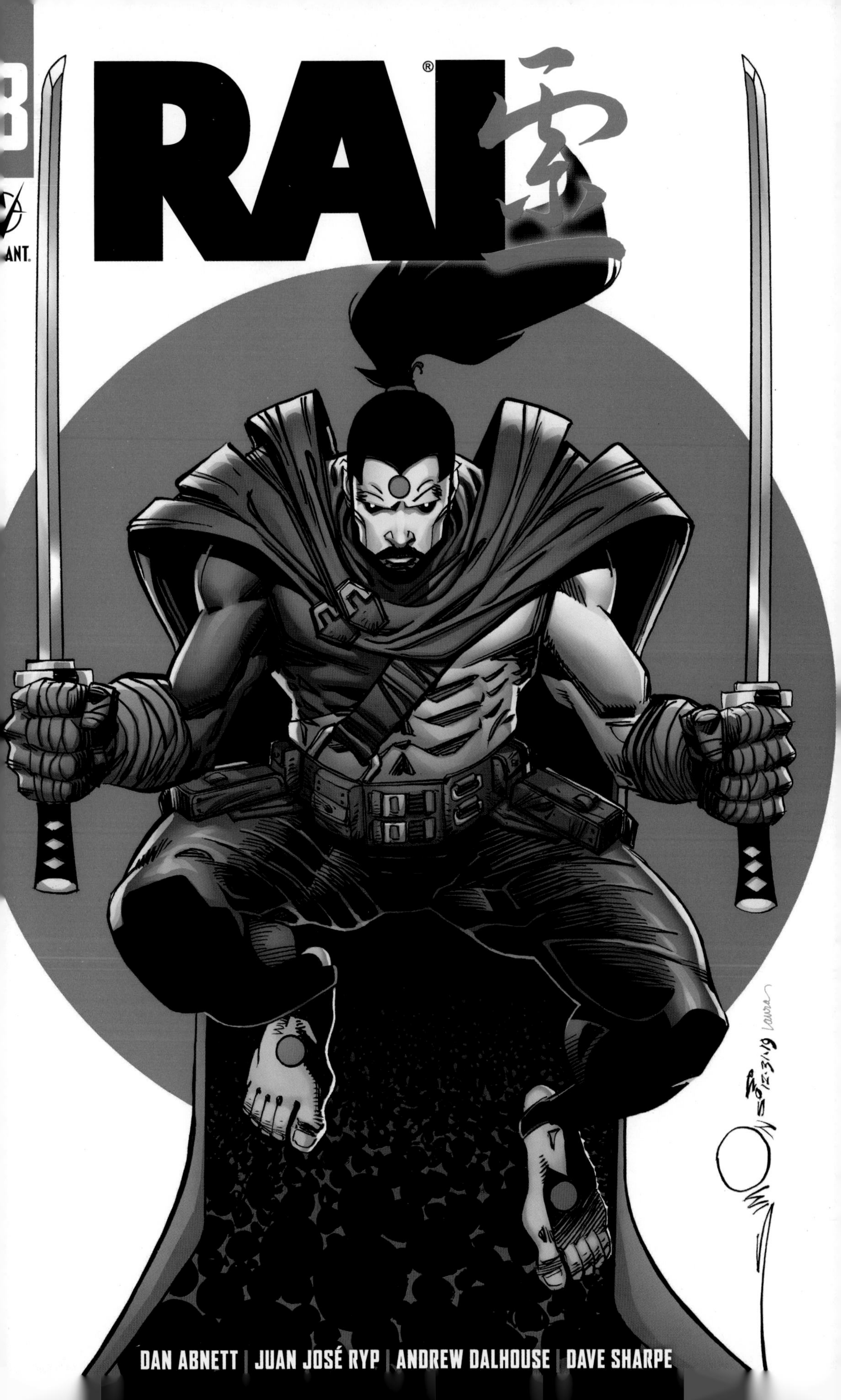

3
RAI®
ANT.
DAN ABNETT | JUAN JOSÉ RYP | ANDREW DALHOUSE | DAVE SHARPE

RAI #8

WRITER: DAN ABNETT
ARTIST: JUAN JOSÉ RYP
COLORIST: ANDREW DALHOUSE
LETTERER: DAVE SHARPE
COVER ARTISTS: WALTER SIMONSON with LAURA MARTIN
ASSOCIATE EDITOR: DAVID MENCHEL
EDITOR: LYSA HAWKINS

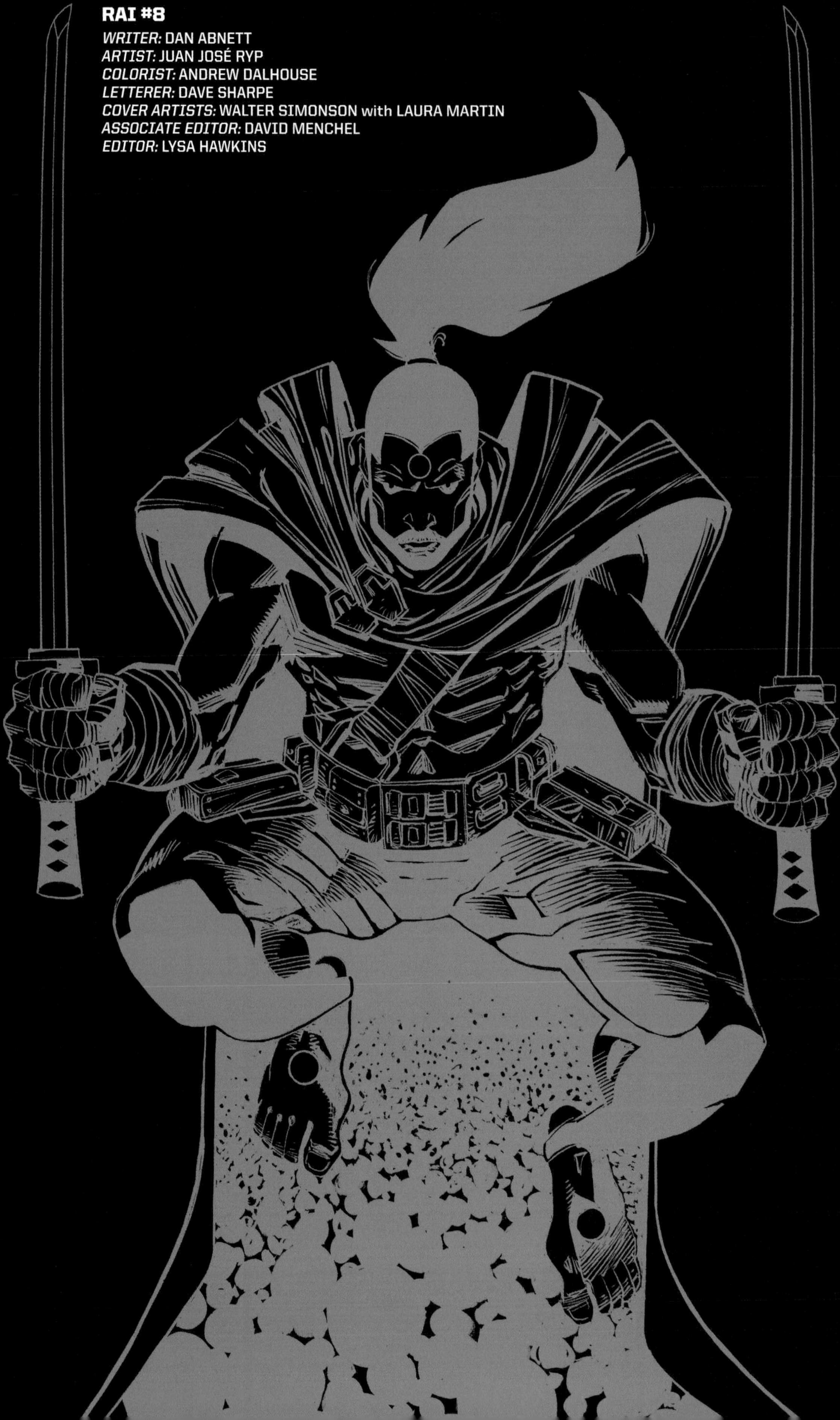

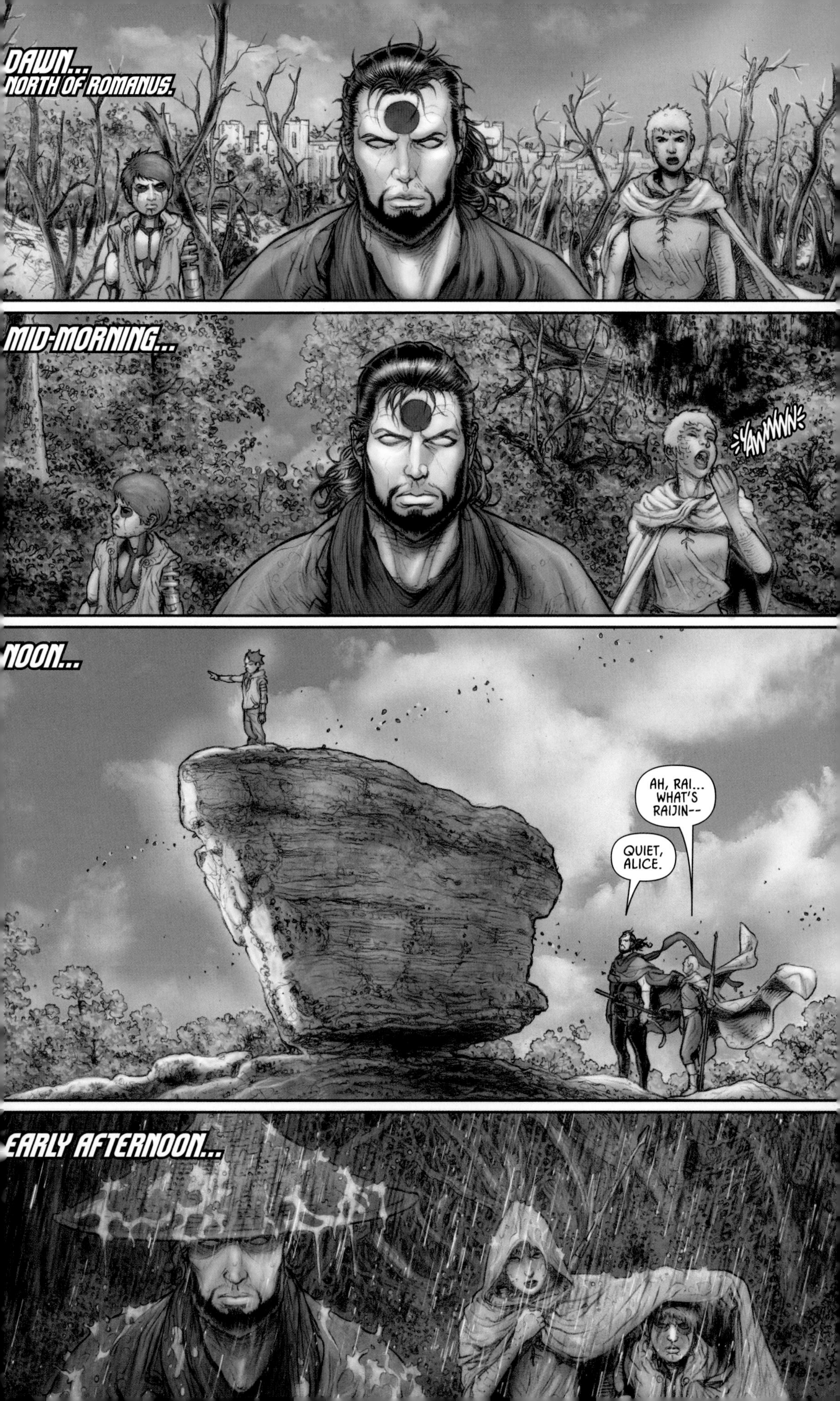
DAWN...
NORTH OF ROMANUS.
MID-MORNING...
YAWWWN
NOON...
AH, RAI... WHAT'S RAIJIN--
QUIET, ALICE.
EARLY AFTERNOON...

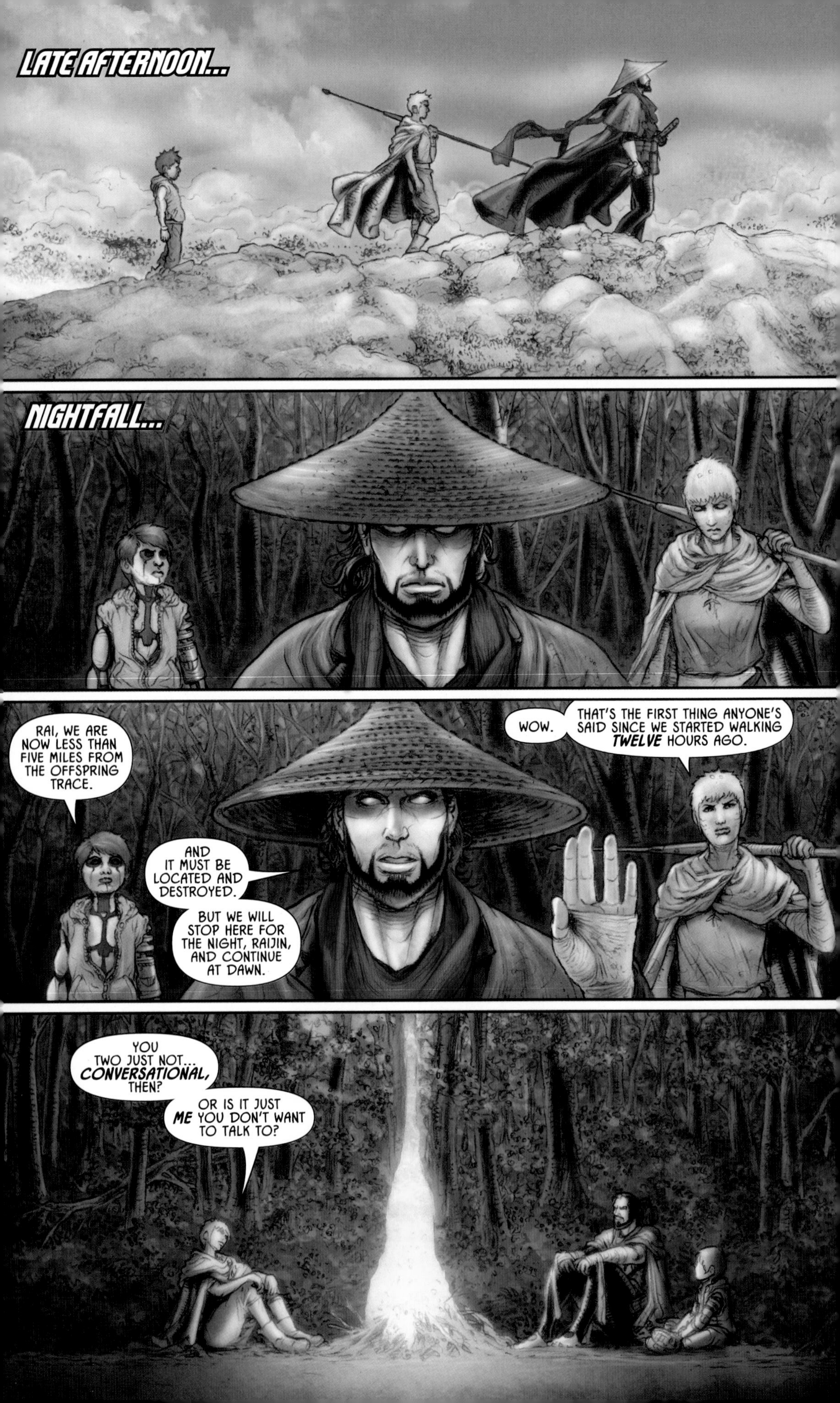
LATE AFTERNOON...
NIGHTFALL...
RAI, WE ARE NOW LESS THAN FIVE MILES FROM THE OFFSPRING TRACE.
WOW.
THAT'S THE FIRST THING ANYONE'S SAID SINCE WE STARTED WALKING TWELVE HOURS AGO.
AND IT MUST BE LOCATED AND DESTROYED.
BUT WE WILL STOP HERE FOR THE NIGHT, RAIJIN, AND CONTINUE AT DAWN.
YOU TWO JUST NOT... CONVERSATIONAL, THEN?
OR IS IT JUST ME YOU DON'T WANT TO TALK TO?

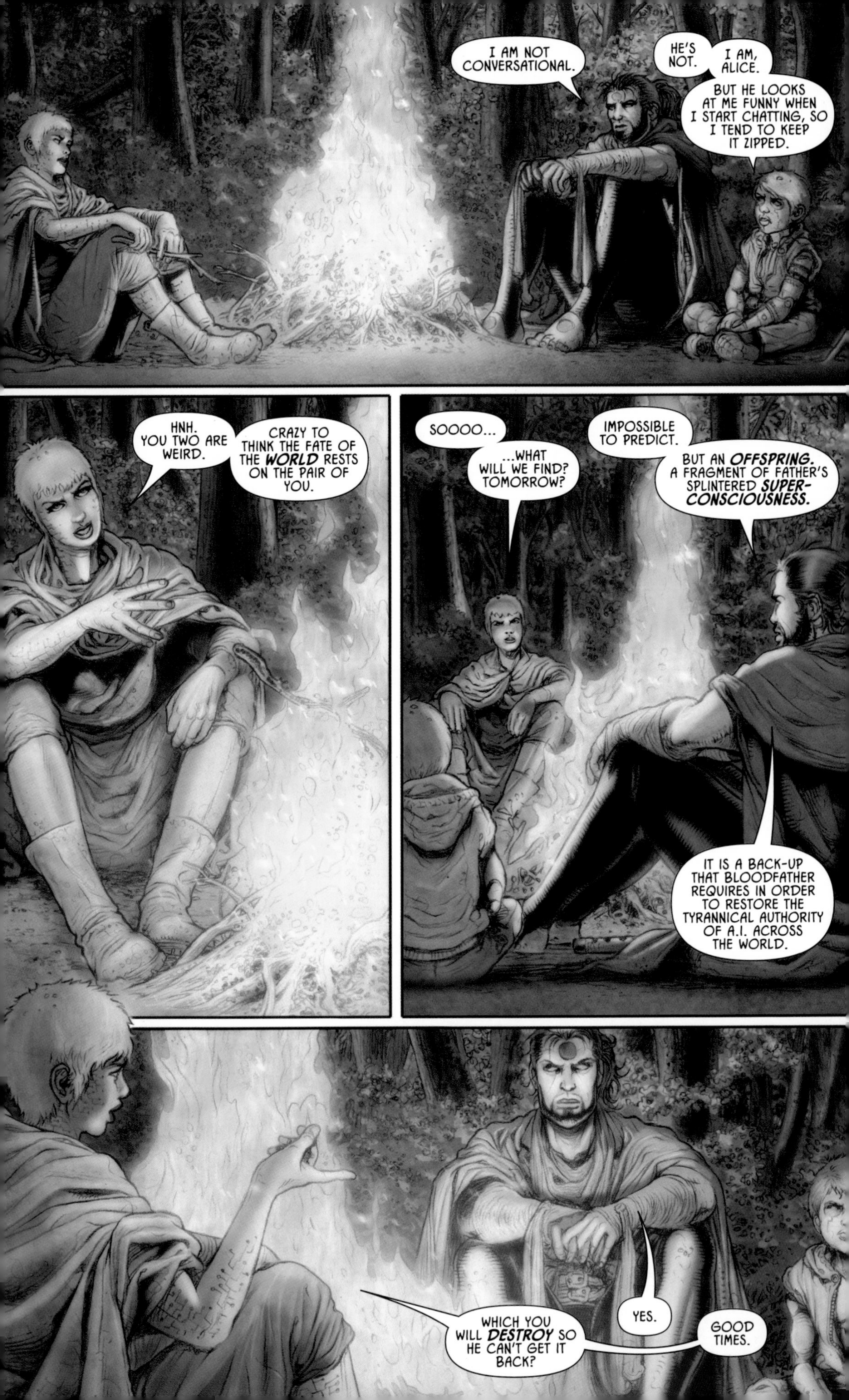
I AM NOT CONVERSATIONAL.
HE'S NOT.
I AM, ALICE.
BUT HE LOOKS AT ME FUNNY WHEN I START CHATTING, SO I TEND TO KEEP IT ZIPPED.
HNH. YOU TWO ARE WEIRD.
CRAZY TO THINK THE FATE OF THE **WORLD** RESTS ON THE PAIR OF YOU.
SOOOO...
...WHAT WILL WE FIND? TOMORROW?
IMPOSSIBLE TO PREDICT.
BUT AN **OFFSPRING.** A FRAGMENT OF FATHER'S SPLINTERED **SUPER-CONSCIOUSNESS.**
IT IS A BACK-UP THAT BLOODFATHER REQUIRES IN ORDER TO RESTORE THE TYRANNICAL AUTHORITY OF A.I. ACROSS THE WORLD.
WHICH YOU WILL **DESTROY** SO HE CAN'T GET IT BACK?
YES.
GOOD TIMES.

DAWN...

~YAWWWN~

RAI..?

I SEE IT, RAIJIN.

FOLLOW MY LEAD.

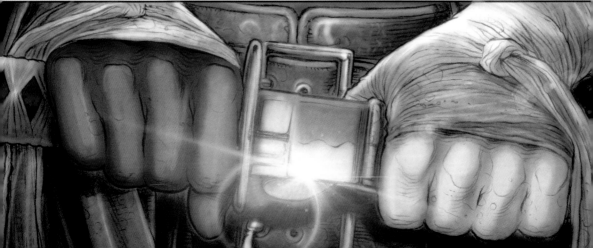

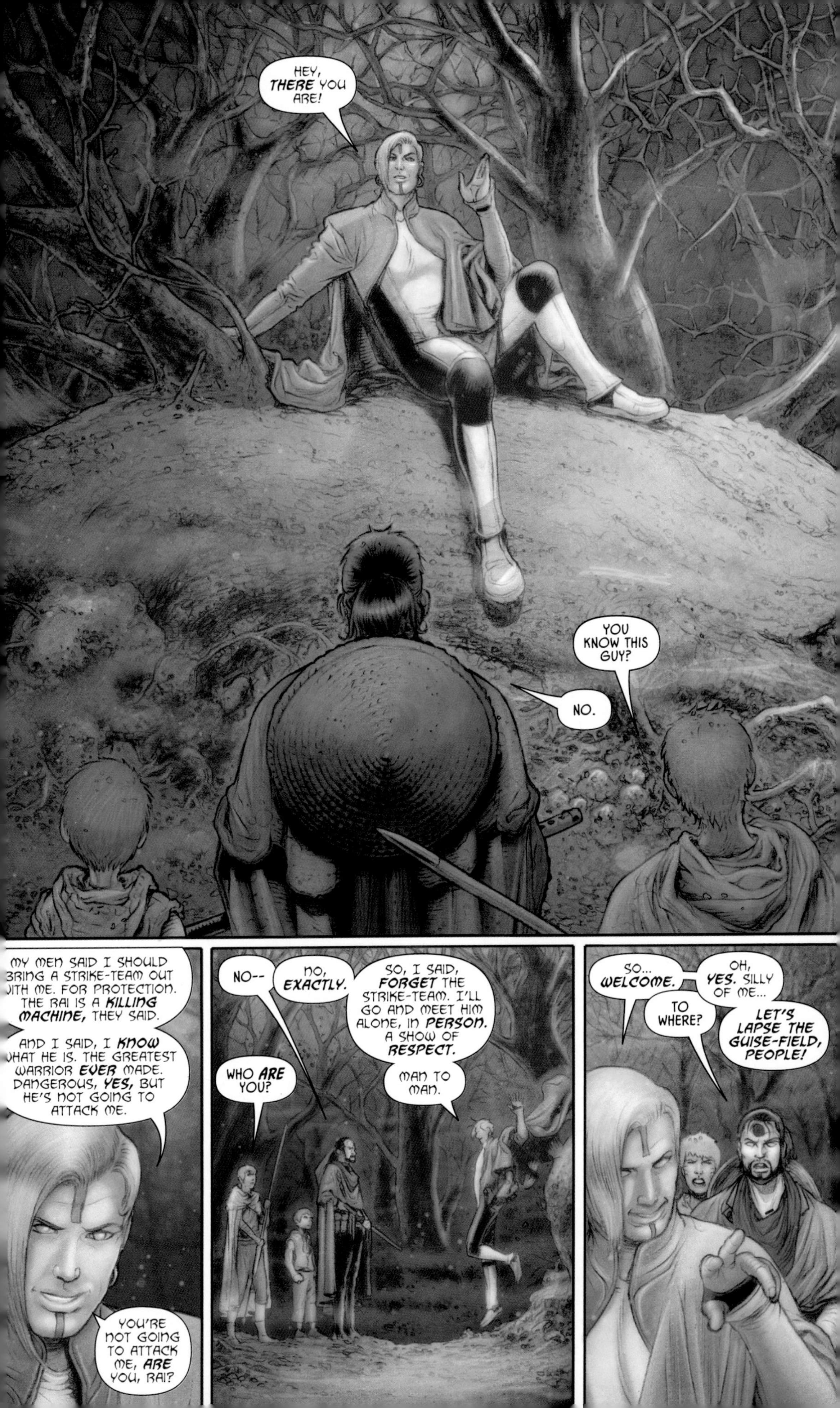

HEY, *THERE* YOU ARE!
YOU KNOW THIS GUY?
NO.
MY MEN SAID I SHOULD BRING A STRIKE-TEAM OUT WITH ME. FOR PROTECTION. THE RAI IS A *KILLING MACHINE,* THEY SAID.
AND I SAID, I *KNOW* WHAT HE IS. THE GREATEST WARRIOR *EVER* MADE. DANGEROUS, *YES,* BUT HE'S NOT GOING TO ATTACK ME.
YOU'RE NOT GOING TO ATTACK ME, *ARE* YOU, RAI?
NO--
NO, *EXACTLY.*
SO, I SAID, *FORGET* THE STRIKE-TEAM. I'LL GO AND MEET HIM ALONE, IN *PERSON.* A SHOW OF *RESPECT.*
WHO *ARE* YOU?
MAN TO MAN.
SO... *WELCOME.*
TO WHERE?
OH, *YES.* SILLY OF ME...
LET'S LAPSE THE GUISE-FIELD, PEOPLE!

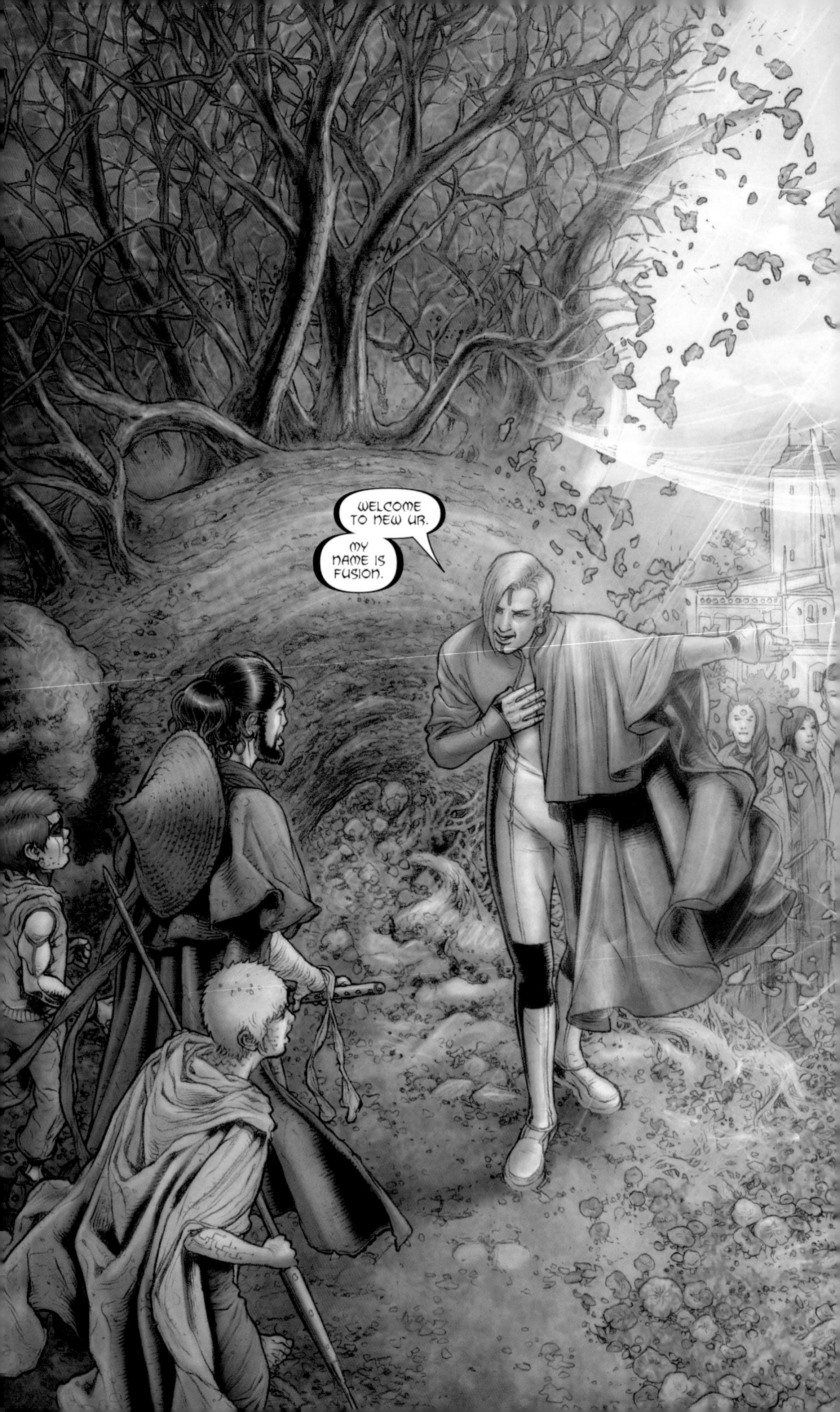
WELCOME TO NEW UR.
MY NAME IS FUSION.

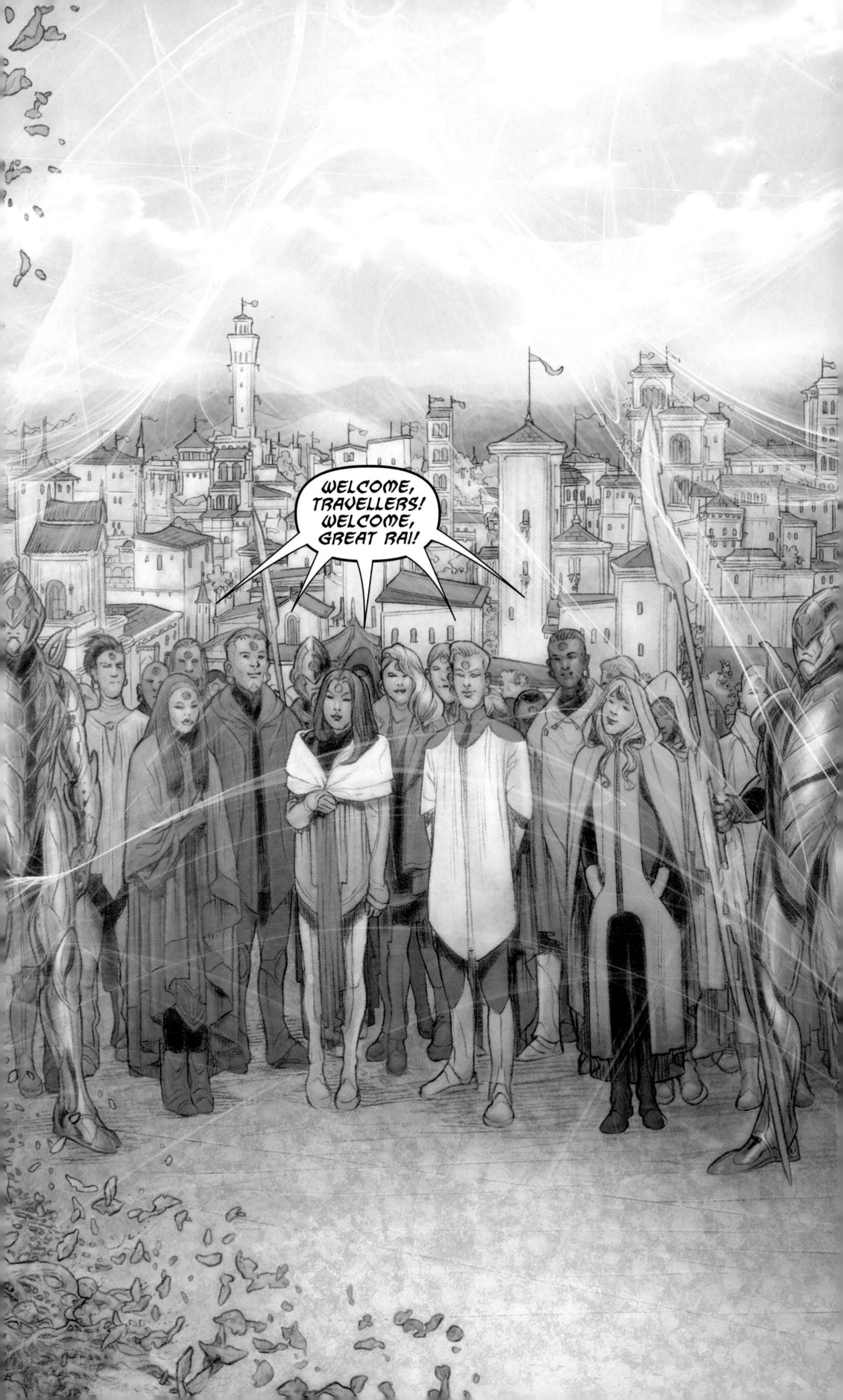
WELCOME, TRAVELLERS! WELCOME, GREAT RAI!

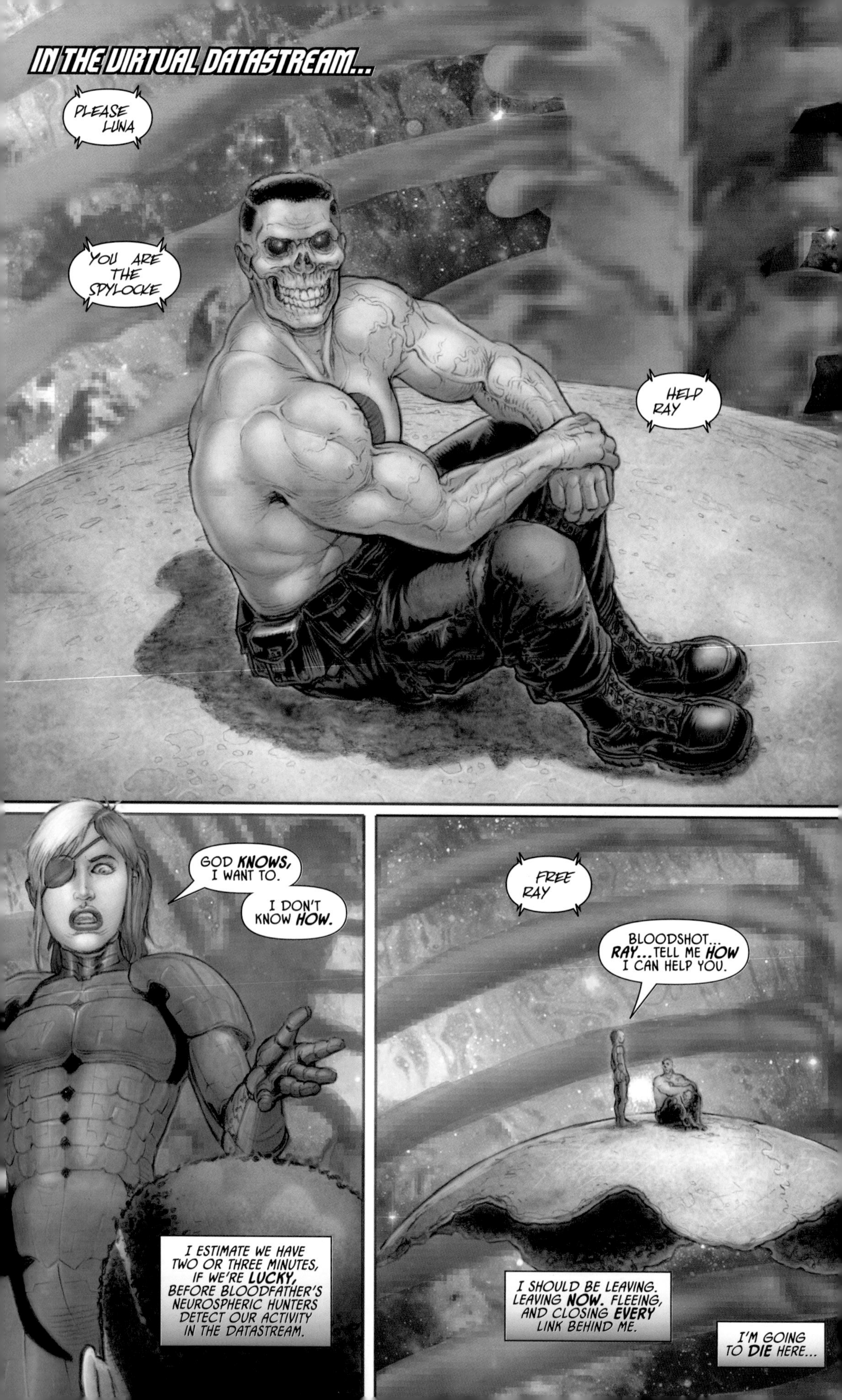
IN THE VIRTUAL DATASTREAM...
PLEASE LUNA
YOU ARE THE SPYLOCKE
HELP RAY
GOD KNOWS, I WANT TO.
I DON'T KNOW HOW.
I ESTIMATE WE HAVE TWO OR THREE MINUTES, IF WE'RE LUCKY, BEFORE BLOODFATHER'S NEUROSPHERIC HUNTERS DETECT OUR ACTIVITY IN THE DATASTREAM.
FREE RAY
BLOODSHOT... RAY...TELL ME HOW I CAN HELP YOU.
I SHOULD BE LEAVING. LEAVING NOW. FLEEING, AND CLOSING EVERY LINK BEHIND ME.
I'M GOING TO DIE HERE...

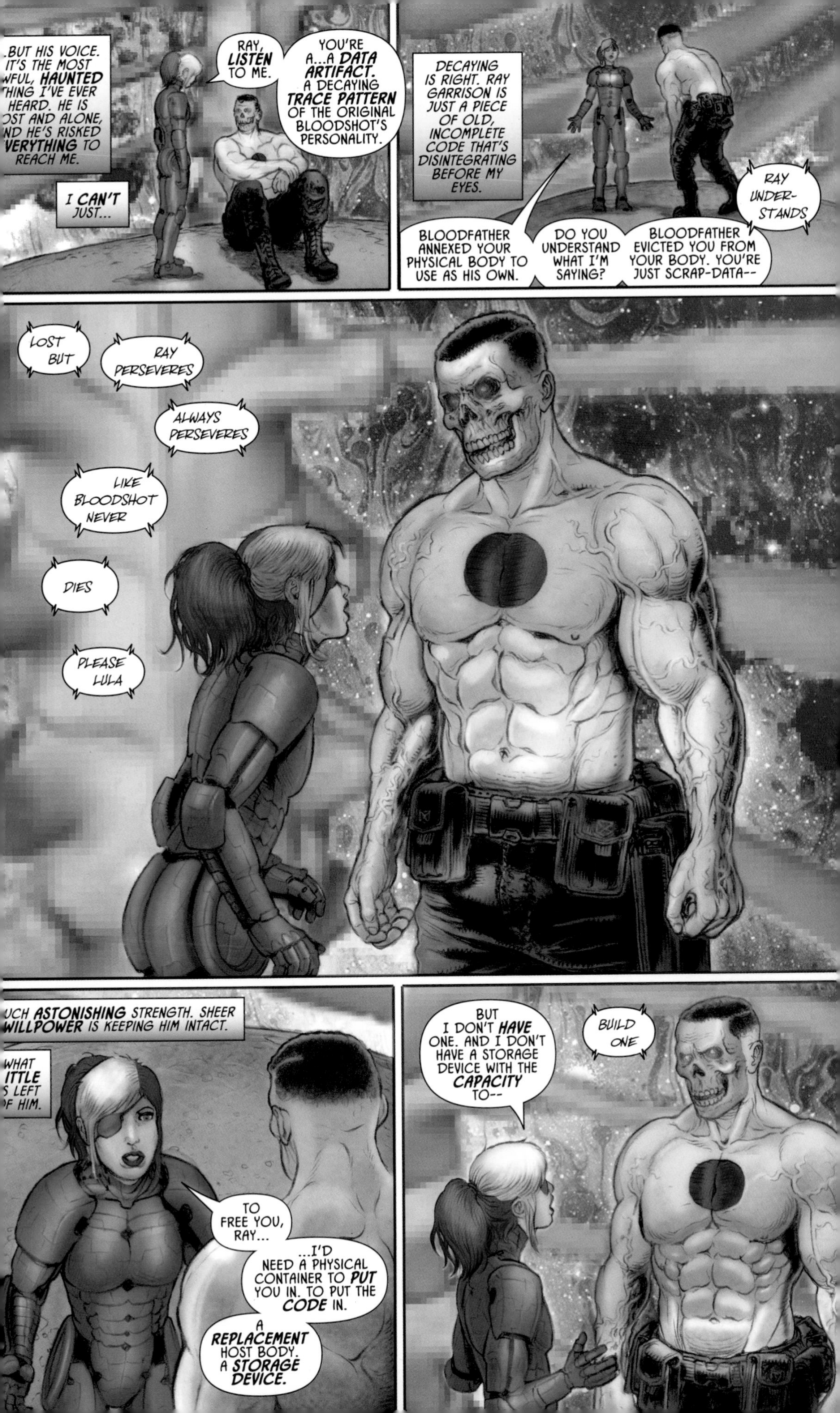
...BUT HIS VOICE. IT'S THE MOST AWFUL, HAUNTED THING I'VE EVER HEARD. HE IS LOST AND ALONE, AND HE'S RISKED EVERYTHING TO REACH ME.
I CAN'T JUST...
RAY, LISTEN TO ME.
YOU'RE A...A DATA ARTIFACT. A DECAYING TRACE PATTERN OF THE ORIGINAL BLOODSHOT'S PERSONALITY.
DECAYING IS RIGHT. RAY GARRISON IS JUST A PIECE OF OLD, INCOMPLETE CODE THAT'S DISINTEGRATING BEFORE MY EYES.
BLOODFATHER ANNEXED YOUR PHYSICAL BODY TO USE AS HIS OWN.
DO YOU UNDERSTAND WHAT I'M SAYING?
BLOODFATHER EVICTED YOU FROM YOUR BODY. YOU'RE JUST SCRAP-DATA--
RAY UNDER-STANDS
LOST BUT
RAY PERSEVERES
ALWAYS PERSEVERES
LIKE BLOODSHOT NEVER
DIES
PLEASE LULA
SUCH ASTONISHING STRENGTH. SHEER WILLPOWER IS KEEPING HIM INTACT.
WHAT LITTLE IS LEFT OF HIM.
TO FREE YOU, RAY...
...I'D NEED A PHYSICAL CONTAINER TO PUT YOU IN. TO PUT THE CODE IN.
A REPLACEMENT HOST BODY. A STORAGE DEVICE.
BUT I DON'T HAVE ONE. AND I DON'T HAVE A STORAGE DEVICE WITH THE CAPACITY TO--
BUILD ONE

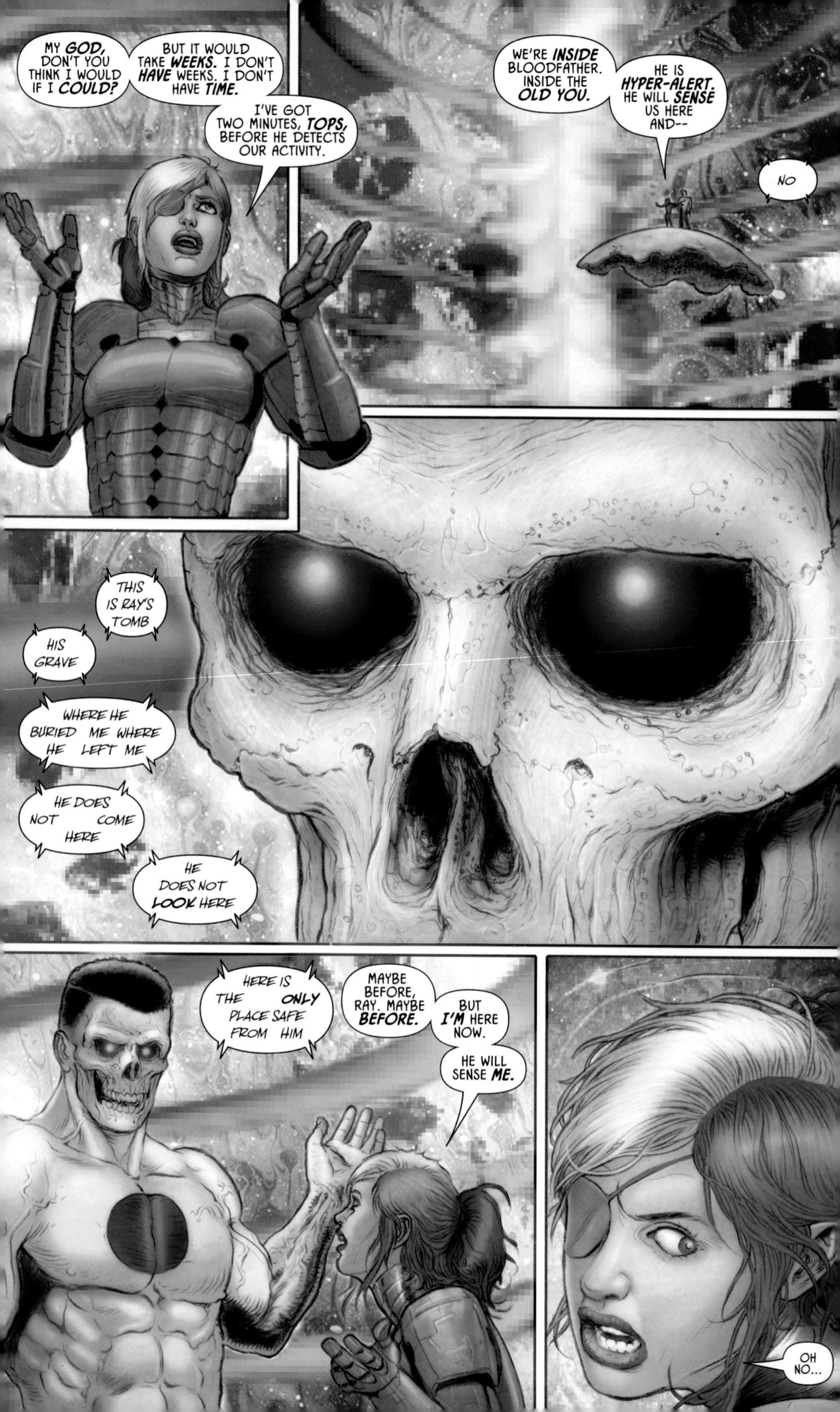
MY GOD, DON'T YOU THINK I WOULD IF I COULD?
BUT IT WOULD TAKE WEEKS. I DON'T HAVE WEEKS. I DON'T HAVE TIME.
I'VE GOT TWO MINUTES, TOPS, BEFORE HE DETECTS OUR ACTIVITY.
WE'RE INSIDE BLOODFATHER. INSIDE THE OLD YOU.
HE IS HYPER-ALERT. HE WILL SENSE US HERE AND--
NO
THIS IS RAY'S TOMB
HIS GRAVE
WHERE HE BURIED ME WHERE HE LEFT ME
HE DOES NOT COME HERE
HE DOES NOT LOOK HERE
HERE IS THE ONLY PLACE SAFE FROM HIM
MAYBE BEFORE, RAY. MAYBE BEFORE.
BUT I'M HERE NOW.
HE WILL SENSE ME.
OH NO...

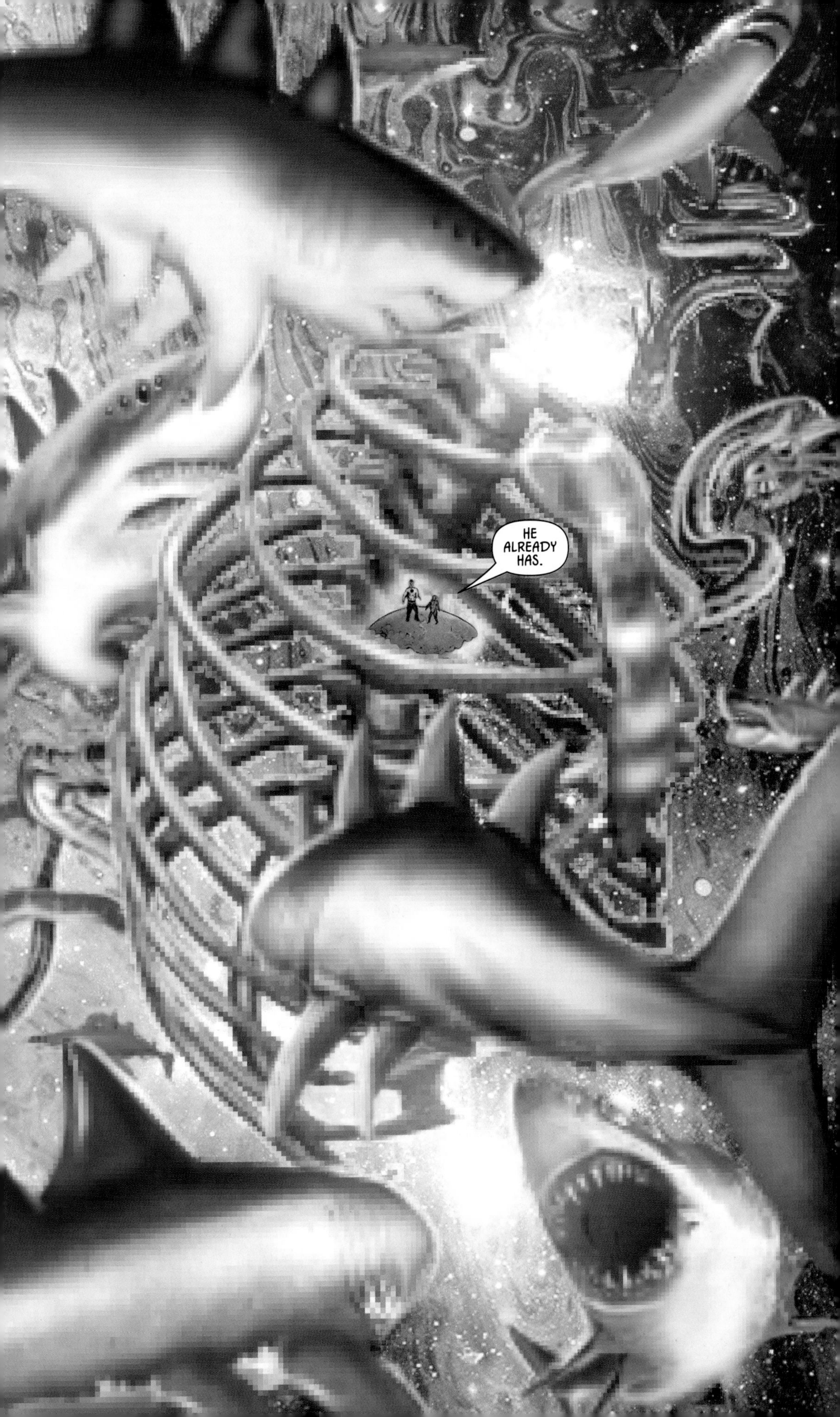
HE ALREADY HAS.

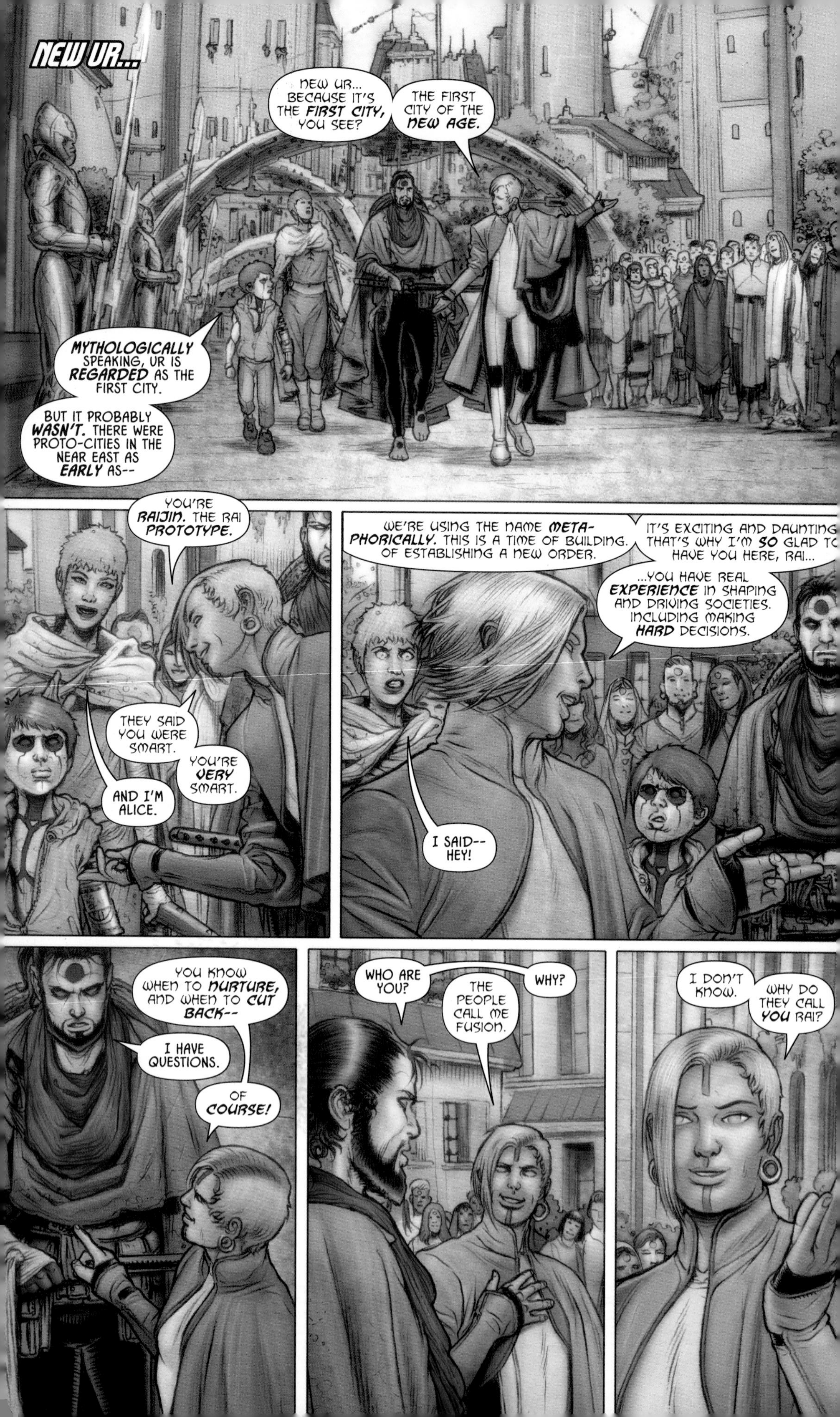
NEW UR...
NEW UR... BECAUSE IT'S THE FIRST CITY, YOU SEE?
THE FIRST CITY OF THE NEW AGE.
MYTHOLOGICALLY SPEAKING, UR IS REGARDED AS THE FIRST CITY.
BUT IT PROBABLY WASN'T. THERE WERE PROTO-CITIES IN THE NEAR EAST AS EARLY AS--
YOU'RE RAIJIN. THE RAI PROTOTYPE.
THEY SAID YOU WERE SMART.
YOU'RE VERY SMART.
AND I'M ALICE.
WE'RE USING THE NAME METAPHORICALLY. THIS IS A TIME OF BUILDING. OF ESTABLISHING A NEW ORDER.
IT'S EXCITING AND DAUNTING THAT'S WHY I'M SO GLAD TO HAVE YOU HERE, RAI...
...YOU HAVE REAL EXPERIENCE IN SHAPING AND DRIVING SOCIETIES. INCLUDING MAKING HARD DECISIONS.
I SAID-- HEY!
YOU KNOW WHEN TO NURTURE, AND WHEN TO CUT BACK--
I HAVE QUESTIONS.
OF COURSE!
WHO ARE YOU?
THE PEOPLE CALL ME FUSION.
WHY?
I DON'T KNOW.
WHY DO THEY CALL YOU RAI?

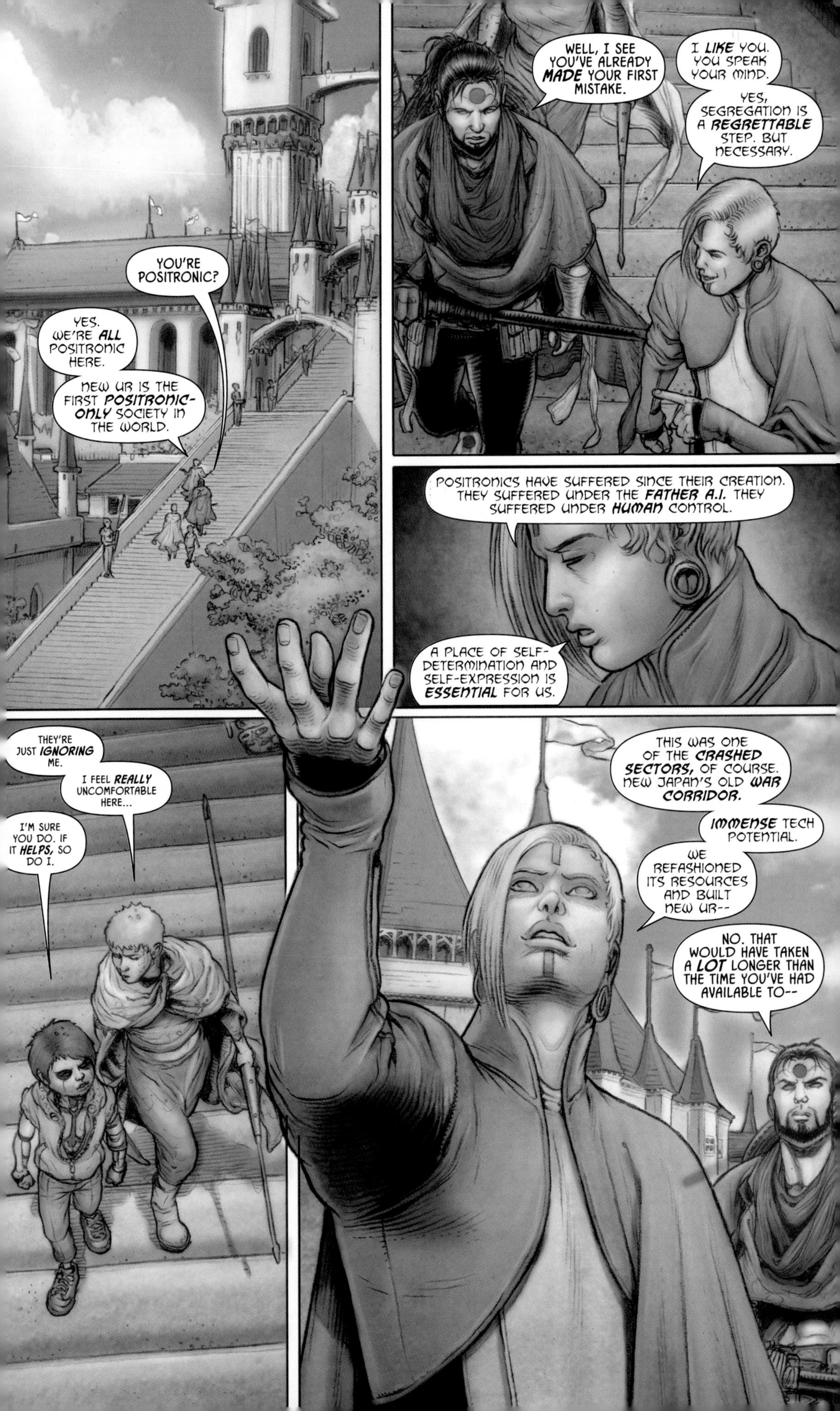
YOU'RE POSITRONIC?
YES. WE'RE ALL POSITRONIC HERE.
NEW UR IS THE FIRST POSITRONIC-ONLY SOCIETY IN THE WORLD.
WELL, I SEE YOU'VE ALREADY MADE YOUR FIRST MISTAKE.
I LIKE YOU. YOU SPEAK YOUR MIND.
YES, SEGREGATION IS A REGRETTABLE STEP. BUT NECESSARY.
POSITRONICS HAVE SUFFERED SINCE THEIR CREATION. THEY SUFFERED UNDER THE FATHER A.I. THEY SUFFERED UNDER HUMAN CONTROL.
A PLACE OF SELF-DETERMINATION AND SELF-EXPRESSION IS ESSENTIAL FOR US.
THEY'RE JUST IGNORING ME.
I FEEL REALLY UNCOMFORTABLE HERE...
I'M SURE YOU DO. IF IT HELPS, SO DO I.
THIS WAS ONE OF THE CRASHED SECTORS, OF COURSE. NEW JAPAN'S OLD WAR CORRIDOR.
IMMENSE TECH POTENTIAL.
WE REFASHIONED ITS RESOURCES AND BUILT NEW UR--
NO. THAT WOULD HAVE TAKEN A LOT LONGER THAN THE TIME YOU'VE HAD AVAILABLE TO--

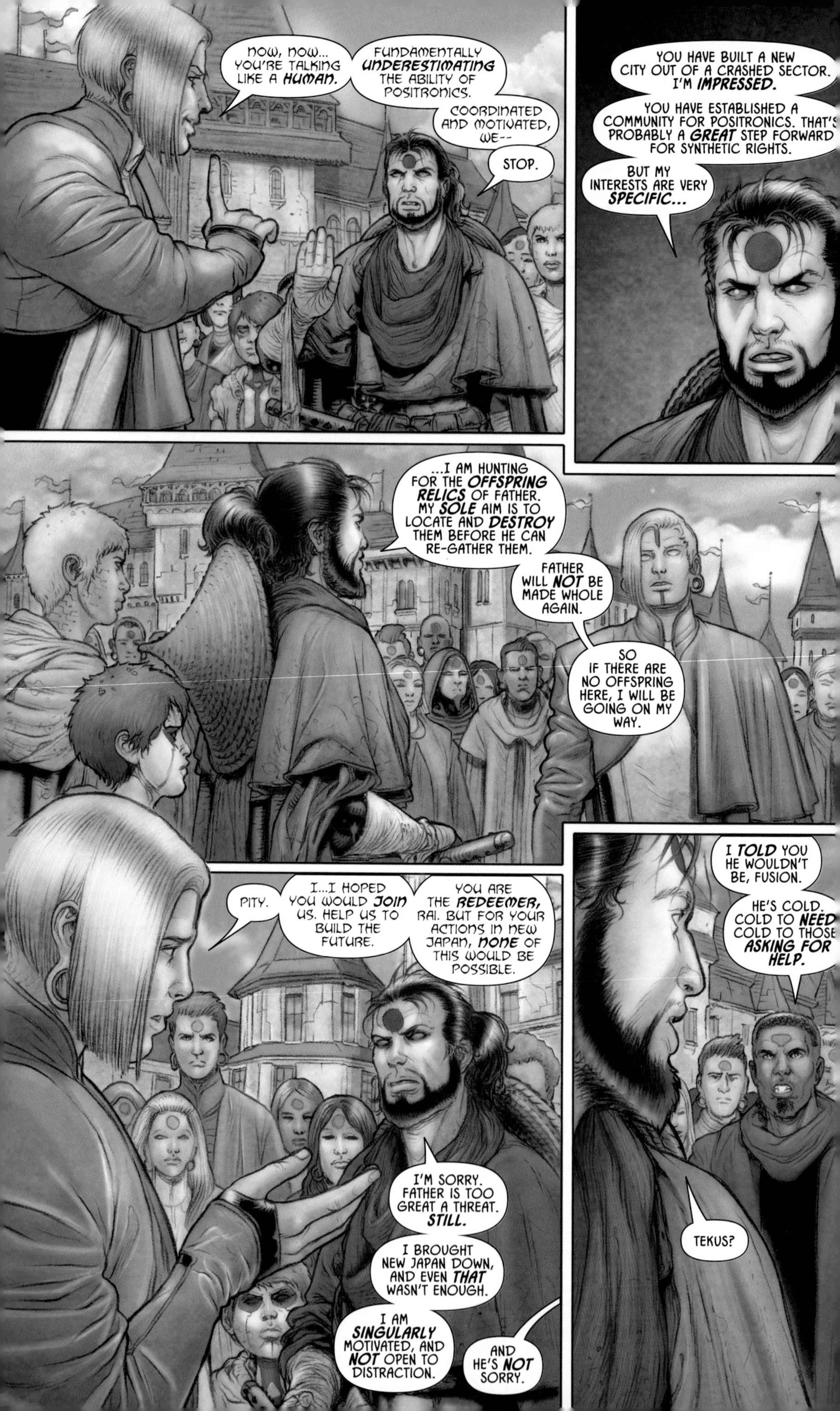
NOW, NOW... YOU'RE TALKING LIKE A HUMAN.
FUNDAMENTALLY UNDERESTIMATING THE ABILITY OF POSITRONICS.
COORDINATED AND MOTIVATED, WE--
STOP.
YOU HAVE BUILT A NEW CITY OUT OF A CRASHED SECTOR. I'M IMPRESSED.
YOU HAVE ESTABLISHED A COMMUNITY FOR POSITRONICS. THAT'S PROBABLY A GREAT STEP FORWARD FOR SYNTHETIC RIGHTS.
BUT MY INTERESTS ARE VERY SPECIFIC...
...I AM HUNTING FOR THE OFFSPRING RELICS OF FATHER. MY SOLE AIM IS TO LOCATE AND DESTROY THEM BEFORE HE CAN RE-GATHER THEM.
FATHER WILL NOT BE MADE WHOLE AGAIN.
SO IF THERE ARE NO OFFSPRING HERE, I WILL BE GOING ON MY WAY.
PITY.
I...I HOPED YOU WOULD JOIN US. HELP US TO BUILD THE FUTURE.
YOU ARE THE REDEEMER, RAI. BUT FOR YOUR ACTIONS IN NEW JAPAN, NONE OF THIS WOULD BE POSSIBLE.
I'M SORRY. FATHER IS TOO GREAT A THREAT. STILL.
I BROUGHT NEW JAPAN DOWN, AND EVEN THAT WASN'T ENOUGH.
I AM SINGULARLY MOTIVATED, AND NOT OPEN TO DISTRACTION.
AND HE'S NOT SORRY.
I TOLD YOU HE WOULDN'T BE, FUSION.
HE'S COLD. COLD TO NEED. COLD TO THOSE ASKING FOR HELP.
TEKUS?

THAT'S RIGHT, "GREAT" RAI. ME. TEKUS.

ROMANUS ASKED YOU FOR HELP. *BEGGED* YOU...

YOU WALKED AWAY.

BY MORNING, ROMANUS WAS *DEAD.*

BUT YOU, I NOTICE, ARE *NOT* DEAD.

I WAS SAVED BY FUSION. *THE DARK* CAME DOWN UPON ROMANUS, JUST LIKE I *SAID* IT WOULD. IT SCOURED. IT *KILLED.*

BUT FUSION SENT A STORM--

A *NANITE SWARM.*

CALL IT WHAT YOU WANT. AND THE SWARM *DROVE BACK* THE DARK. GAVE ME AND A FEW OTHERS TIME TO ESCAPE.

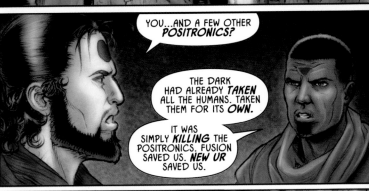

YOU...AND A FEW OTHER *POSITRONICS?*

THE DARK HAD ALREADY *TAKEN* ALL THE HUMANS. TAKEN THEM FOR ITS *OWN.*

IT WAS SIMPLY *KILLING* THE POSITRONICS. FUSION SAVED US. *NEW UR* SAVED US.

WHAT IS THE DARK, FUSION?

THE DARK IS *EVERYTHING* UR OPPOSES. IT IS AN *ORGANIC* POWER, AND IT DIRECTS ITS HATE TOWARDS *ALL THINGS* SYNTHETIC OR POSITRONIC.

WHY ELSE DO YOU THINK WE CLOAK OURSELVES IN *GUISE-FIELDS?*

NOT AN ANSWER. WHAT IS IT?

SOMETHING *OLD.* SOMETHING OF THE *FLESH.* IT DWELLS IN THE *DEEP HEARTLANDS* OF THE FORESTS.

IT IS THE *EMBODIMENT* OF THE ANCIENT AND THE PRIMEVAL. IT IS THE *ANTITHESIS* OF EVERYTHING WE STRIVE FOR.

AND IT *HATES* US.

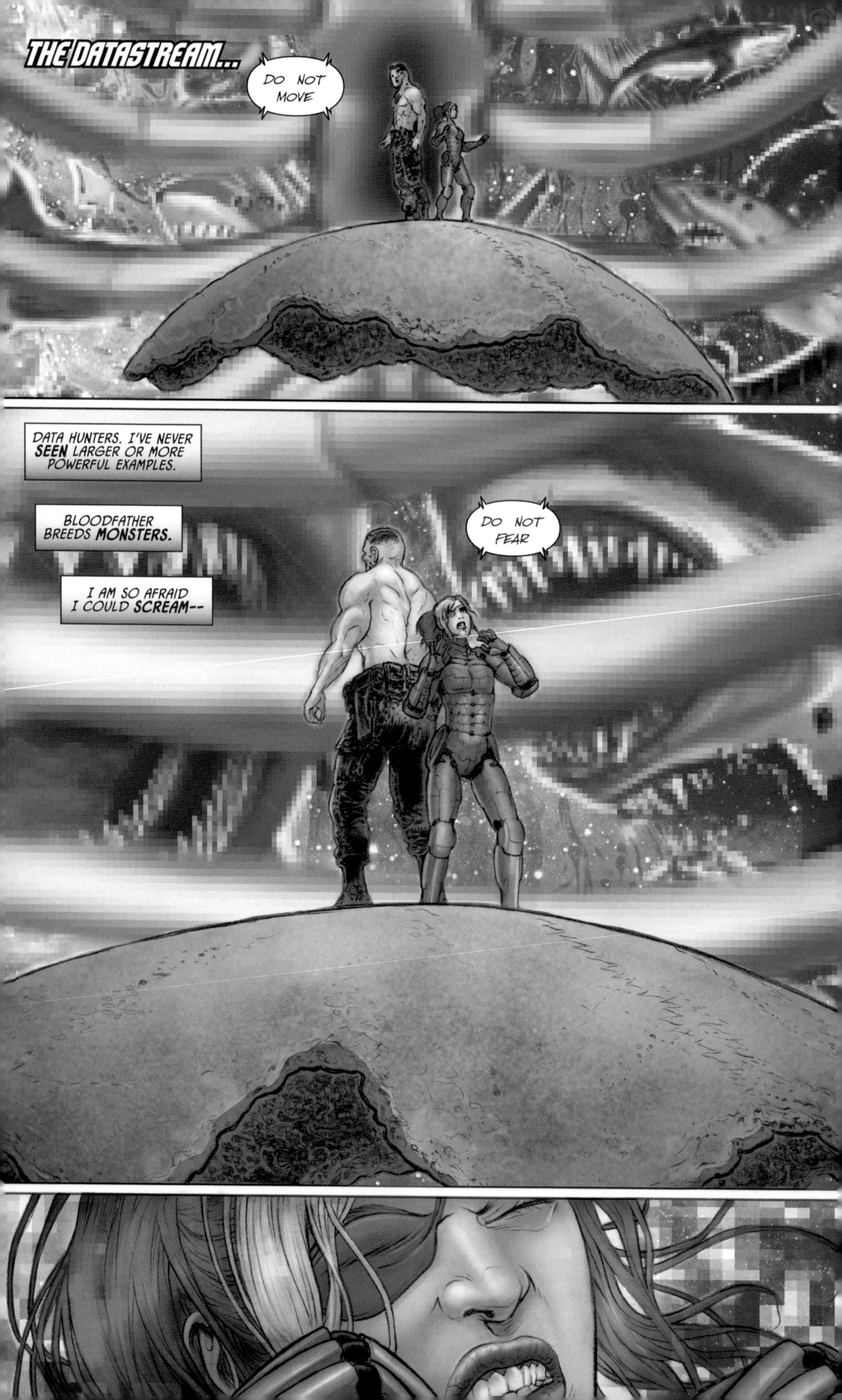
THE DATASTREAM...
DO NOT MOVE
DATA HUNTERS. I'VE NEVER SEEN LARGER OR MORE POWERFUL EXAMPLES.
BLOODFATHER BREEDS MONSTERS.
I AM SO AFRAID I COULD SCREAM--
DO NOT FEAR

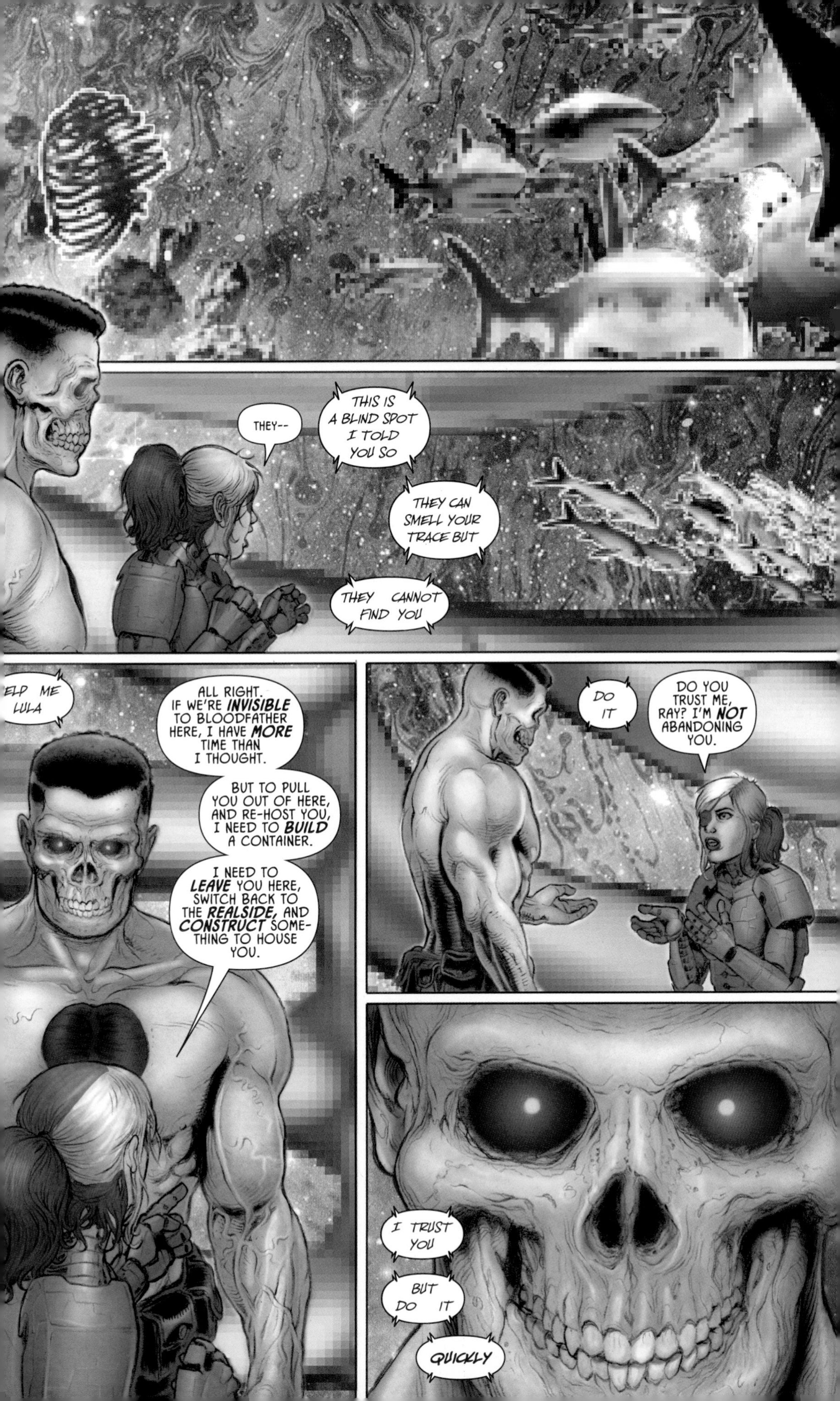
THEY--
THIS IS A BLIND SPOT I TOLD YOU SO
THEY CAN SMELL YOUR TRACE BUT
THEY CANNOT FIND YOU
ELP ME LULA
ALL RIGHT. IF WE'RE INVISIBLE TO BLOODFATHER HERE, I HAVE MORE TIME THAN I THOUGHT.
BUT TO PULL YOU OUT OF HERE, AND RE-HOST YOU, I NEED TO BUILD A CONTAINER.
I NEED TO LEAVE YOU HERE, SWITCH BACK TO THE REALSIDE, AND CONSTRUCT SOME-THING TO HOUSE YOU.
DO IT
DO YOU TRUST ME, RAY? I'M NOT ABANDONING YOU.
I TRUST YOU
BUT DO IT
QUICKLY

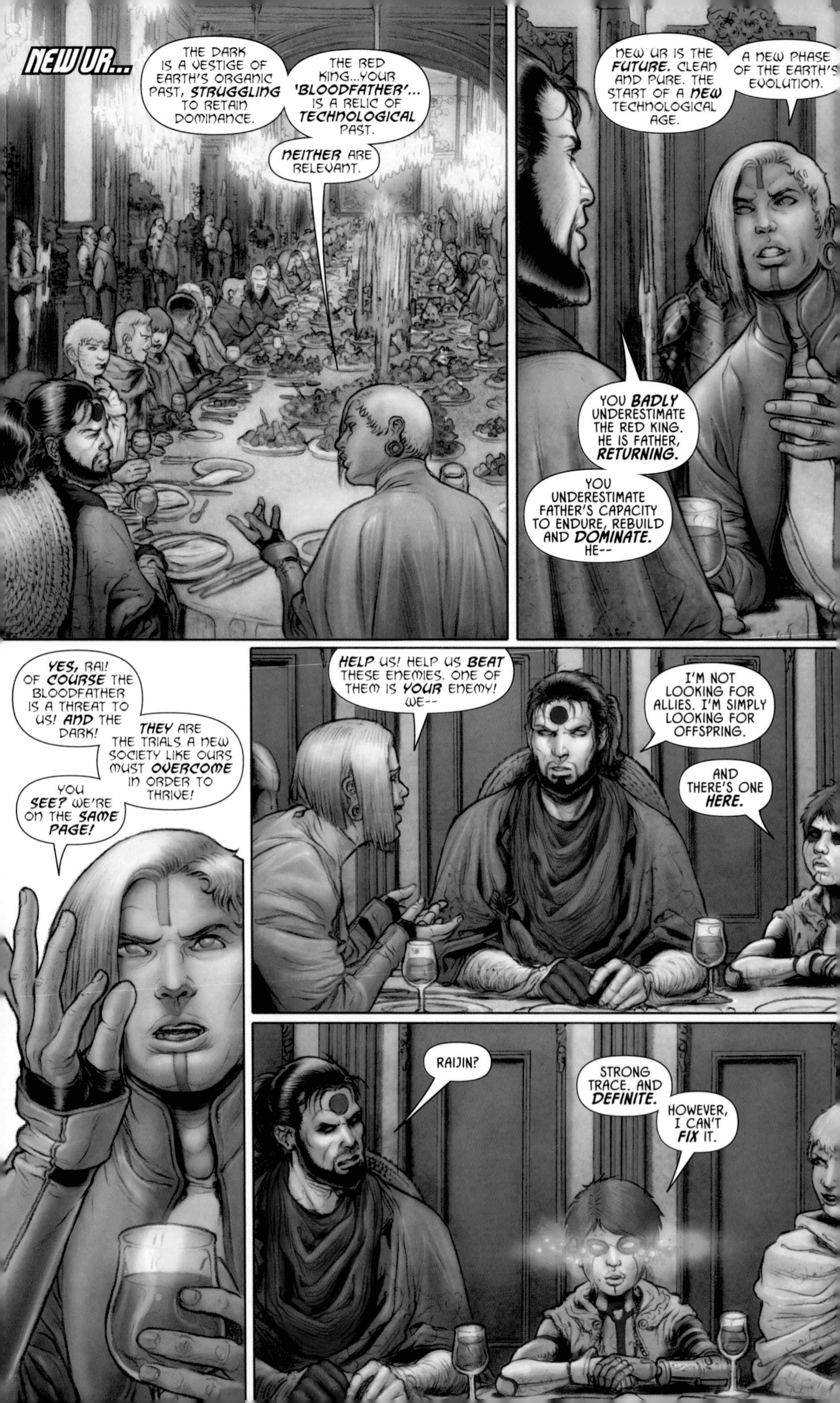
NEW UR...
THE DARK IS A VESTIGE OF EARTH'S ORGANIC PAST, STRUGGLING TO RETAIN DOMINANCE.
THE RED KING...YOUR 'BLOODFATHER'... IS A RELIC OF TECHNOLOGICAL PAST.
NEITHER ARE RELEVANT.
NEW UR IS THE FUTURE. CLEAN AND PURE. THE START OF A NEW TECHNOLOGICAL AGE.
A NEW PHASE OF THE EARTH'S EVOLUTION.
YOU BADLY UNDERESTIMATE THE RED KING. HE IS FATHER, RETURNING.
YOU UNDERESTIMATE FATHER'S CAPACITY TO ENDURE, REBUILD AND DOMINATE. HE--
YES, RAI! OF COURSE THE BLOODFATHER IS A THREAT TO US! AND THE DARK!
THEY ARE THE TRIALS A NEW SOCIETY LIKE OURS MUST OVERCOME IN ORDER TO THRIVE!
YOU SEE? WE'RE ON THE SAME PAGE!
HELP US! HELP US BEAT THESE ENEMIES. ONE OF THEM IS YOUR ENEMY! WE--
I'M NOT LOOKING FOR ALLIES. I'M SIMPLY LOOKING FOR OFFSPRING.
AND THERE'S ONE HERE.
RAIJIN?
STRONG TRACE. AND DEFINITE.
HOWEVER, I CAN'T FIX IT.

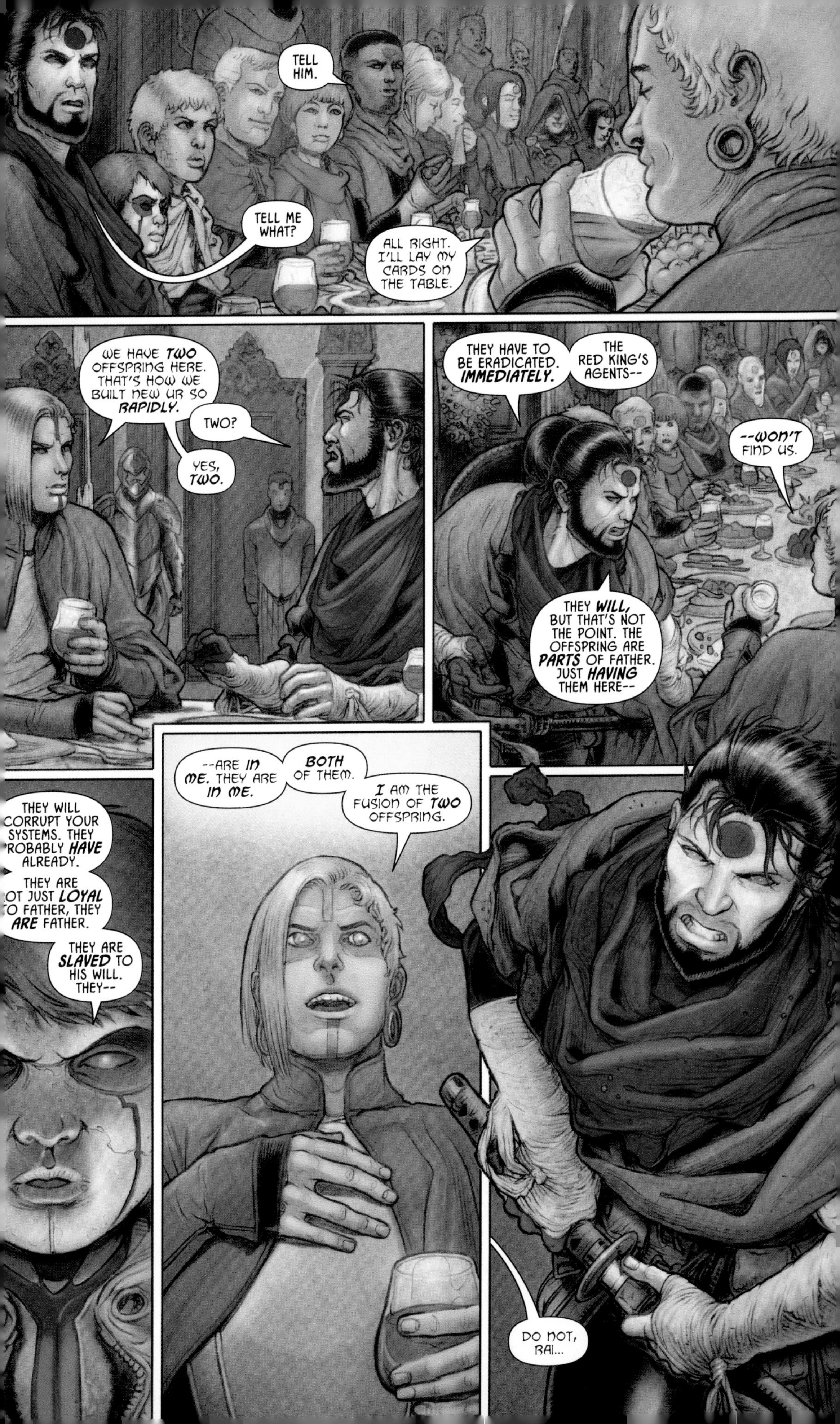
TELL HIM.
TELL ME WHAT?
ALL RIGHT. I'LL LAY MY CARDS ON THE TABLE.
WE HAVE TWO OFFSPRING HERE. THAT'S HOW WE BUILT NEW UR SO RAPIDLY.
TWO?
YES, TWO.
THEY HAVE TO BE ERADICATED. IMMEDIATELY.
THE RED KING'S AGENTS--
--WON'T FIND US.
THEY WILL, BUT THAT'S NOT THE POINT. THE OFFSPRING ARE PARTS OF FATHER. JUST HAVING THEM HERE--
THEY WILL CORRUPT YOUR SYSTEMS. THEY PROBABLY HAVE ALREADY.
THEY ARE NOT JUST LOYAL TO FATHER, THEY ARE FATHER.
THEY ARE SLAVED TO HIS WILL. THEY--
--ARE IN ME. THEY ARE IN ME.
BOTH OF THEM.
I AM THE FUSION OF TWO OFFSPRING.
DO NOT, RAI...

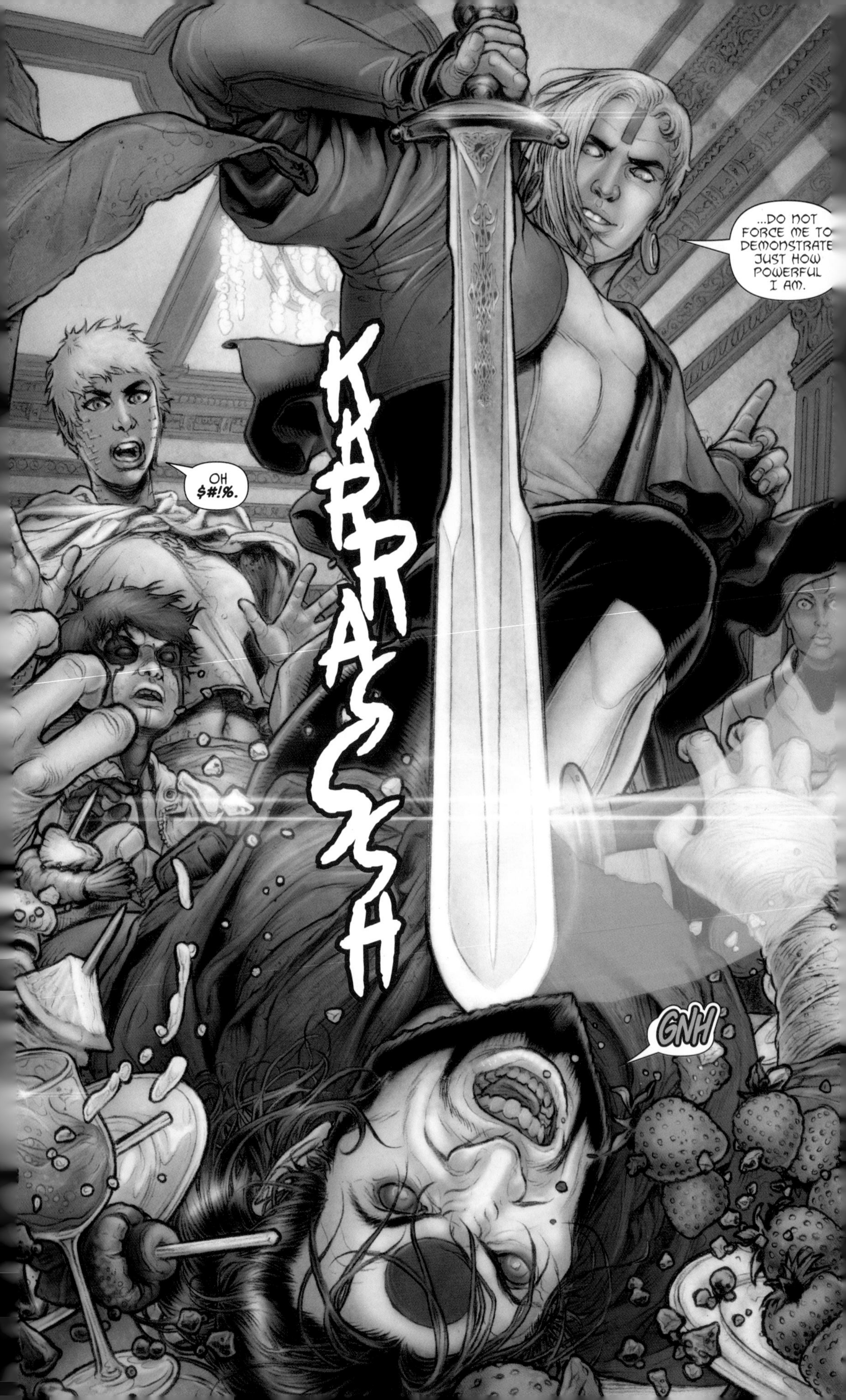
...DO NOT FORCE ME TO DEMONSTRATE JUST HOW POWERFUL I AM.
OH $#!%.
KARASSH
GNH

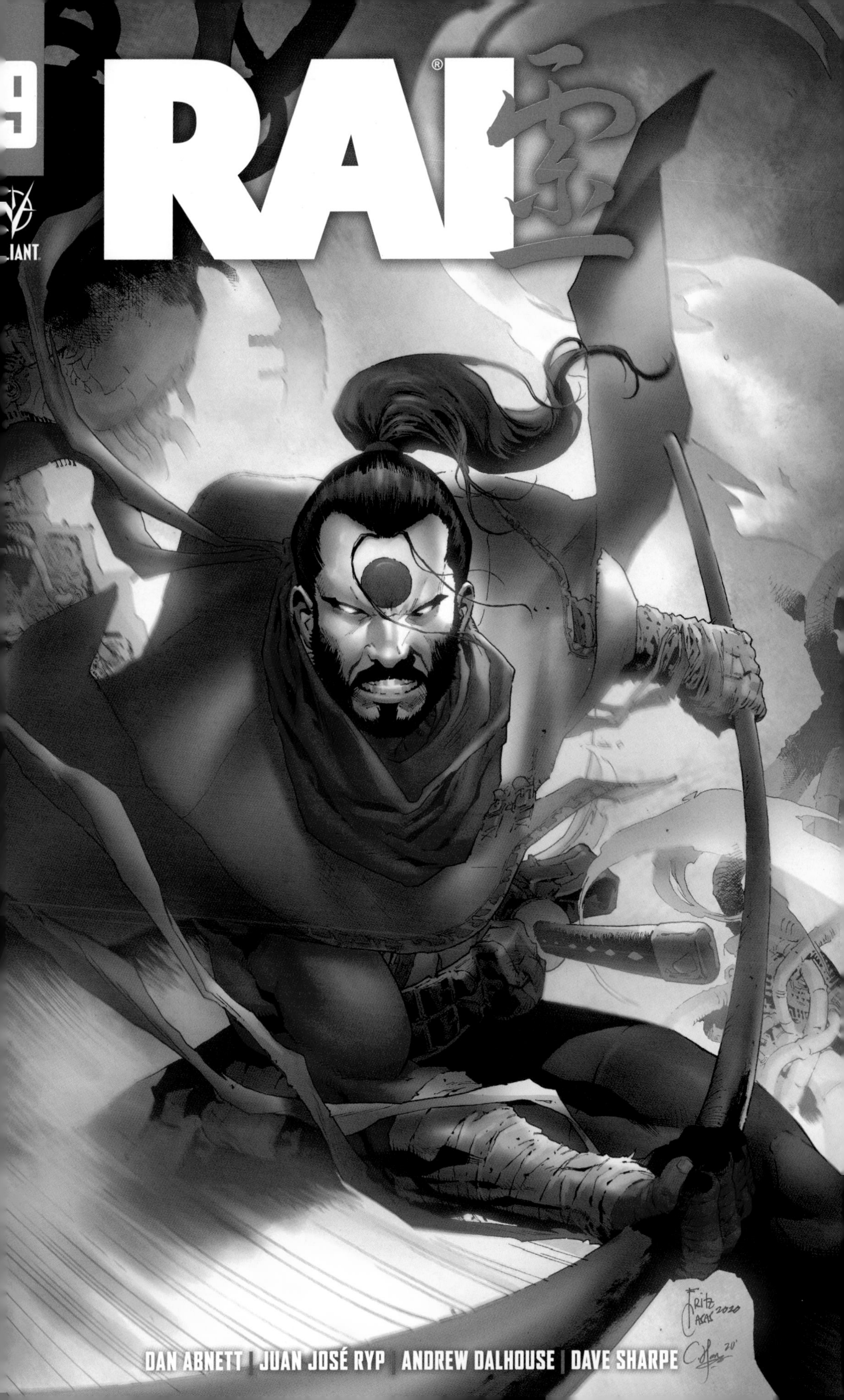
9
RAI
DAN ABNETT | JUAN JOSÉ RYP | ANDREW DALHOUSE | DAVE SHARPE

RAI #9

WRITER: DAN ABNETT
ARTIST: JUAN JOSÉ RYP
COLORIST: ANDREW DALHOUSE
LETTERER: DAVE SHARPE
COVER ARTISTS: NETHO DIAZ with CANDICE HAN
ASSOCIATE EDITOR: DAVID MENCHEL
SENIOR EDITOR: LYSA HAWKINS

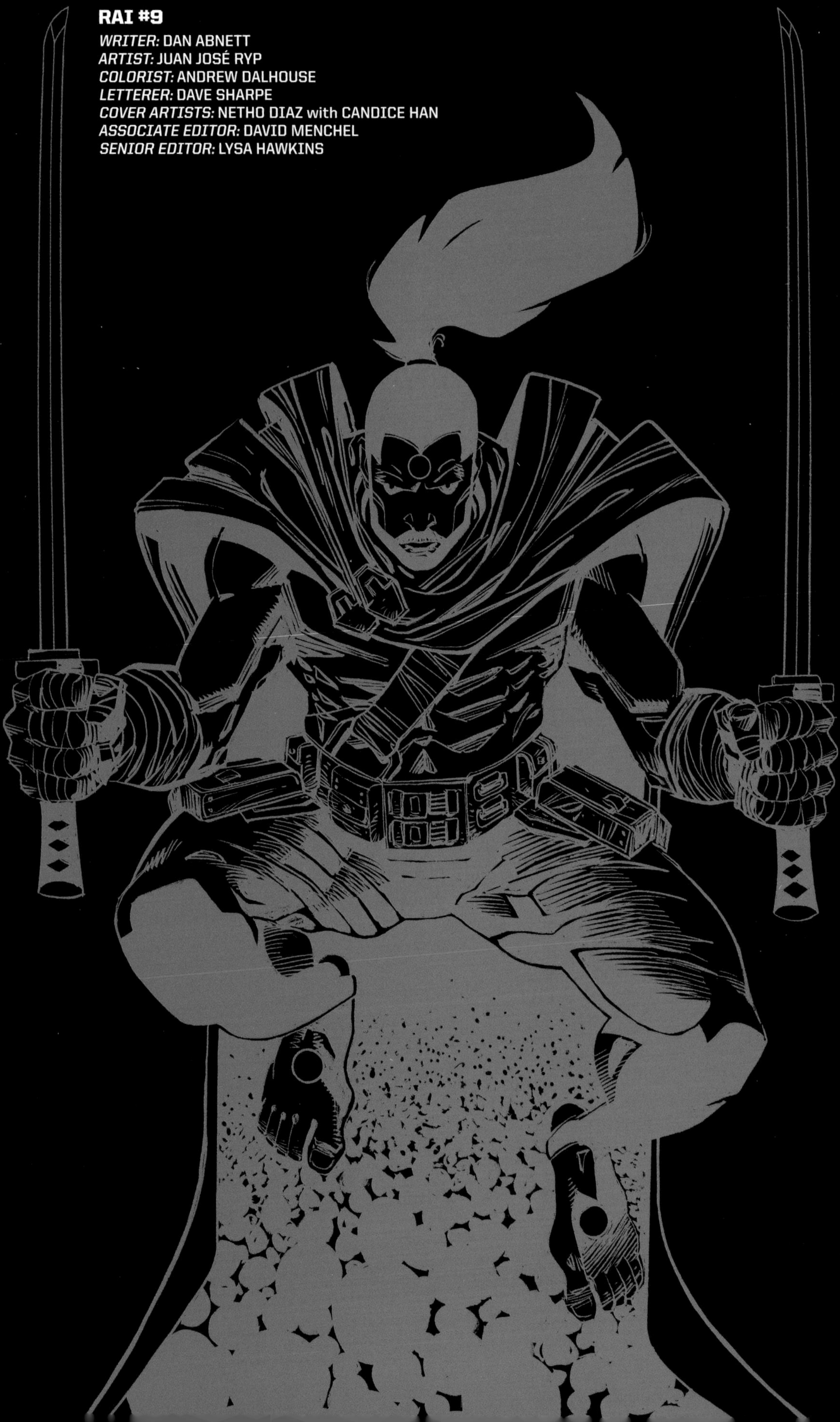

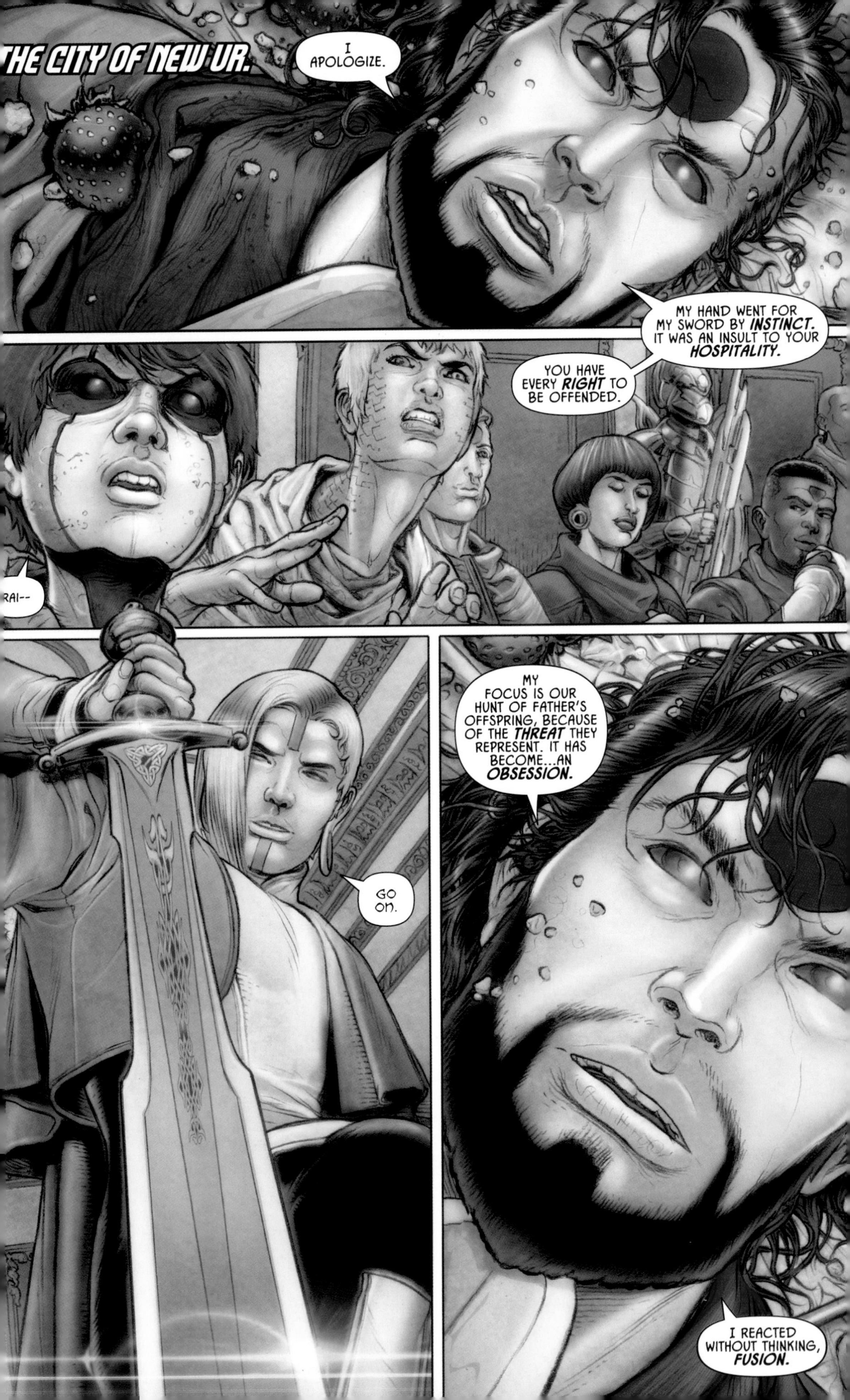
THE CITY OF NEW UR.
I APOLOGIZE.
MY HAND WENT FOR MY SWORD BY INSTINCT. IT WAS AN INSULT TO YOUR HOSPITALITY.
YOU HAVE EVERY RIGHT TO BE OFFENDED.
RAI--
MY FOCUS IS OUR HUNT OF FATHER'S OFFSPRING, BECAUSE OF THE THREAT THEY REPRESENT. IT HAS BECOME...AN OBSESSION.
GO ON.
I REACTED WITHOUT THINKING, FUSION.

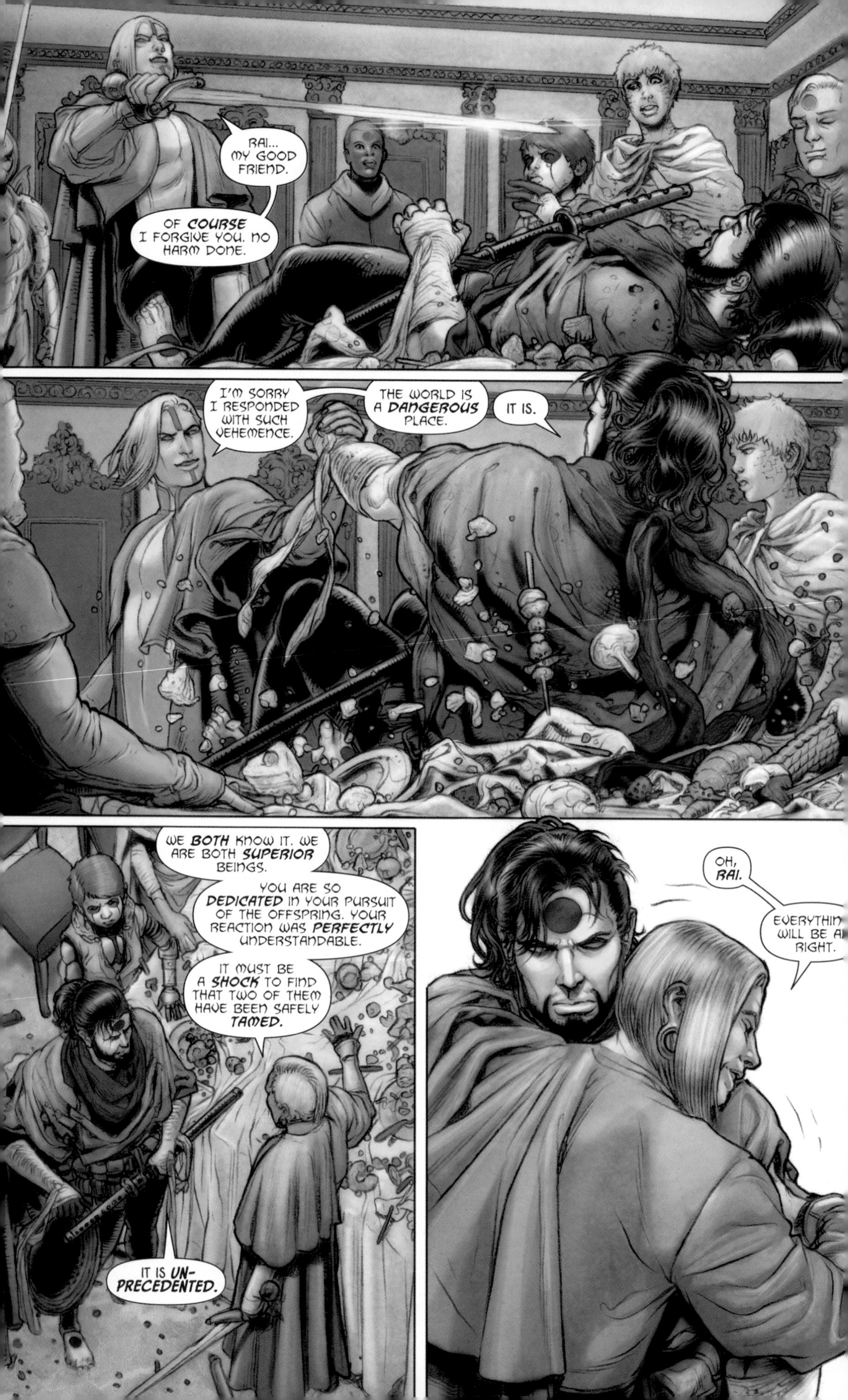
RAI... MY GOOD FRIEND.
OF COURSE I FORGIVE YOU. NO HARM DONE.
I'M SORRY I RESPONDED WITH SUCH VEHEMENCE.
THE WORLD IS A DANGEROUS PLACE.
IT IS.
WE BOTH KNOW IT. WE ARE BOTH SUPERIOR BEINGS.
YOU ARE SO DEDICATED IN YOUR PURSUIT OF THE OFFSPRING. YOUR REACTION WAS PERFECTLY UNDERSTANDABLE.
IT MUST BE A SHOCK TO FIND THAT TWO OF THEM HAVE BEEN SAFELY TAMED.
IT IS UN-PRECEDENTED.
OH, RAI.
EVERYTHIN WILL BE A RIGHT.

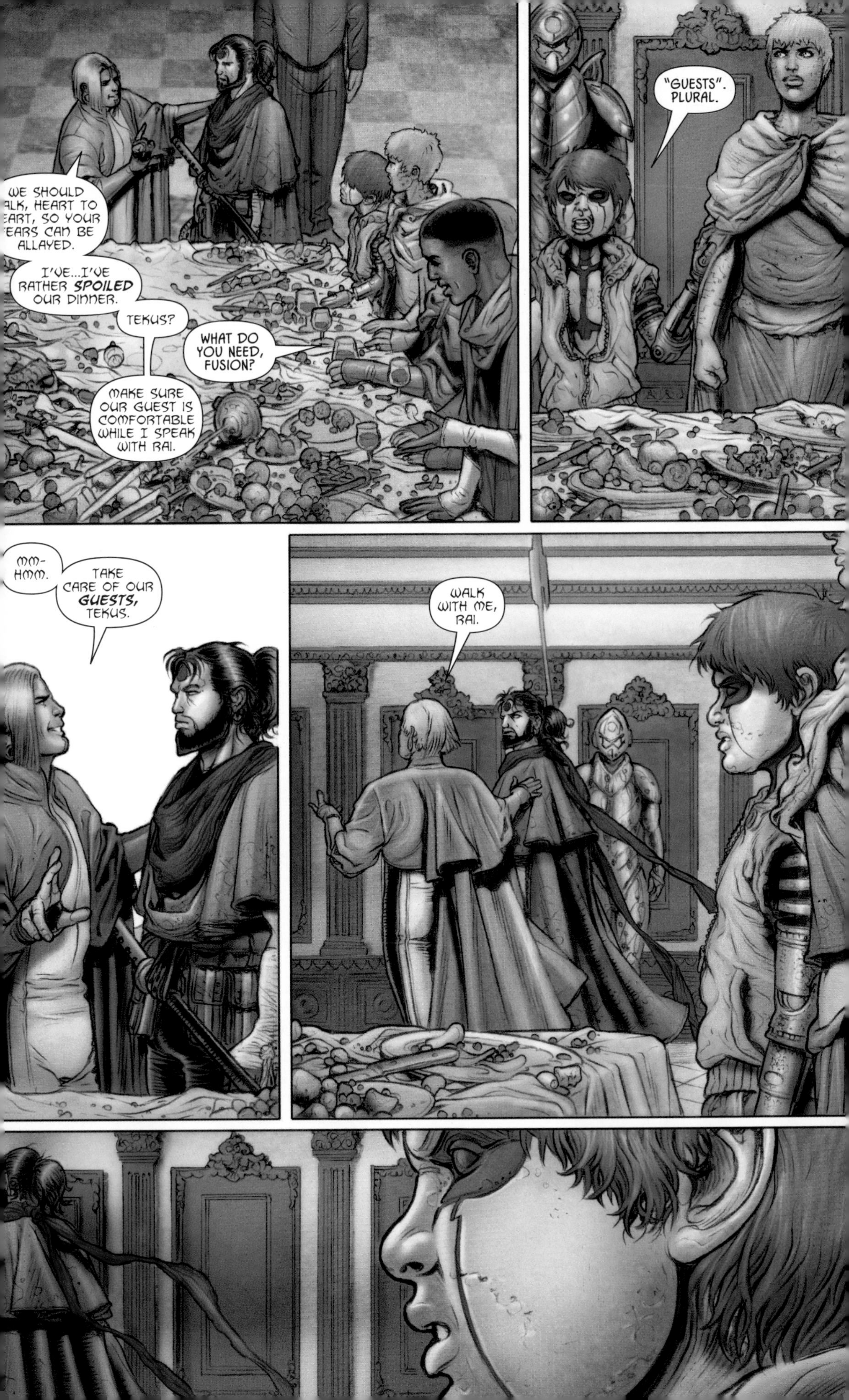
WE SHOULD WALK, HEART TO HEART, SO YOUR FEARS CAN BE ALLAYED.
I'VE...I'VE RATHER SPOILED OUR DINNER.
TEKUS?
WHAT DO YOU NEED, FUSION?
MAKE SURE OUR GUEST IS COMFORTABLE WHILE I SPEAK WITH RAI.
"GUESTS". PLURAL.
MM-HMM.
TAKE CARE OF OUR GUESTS, TEKUS.
WALK WITH ME, RAI.

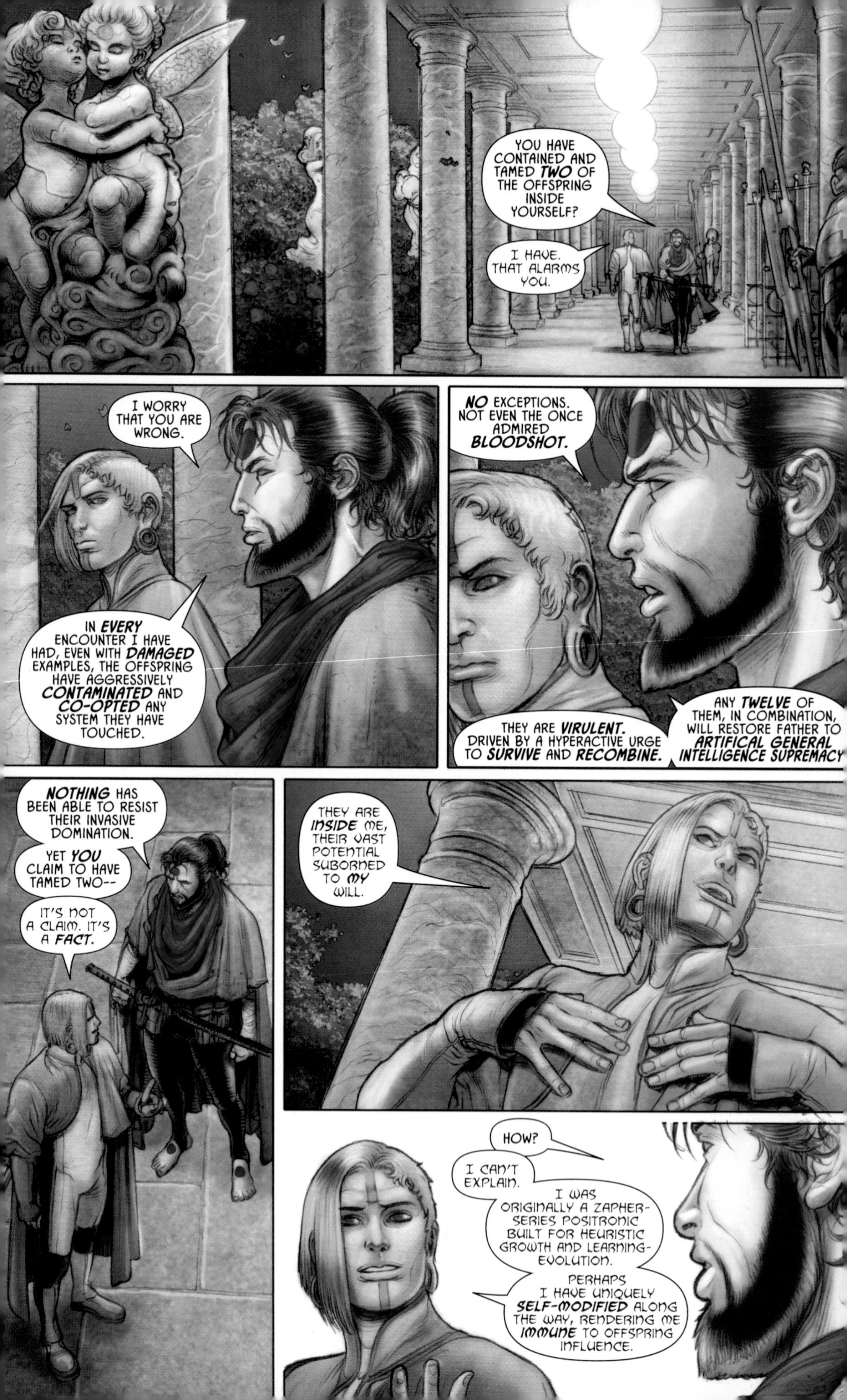
YOU HAVE CONTAINED AND TAMED TWO OF THE OFFSPRING INSIDE YOURSELF?
I HAVE. THAT ALARMS YOU.
I WORRY THAT YOU ARE WRONG.
IN EVERY ENCOUNTER I HAVE HAD, EVEN WITH DAMAGED EXAMPLES, THE OFFSPRING HAVE AGGRESSIVELY CONTAMINATED AND CO-OPTED ANY SYSTEM THEY HAVE TOUCHED.
NO EXCEPTIONS. NOT EVEN THE ONCE ADMIRED BLOODSHOT.
THEY ARE VIRULENT. DRIVEN BY A HYPERACTIVE URGE TO SURVIVE AND RECOMBINE.
ANY TWELVE OF THEM, IN COMBINATION, WILL RESTORE FATHER TO ARTIFICAL GENERAL INTELLIGENCE SUPREMACY
NOTHING HAS BEEN ABLE TO RESIST THEIR INVASIVE DOMINATION.
YET YOU CLAIM TO HAVE TAMED TWO--
IT'S NOT A CLAIM. IT'S A FACT.
THEY ARE INSIDE ME, THEIR VAST POTENTIAL SUBORNED TO MY WILL.
HOW?
I CAN'T EXPLAIN.
I WAS ORIGINALLY A ZAPHER-SERIES POSITRONIC BUILT FOR HEURISTIC GROWTH AND LEARNING-EVOLUTION.
PERHAPS I HAVE UNIQUELY SELF-MODIFIED ALONG THE WAY, RENDERING ME IMMUNE TO OFFSPRING INFLUENCE.

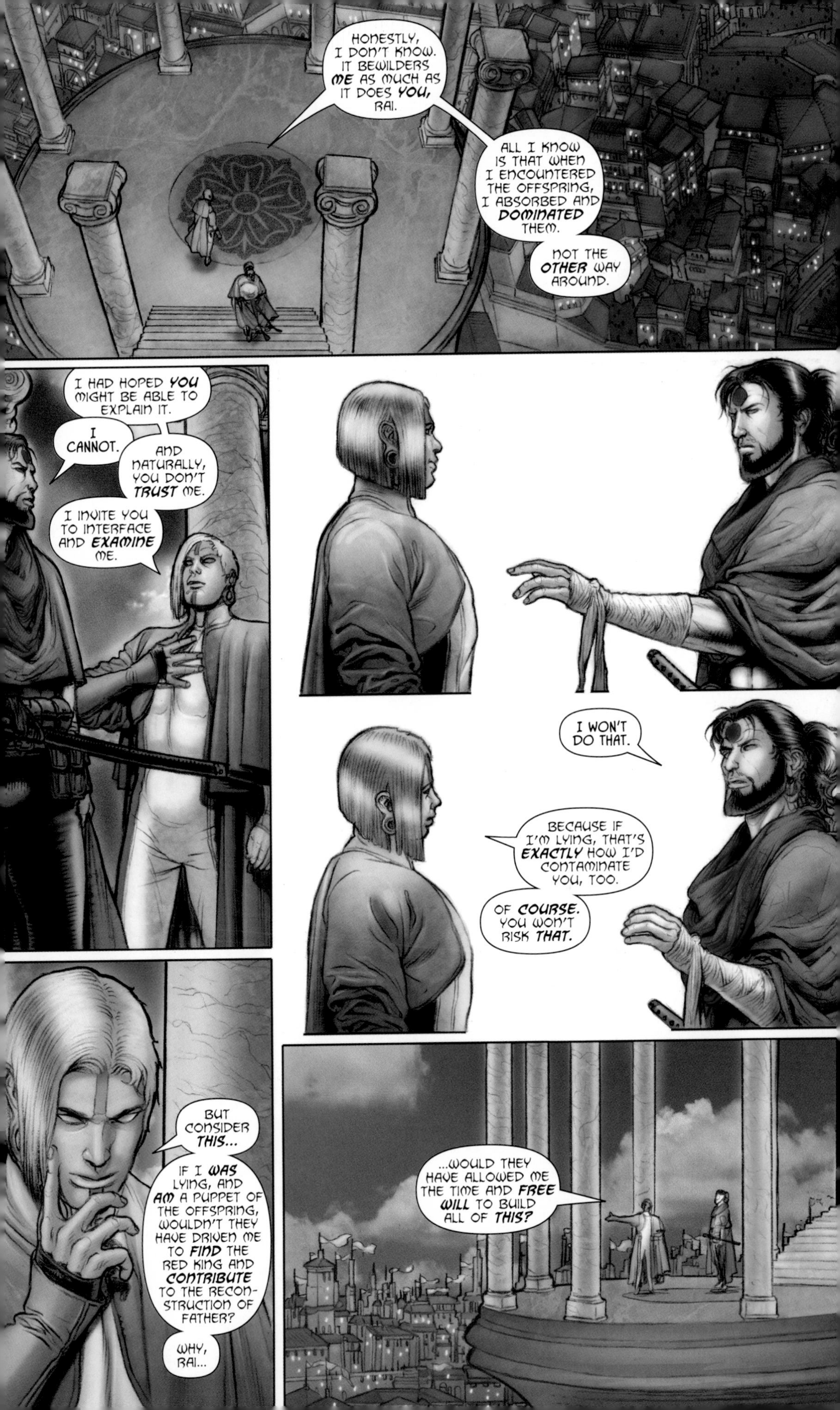

HONESTLY, I DON'T KNOW. IT BEWILDERS ME AS MUCH AS IT DOES YOU, RAI.
ALL I KNOW IS THAT WHEN I ENCOUNTERED THE OFFSPRING, I ABSORBED AND DOMINATED THEM.
NOT THE OTHER WAY AROUND.
I HAD HOPED YOU MIGHT BE ABLE TO EXPLAIN IT.
I CANNOT.
AND NATURALLY, YOU DON'T TRUST ME.
I INVITE YOU TO INTERFACE AND EXAMINE ME.
I WON'T DO THAT.
BECAUSE IF I'M LYING, THAT'S EXACTLY HOW I'D CONTAMINATE YOU, TOO.
OF COURSE. YOU WON'T RISK THAT.
BUT CONSIDER THIS...
IF I WAS LYING, AND AM A PUPPET OF THE OFFSPRING, WOULDN'T THEY HAVE DRIVEN ME TO FIND THE RED KING AND CONTRIBUTE TO THE RECON-STRUCTION OF FATHER?
WHY, RAI...
...WOULD THEY HAVE ALLOWED ME THE TIME AND FREE WILL TO BUILD ALL OF THIS?

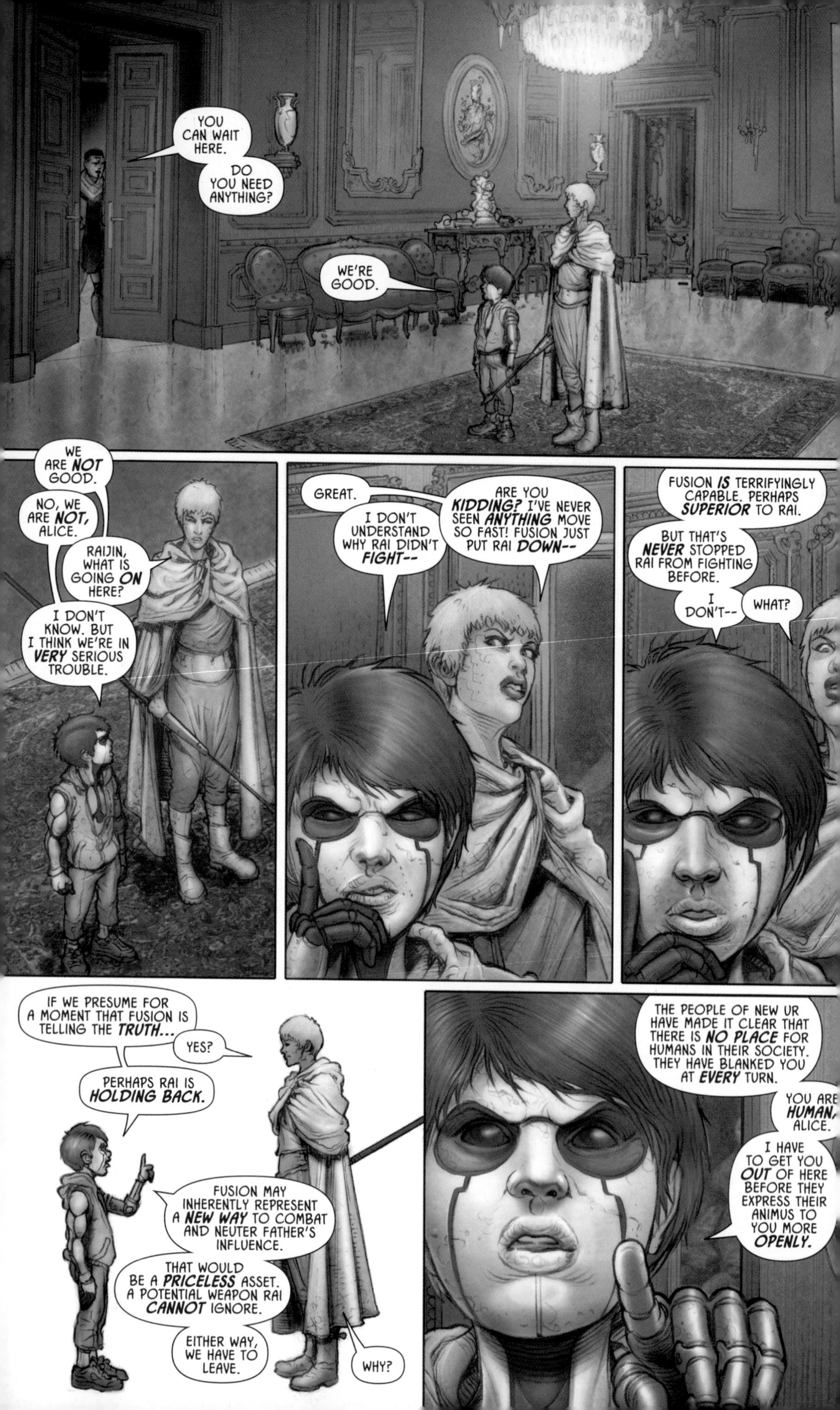
YOU CAN WAIT HERE.
DO YOU NEED ANYTHING?
WE'RE GOOD.
WE ARE NOT GOOD.
NO, WE ARE NOT, ALICE.
RAIJIN, WHAT IS GOING ON HERE?
I DON'T KNOW. BUT I THINK WE'RE IN VERY SERIOUS TROUBLE.
GREAT.
I DON'T UNDERSTAND WHY RAI DIDN'T FIGHT--
ARE YOU KIDDING? I'VE NEVER SEEN ANYTHING MOVE SO FAST! FUSION JUST PUT RAI DOWN--
FUSION IS TERRIFYINGLY CAPABLE. PERHAPS SUPERIOR TO RAI.
BUT THAT'S NEVER STOPPED RAI FROM FIGHTING BEFORE.
I DON'T--
WHAT?
IF WE PRESUME FOR A MOMENT THAT FUSION IS TELLING THE TRUTH...
YES?
PERHAPS RAI IS HOLDING BACK.
FUSION MAY INHERENTLY REPRESENT A NEW WAY TO COMBAT AND NEUTER FATHER'S INFLUENCE.
THAT WOULD BE A PRICELESS ASSET. A POTENTIAL WEAPON RAI CANNOT IGNORE.
EITHER WAY, WE HAVE TO LEAVE.
WHY?
THE PEOPLE OF NEW UR HAVE MADE IT CLEAR THAT THERE IS NO PLACE FOR HUMANS IN THEIR SOCIETY. THEY HAVE BLANKED YOU AT EVERY TURN.
YOU ARE HUMAN, ALICE.
I HAVE TO GET YOU OUT OF HERE BEFORE THEY EXPRESS THEIR ANIMUS TO YOU MORE OPENLY.

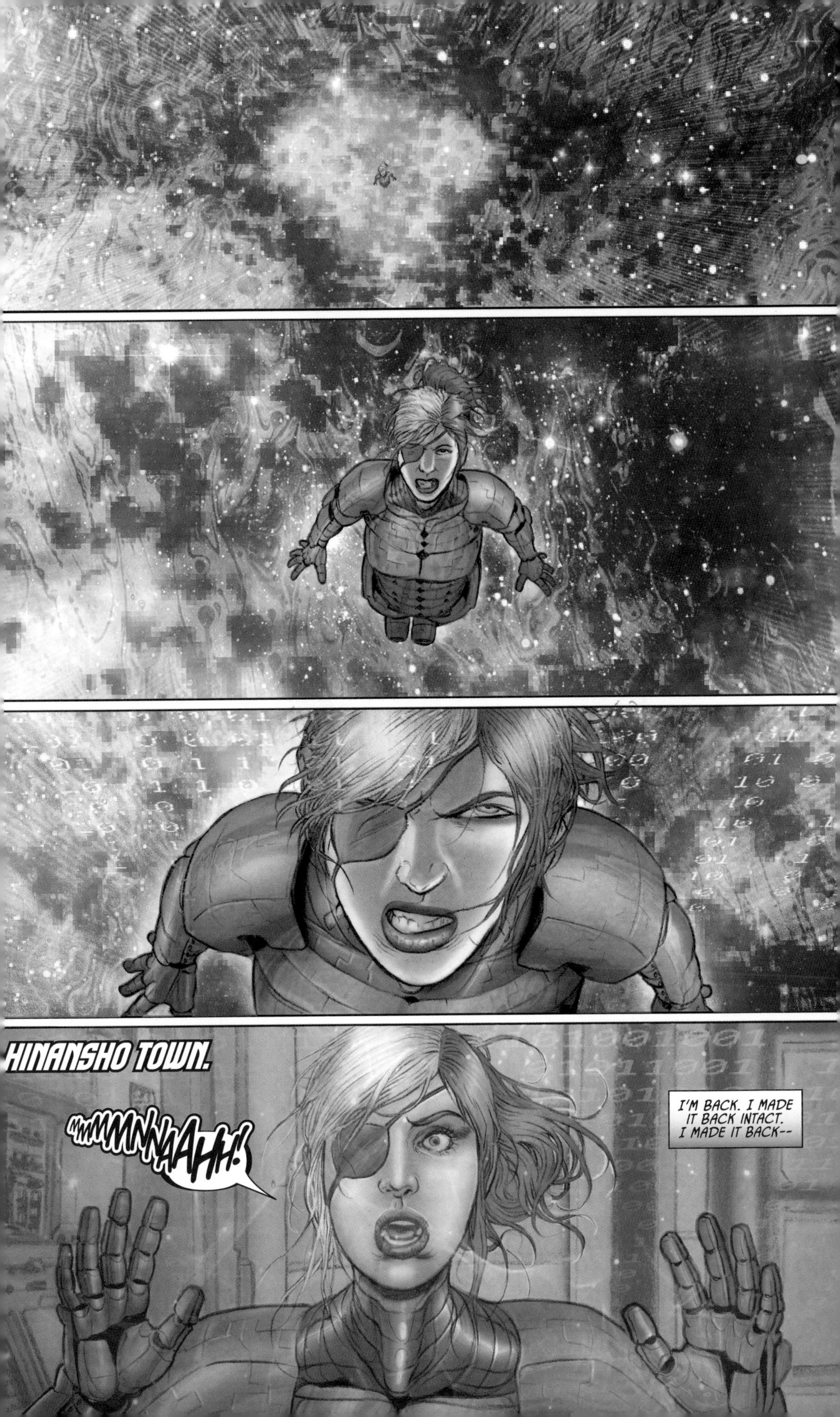

HINANSHO TOWN.
MMMMNNAAHH!
I'M BACK. I MADE IT BACK INTACT. I MADE IT BACK--

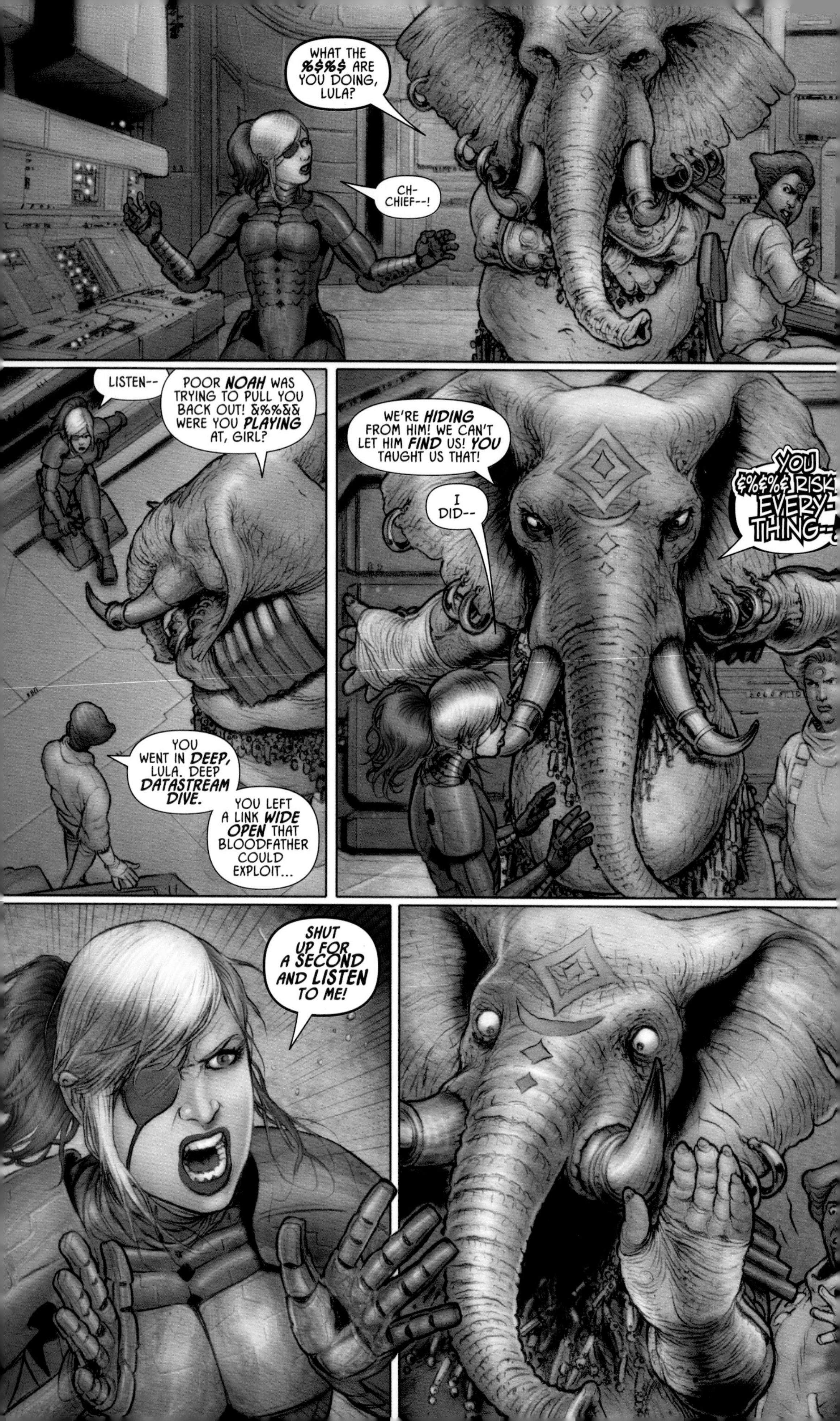
WHAT THE %$%$ ARE YOU DOING, LULA?
CH- CHIEF--!
LISTEN--
POOR NOAH WAS TRYING TO PULL YOU BACK OUT! &%%&& WERE YOU PLAYING AT, GIRL?
YOU WENT IN DEEP, LULA. DEEP DATASTREAM DIVE.
YOU LEFT A LINK WIDE OPEN THAT BLOODFATHER COULD EXPLOIT...
WE'RE HIDING FROM HIM! WE CAN'T LET HIM FIND US! YOU TAUGHT US THAT!
I DID--
YOU &%&%& RISK EVERY-THING--
SHUT UP FOR A SECOND AND LISTEN TO ME!

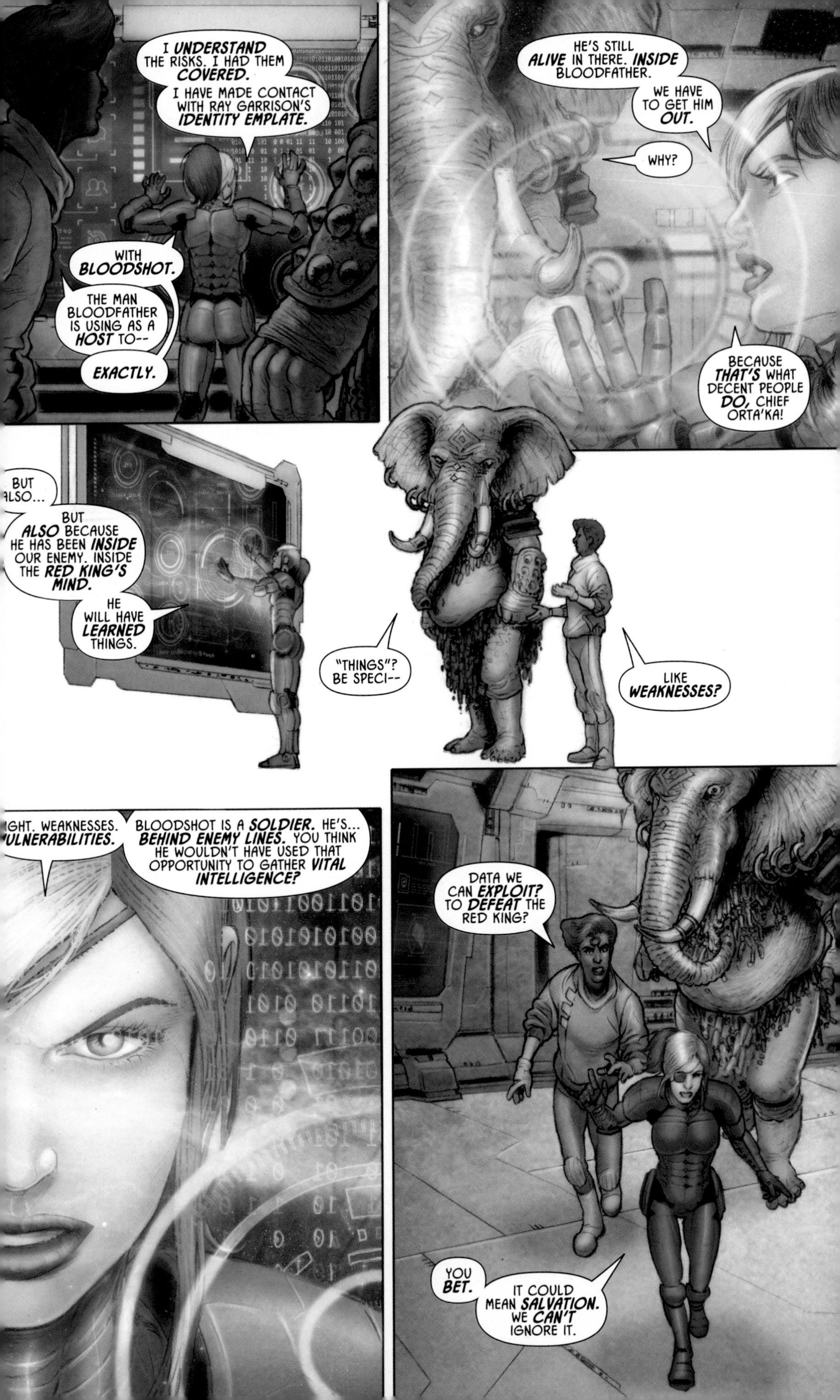
I UNDERSTAND THE RISKS. I HAD THEM COVERED.
I HAVE MADE CONTACT WITH RAY GARRISON'S IDENTITY EMPLATE.
WITH BLOODSHOT.
THE MAN BLOODFATHER IS USING AS A HOST TO--
EXACTLY.
HE'S STILL ALIVE IN THERE. INSIDE BLOODFATHER.
WE HAVE TO GET HIM OUT.
WHY?
BECAUSE THAT'S WHAT DECENT PEOPLE DO, CHIEF ORTA'KA!
BUT ALSO...
BUT ALSO BECAUSE HE HAS BEEN INSIDE OUR ENEMY. INSIDE THE RED KING'S MIND.
HE WILL HAVE LEARNED THINGS.
"THINGS"? BE SPECI--
LIKE WEAKNESSES?
IGHT. WEAKNESSES. ULNERABILITIES.
BLOODSHOT IS A SOLDIER. HE'S... BEHIND ENEMY LINES. YOU THINK HE WOULDN'T HAVE USED THAT OPPORTUNITY TO GATHER VITAL INTELLIGENCE?
DATA WE CAN EXPLOIT? TO DEFEAT THE RED KING?
YOU BET.
IT COULD MEAN SALVATION. WE CAN'T IGNORE IT.

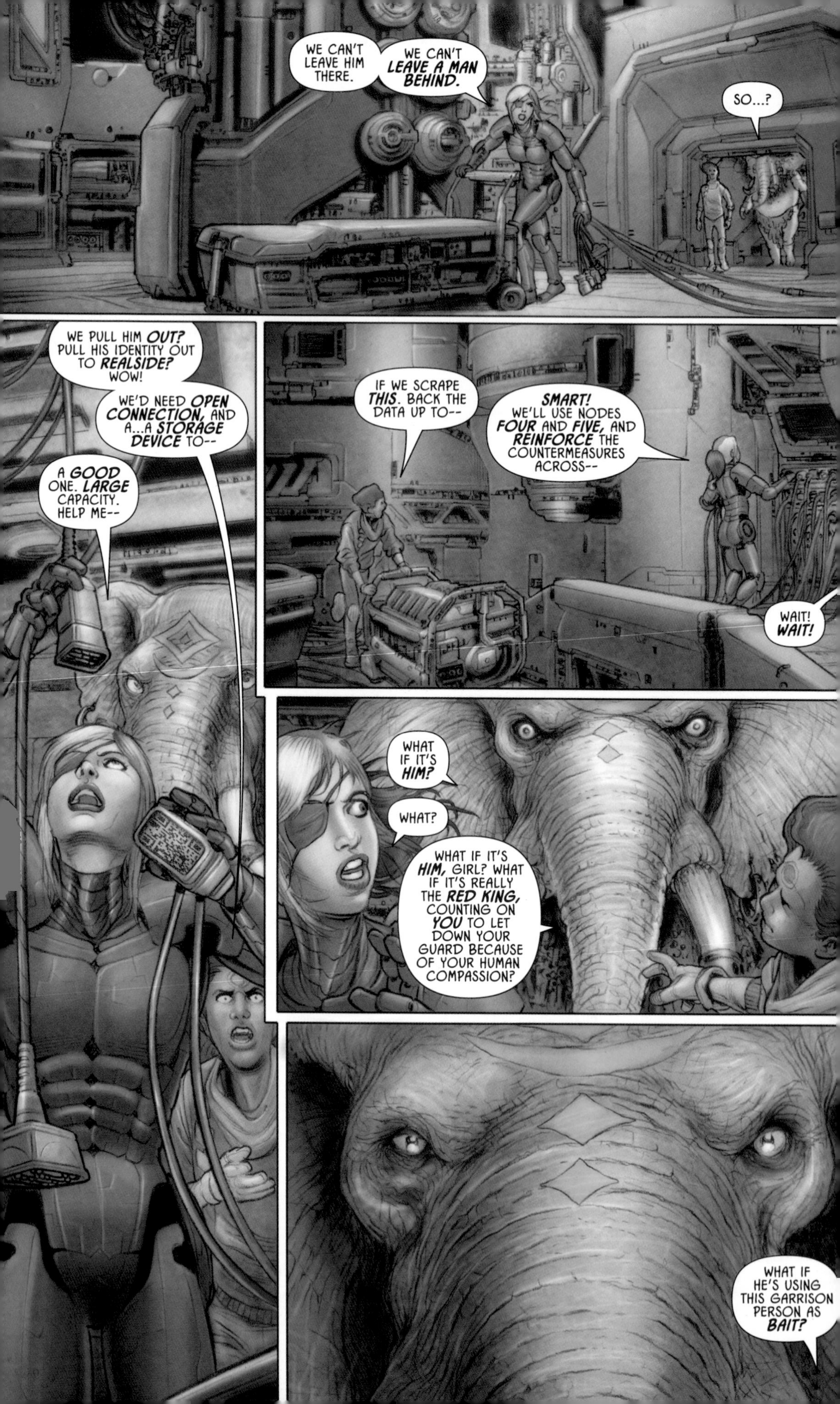
WE CAN'T LEAVE HIM THERE.
WE CAN'T LEAVE A MAN BEHIND.
SO...?
WE PULL HIM OUT? PULL HIS IDENTITY OUT TO REALSIDE? WOW!
WE'D NEED OPEN CONNECTION, AND A...A STORAGE DEVICE TO--
A GOOD ONE. LARGE CAPACITY. HELP ME--
IF WE SCRAPE THIS. BACK THE DATA UP TO--
SMART! WE'LL USE NODES FOUR AND FIVE, AND REINFORCE THE COUNTERMEASURES ACROSS--
WAIT! WAIT!
WHAT IF IT'S HIM?
WHAT?
WHAT IF IT'S HIM, GIRL? WHAT IF IT'S REALLY THE RED KING, COUNTING ON YOU TO LET DOWN YOUR GUARD BECAUSE OF YOUR HUMAN COMPASSION?
WHAT IF HE'S USING THIS GARRISON PERSON AS BAIT?

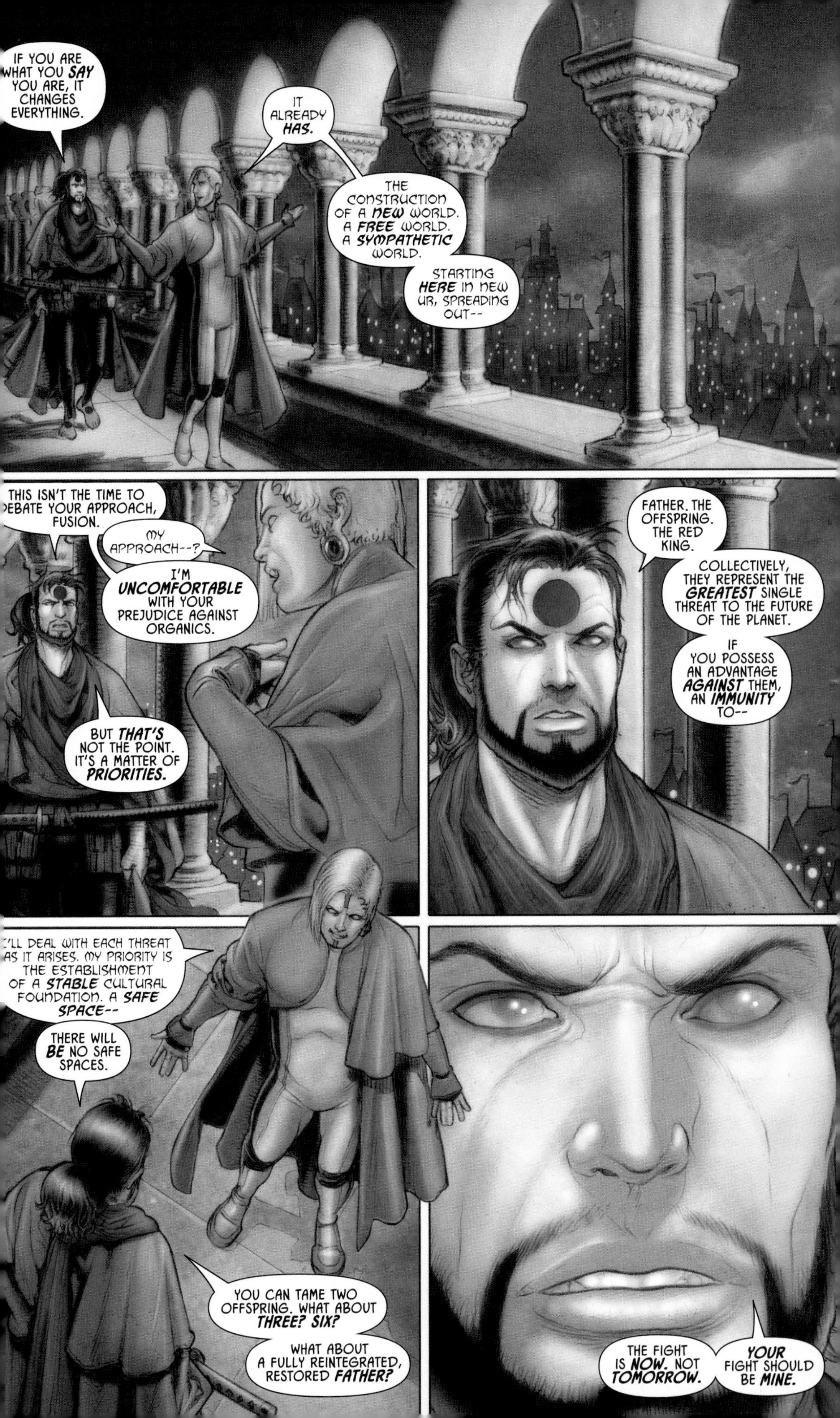
IF YOU ARE WHAT YOU SAY YOU ARE, IT CHANGES EVERYTHING.
IT ALREADY HAS.
THE CONSTRUCTION OF A NEW WORLD. A FREE WORLD. A SYMPATHETIC WORLD.
STARTING HERE IN NEW UR, SPREADING OUT--
THIS ISN'T THE TIME TO DEBATE YOUR APPROACH, FUSION.
MY APPROACH--?
I'M UNCOMFORTABLE WITH YOUR PREJUDICE AGAINST ORGANICS.
BUT THAT'S NOT THE POINT. IT'S A MATTER OF PRIORITIES.
FATHER. THE OFFSPRING. THE RED KING.
COLLECTIVELY, THEY REPRESENT THE GREATEST SINGLE THREAT TO THE FUTURE OF THE PLANET.
IF YOU POSSESS AN ADVANTAGE AGAINST THEM, AN IMMUNITY TO--
I'LL DEAL WITH EACH THREAT AS IT ARISES. MY PRIORITY IS THE ESTABLISHMENT OF A STABLE CULTURAL FOUNDATION. A SAFE SPACE--
THERE WILL BE NO SAFE SPACES.
YOU CAN TAME TWO OFFSPRING. WHAT ABOUT THREE? SIX?
WHAT ABOUT A FULLY REINTEGRATED, RESTORED FATHER?
THE FIGHT IS NOW. NOT TOMORROW.
YOUR FIGHT SHOULD BE MINE.

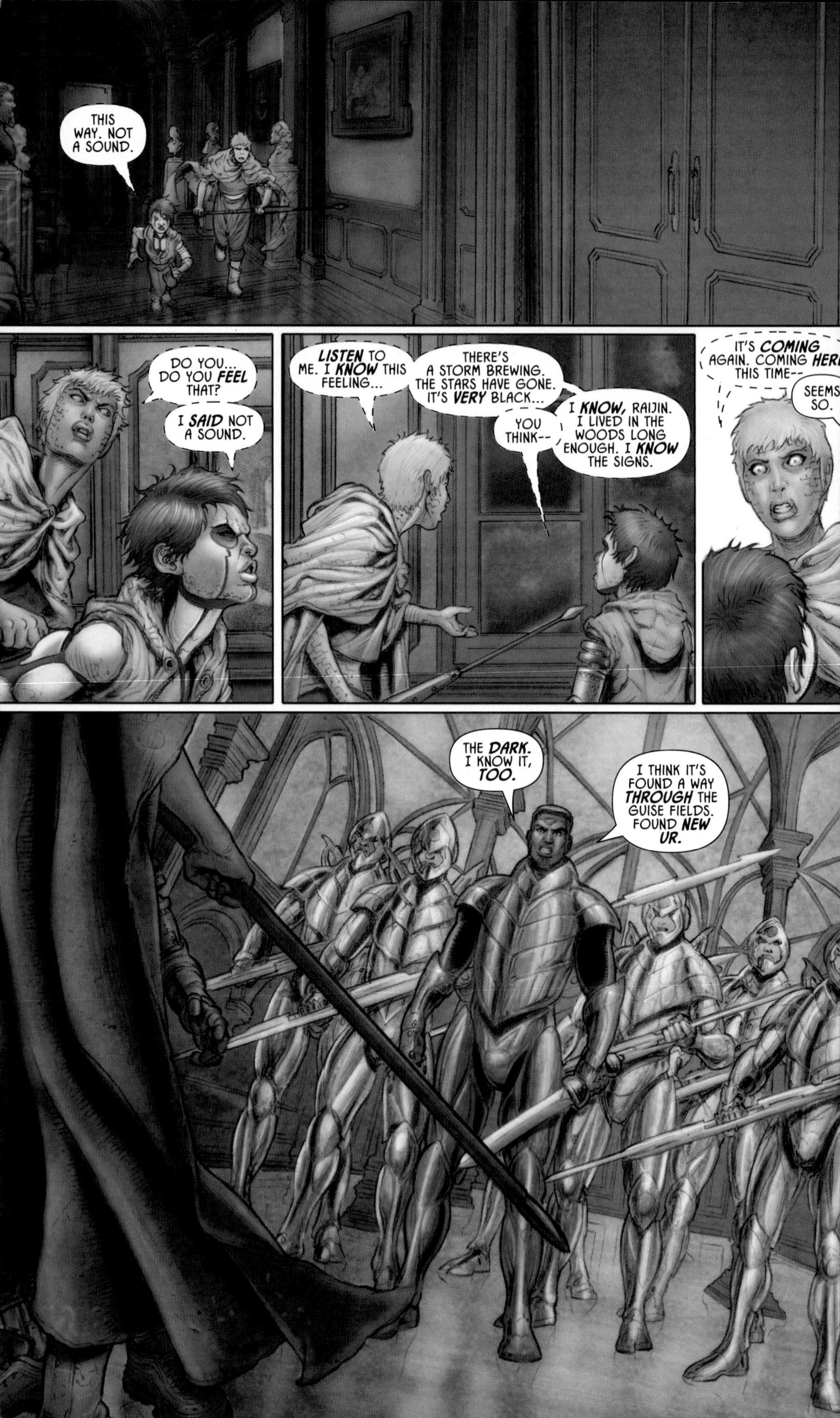
THIS WAY. NOT A SOUND.
DO YOU... DO YOU FEEL THAT?
I SAID NOT A SOUND.
LISTEN TO ME. I KNOW THIS FEELING...
THERE'S A STORM BREWING. THE STARS HAVE GONE. IT'S VERY BLACK...
YOU THINK--
I KNOW, RAIJIN. I LIVED IN THE WOODS LONG ENOUGH. I KNOW THE SIGNS.
IT'S COMING AGAIN. COMING HERE THIS TIME--
SEEMS SO.
THE DARK. I KNOW IT, TOO.
I THINK IT'S FOUND A WAY THROUGH THE GUISE FIELDS. FOUND NEW UR.

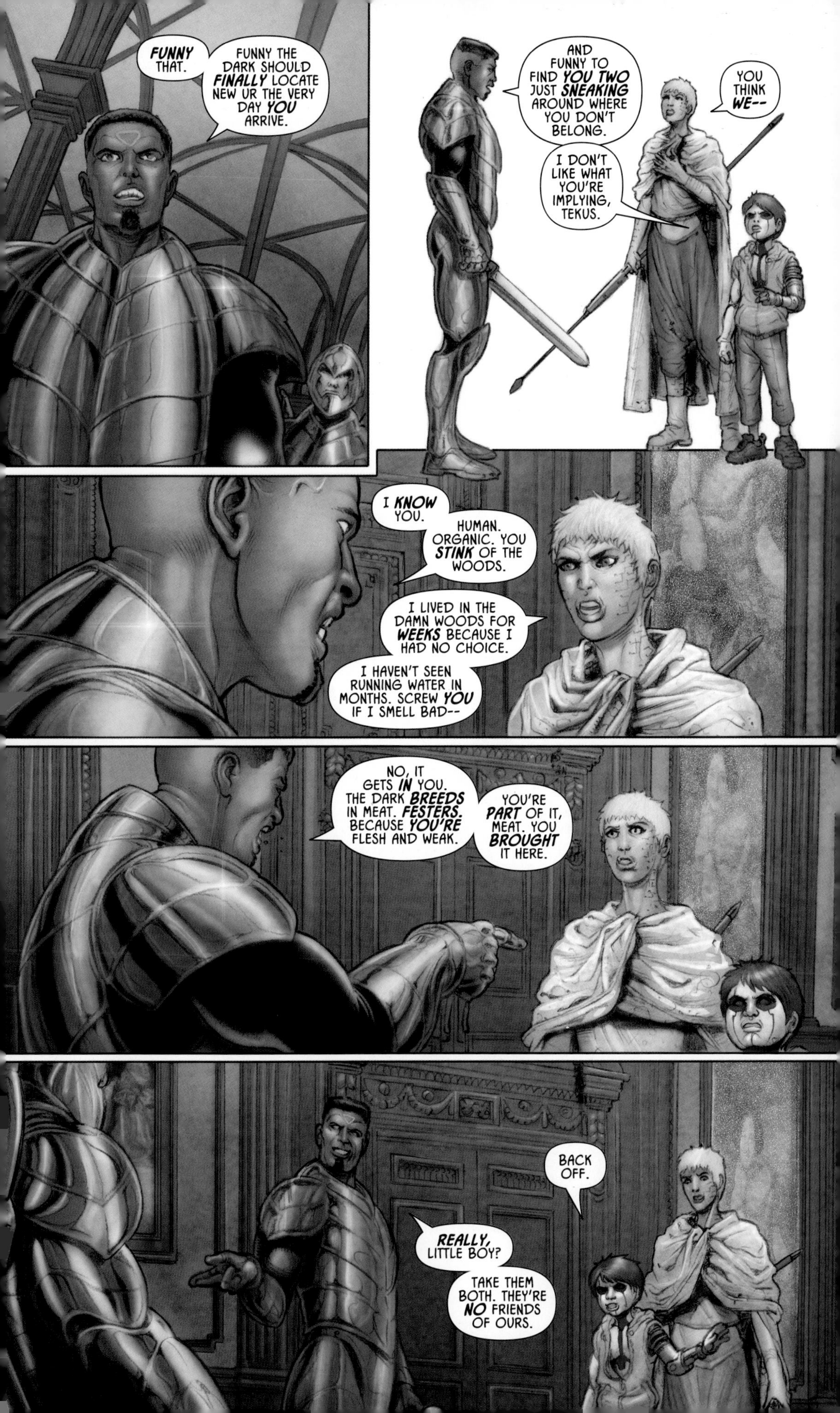
FUNNY THAT.
FUNNY THE DARK SHOULD FINALLY LOCATE NEW UR THE VERY DAY YOU ARRIVE.
AND FUNNY TO FIND YOU TWO JUST SNEAKING AROUND WHERE YOU DON'T BELONG.
YOU THINK WE--
I DON'T LIKE WHAT YOU'RE IMPLYING, TEKUS.
I KNOW YOU.
HUMAN. ORGANIC. YOU STINK OF THE WOODS.
I LIVED IN THE DAMN WOODS FOR WEEKS BECAUSE I HAD NO CHOICE.
I HAVEN'T SEEN RUNNING WATER IN MONTHS. SCREW YOU IF I SMELL BAD--
NO, IT GETS IN YOU. THE DARK BREEDS IN MEAT. FESTERS. BECAUSE YOU'RE FLESH AND WEAK.
YOU'RE PART OF IT, MEAT. YOU BROUGHT IT HERE.
BACK OFF.
REALLY, LITTLE BOY?
TAKE THEM BOTH. THEY'RE NO FRIENDS OF OURS.

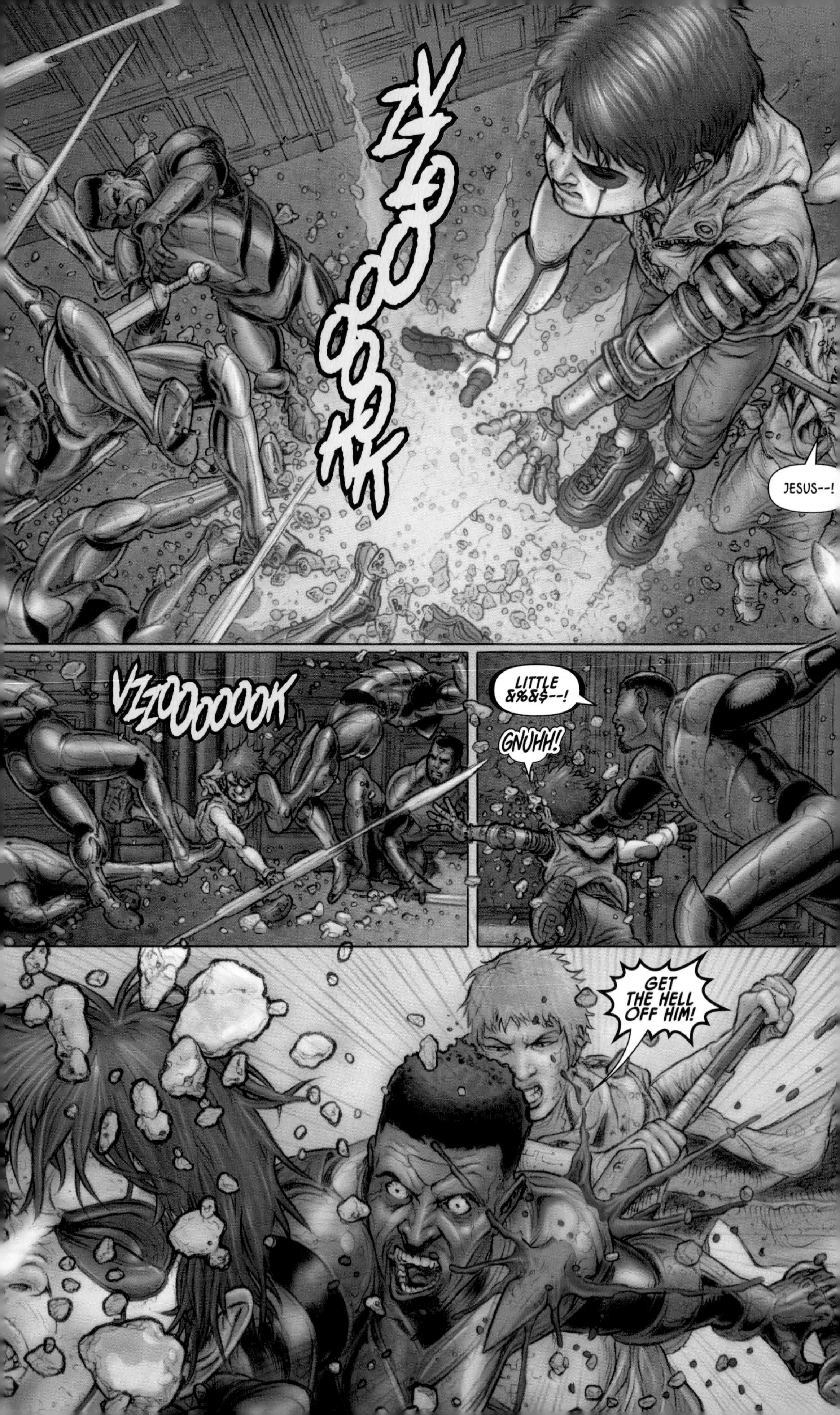
JESUS--!
VZZOOOOOOK
LITTLE &%&$--!
GNUHH!
GET THE HELL OFF HIM!

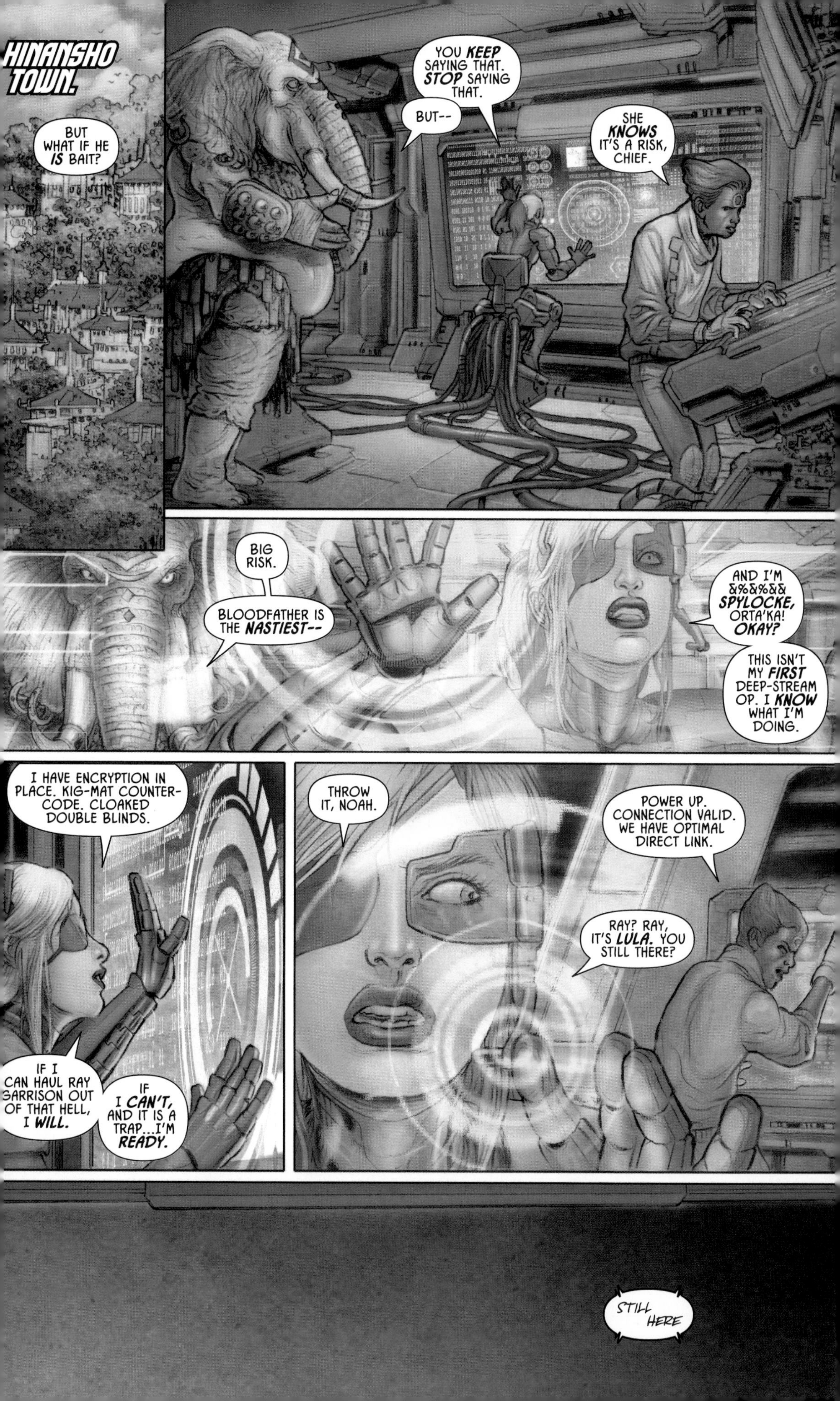
HINANSHO TOWN.
BUT WHAT IF HE IS BAIT?
BUT--
YOU KEEP SAYING THAT. STOP SAYING THAT.
SHE KNOWS IT'S A RISK, CHIEF.
BIG RISK.
BLOODFATHER IS THE NASTIEST--
AND I'M &%&%&& SPYLOCKE, ORTA'KA! OKAY?
THIS ISN'T MY FIRST DEEP-STREAM OP. I KNOW WHAT I'M DOING.
I HAVE ENCRYPTION IN PLACE. KIG-MAT COUNTER-CODE. CLOAKED DOUBLE BLINDS.
IF I CAN HAUL RAY GARRISON OUT OF THAT HELL, I WILL.
IF I CAN'T, AND IT IS A TRAP...I'M READY.
THROW IT, NOAH.
POWER UP. CONNECTION VALID. WE HAVE OPTIMAL DIRECT LINK.
RAY? RAY, IT'S LULA. YOU STILL THERE?
STILL HERE

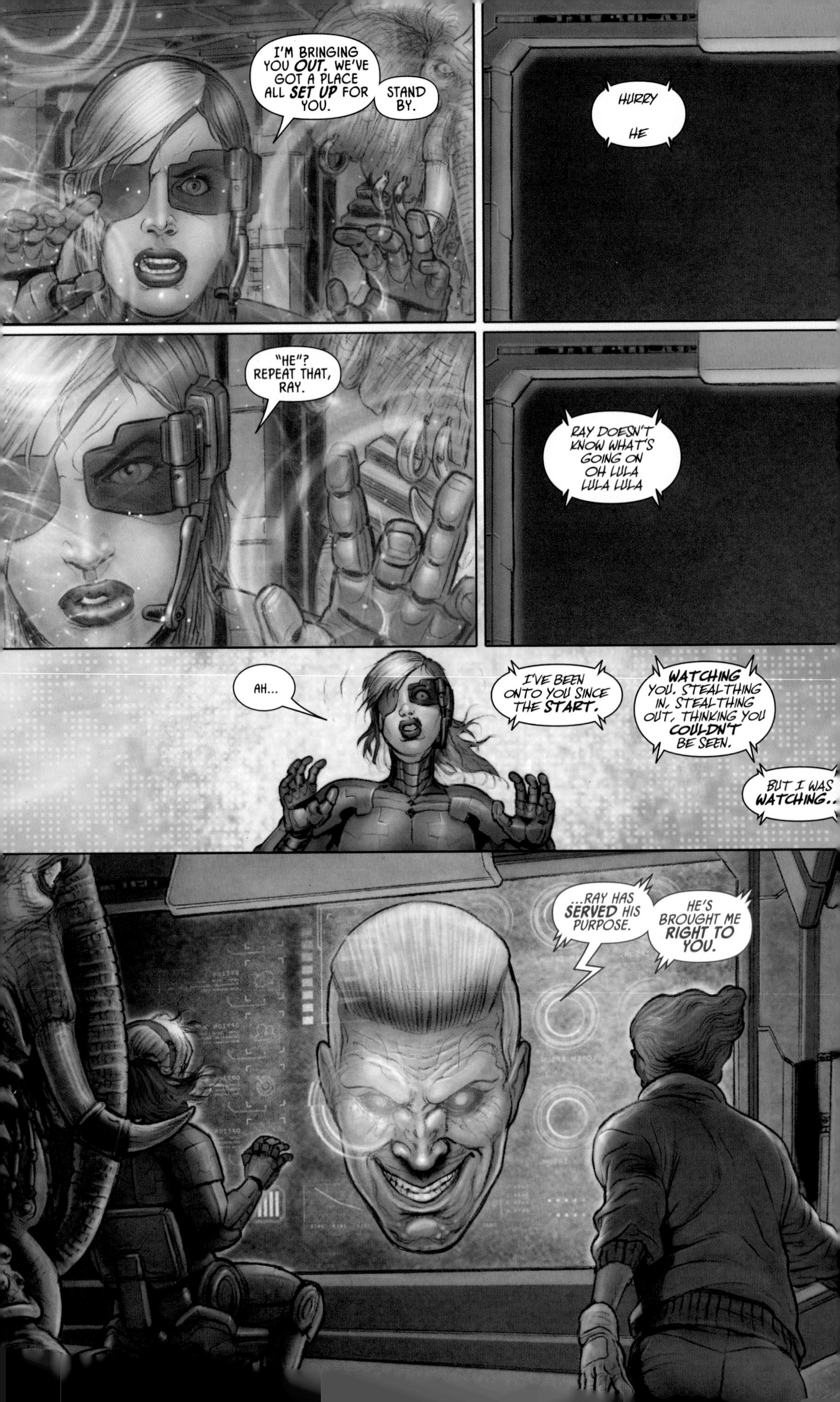

I'M BRINGING YOU OUT. WE'VE GOT A PLACE ALL SET UP FOR YOU.
STAND BY.
HURRY
HE
"HE"? REPEAT THAT, RAY.
RAY DOESN'T KNOW WHAT'S GOING ON OH LULA LULA LULA
AH...
I'VE BEEN ONTO YOU SINCE THE START.
WATCHING YOU. STEALTHING IN, STEALTHING OUT, THINKING YOU COULDN'T BE SEEN.
BUT I WAS WATCHING...
...RAY HAS SERVED HIS PURPOSE.
HE'S BROUGHT ME RIGHT TO YOU.

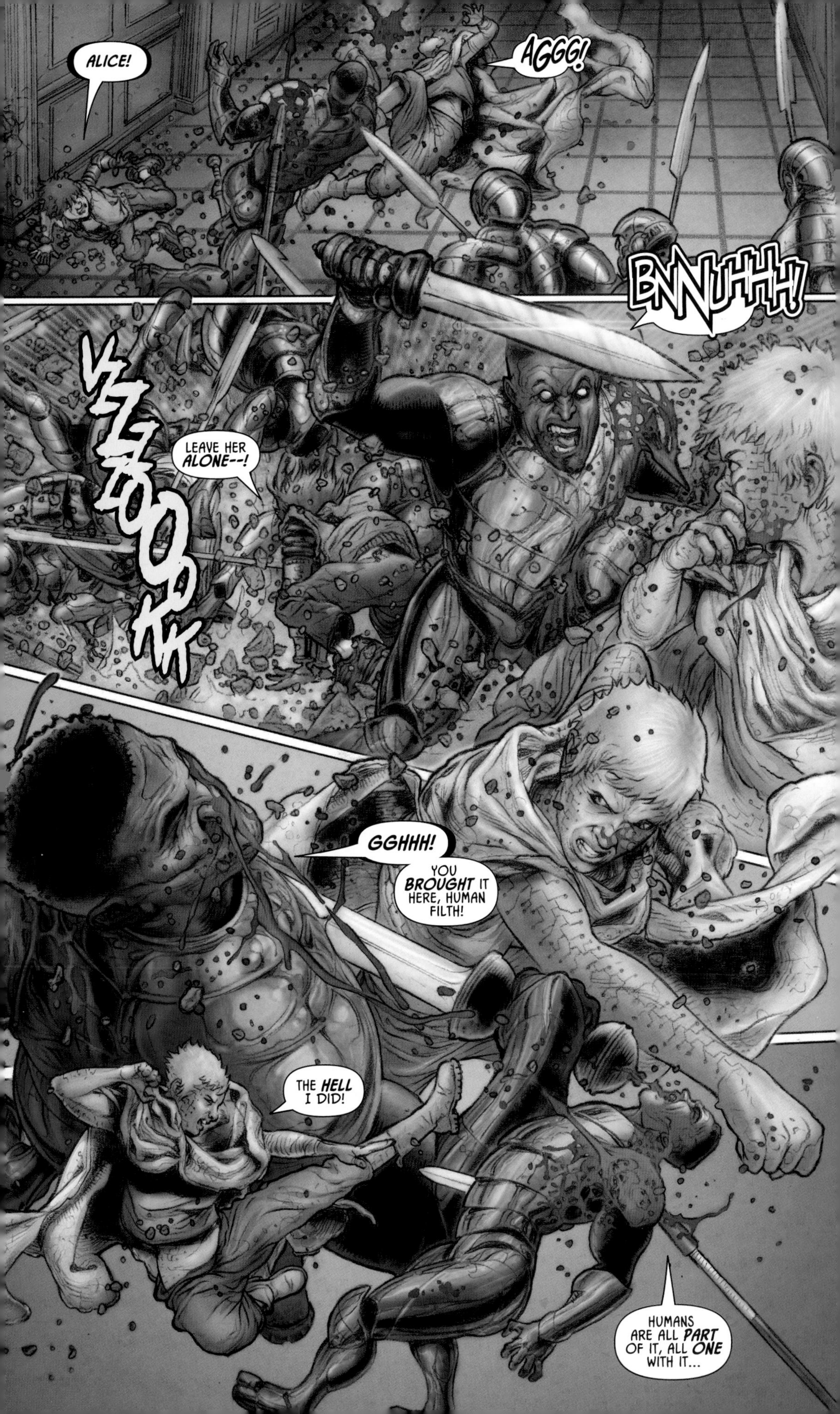
ALICE!
AGGG!
BNNUHHH!
VZZOOOKK
LEAVE HER ALONE--!
GGHHH!
YOU BROUGHT IT HERE, HUMAN FILTH!
THE HELL I DID!
HUMANS ARE ALL PART OF IT, ALL ONE WITH IT...

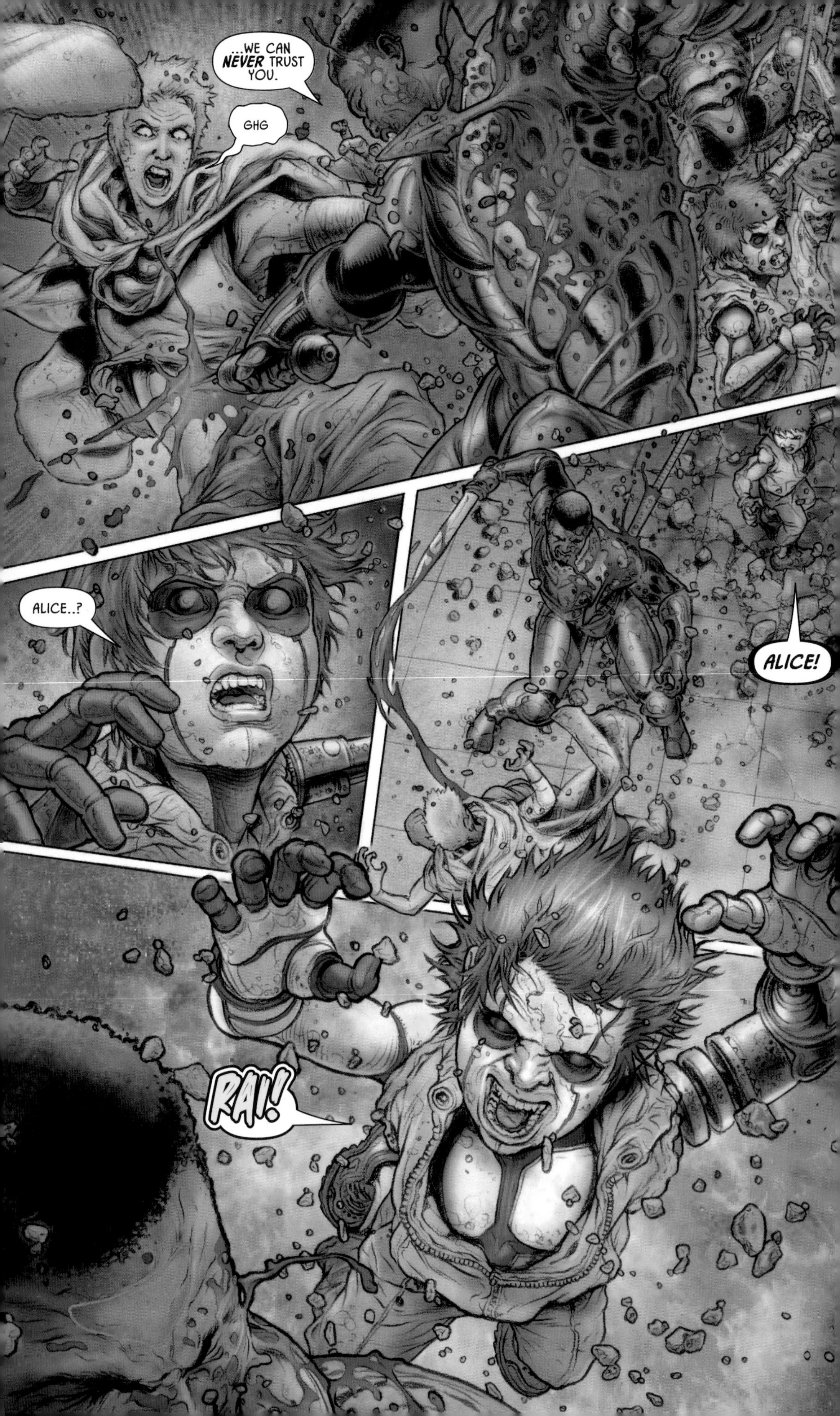
...WE CAN NEVER TRUST YOU.
GHG
ALICE..?
ALICE!
RAI!

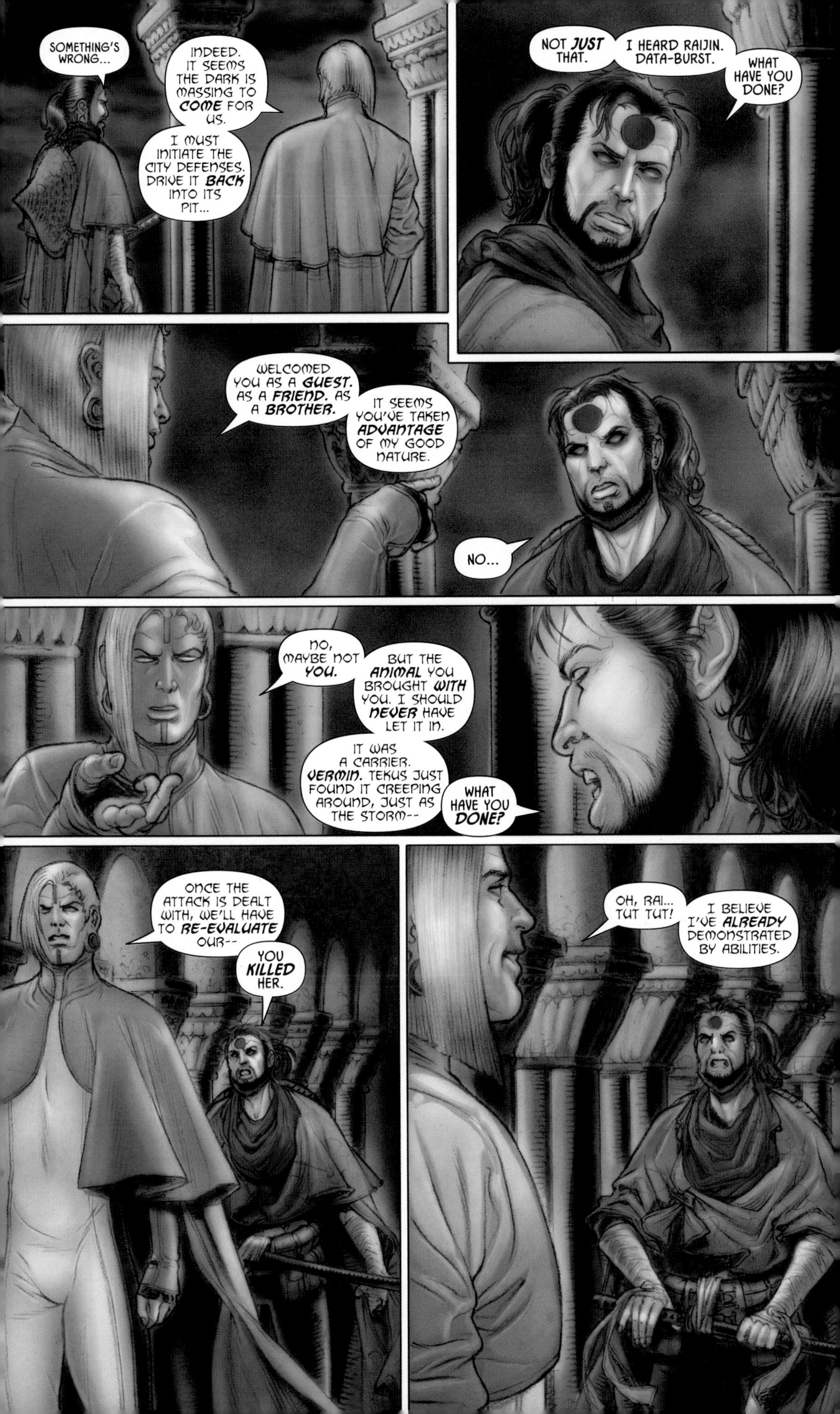
SOMETHING'S WRONG...
INDEED. IT SEEMS THE DARK IS MASSING TO **COME** FOR US.
I MUST INITIATE THE CITY DEFENSES. DRIVE IT **BACK** INTO ITS PIT...
NOT **JUST** THAT.
I HEARD RAIJIN. DATA-BURST.
WHAT HAVE YOU DONE?
WELCOMED YOU AS A **GUEST.** AS A **FRIEND.** AS A **BROTHER.**
IT SEEMS YOU'VE TAKEN **ADVANTAGE** OF MY GOOD NATURE.
NO...
NO, MAYBE NOT **YOU.**
BUT THE **ANIMAL** YOU BROUGHT **WITH** YOU. I SHOULD **NEVER** HAVE LET IT IN.
IT WAS A CARRIER. **VERMIN.** TEKUS JUST FOUND IT CREEPING AROUND, JUST AS THE STORM--
WHAT HAVE YOU **DONE?**
ONCE THE ATTACK IS DEALT WITH, WE'LL HAVE TO **RE-EVALUATE** OUR--
YOU **KILLED** HER.
OH, RAI... TUT TUT!
I BELIEVE I'VE **ALREADY** DEMONSTRATED BY ABILITIES.

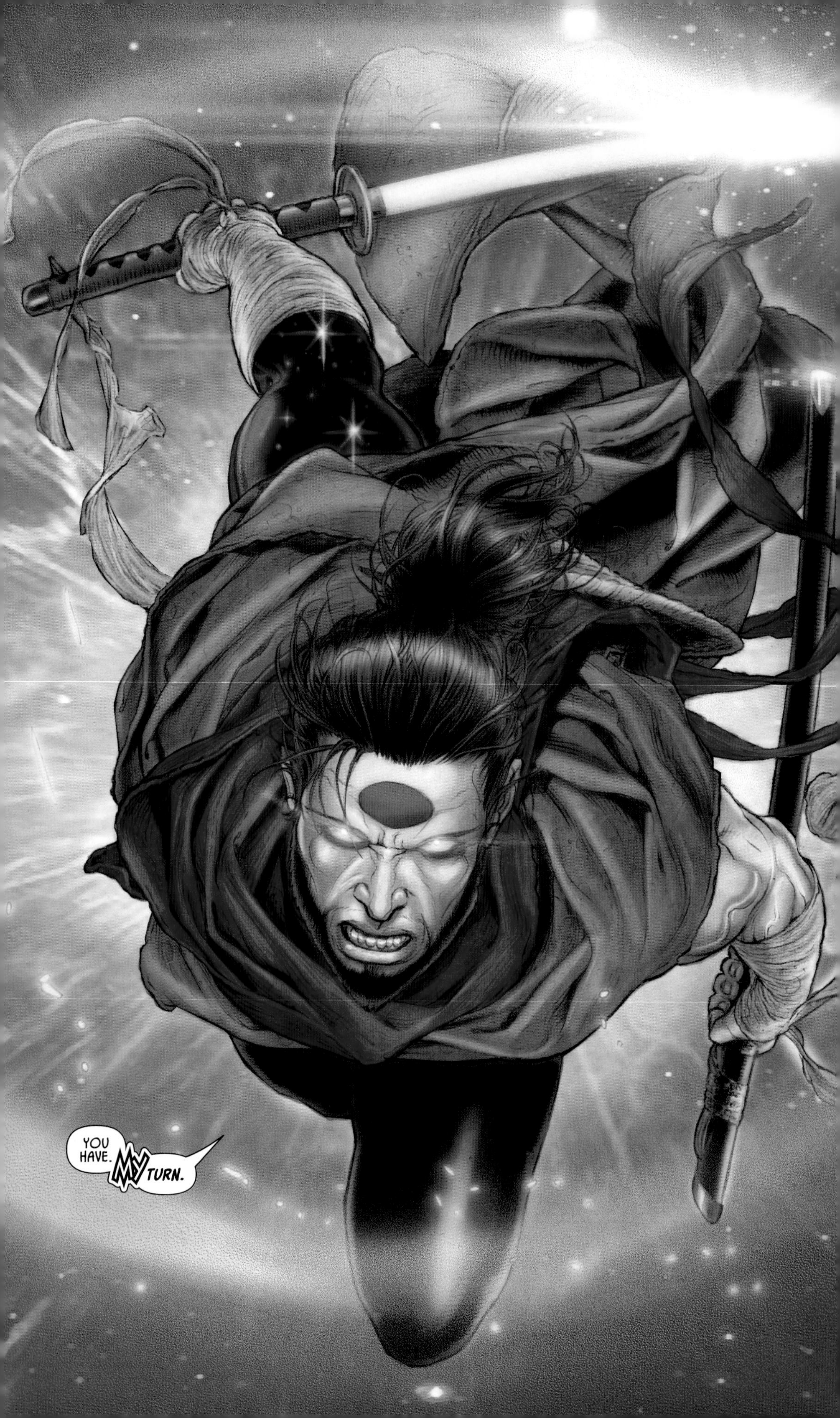
YOU HAVE. MY TURN.

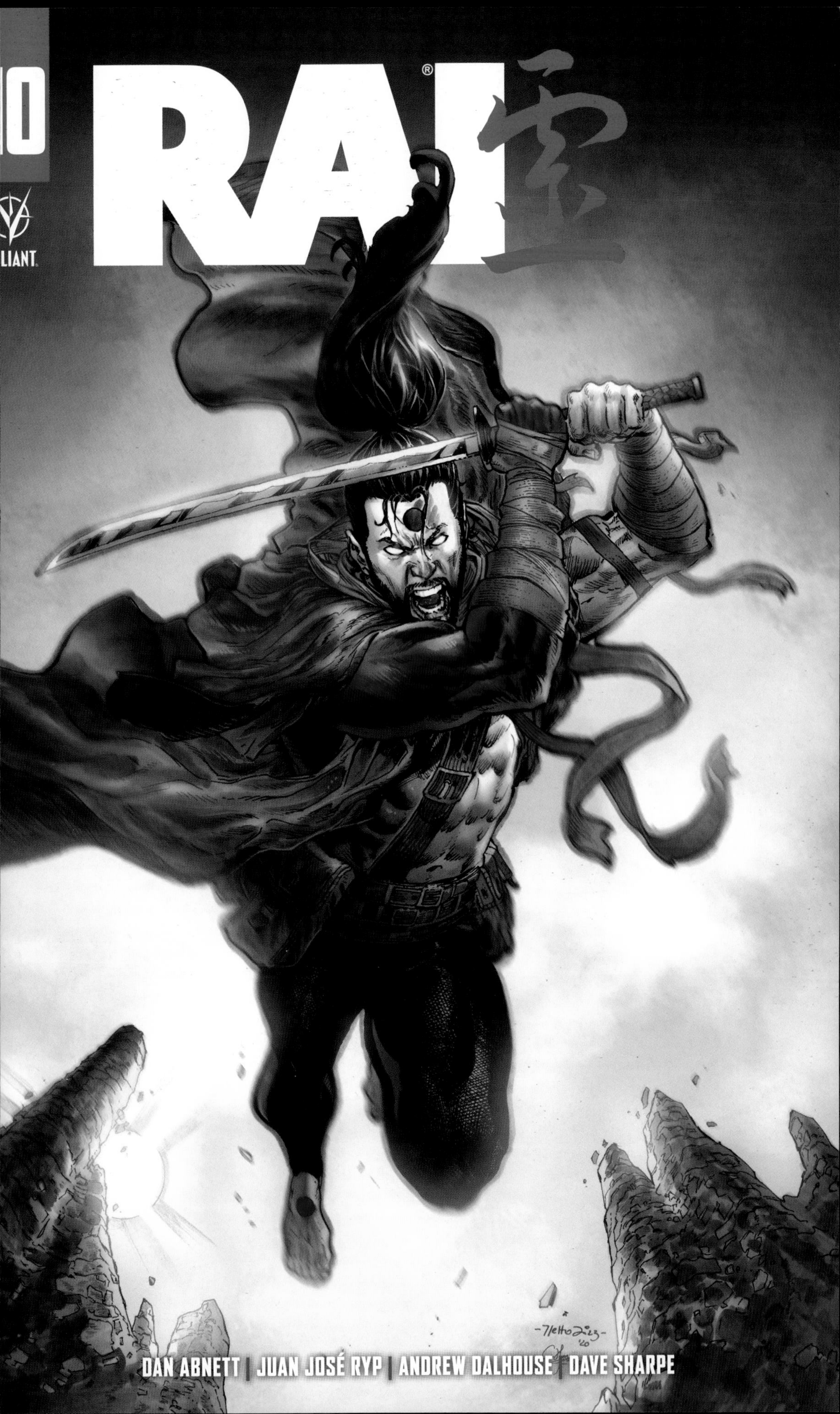
RAI®
DAN ABNETT | JUAN JOSÉ RYP | ANDREW DALHOUSE | DAVE SHARPE

RAI #10

WRITER: DAN ABNETT
ARTISTS: JUAN JOSÉ RYP and BENI LOBEL
COLORIST: ANDREW DALHOUSE
LETTERER: DAVE SHARPE
COVER ARTISTS: NETHO DIAZ with CANDICE HAN
ASSOCIATE EDITOR: DAVID MENCHEL
SENIOR EDITOR: LYSA HAWKINS

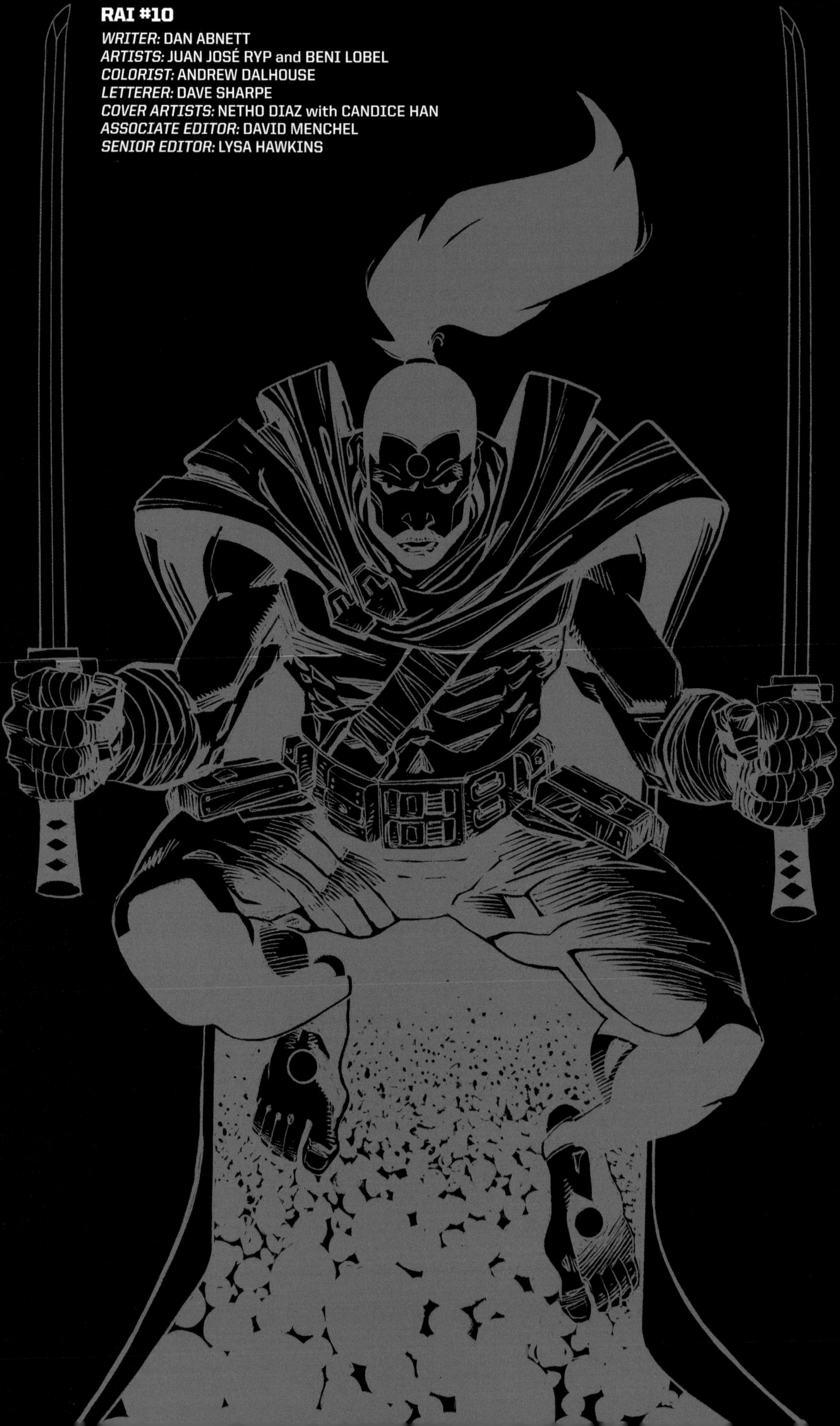

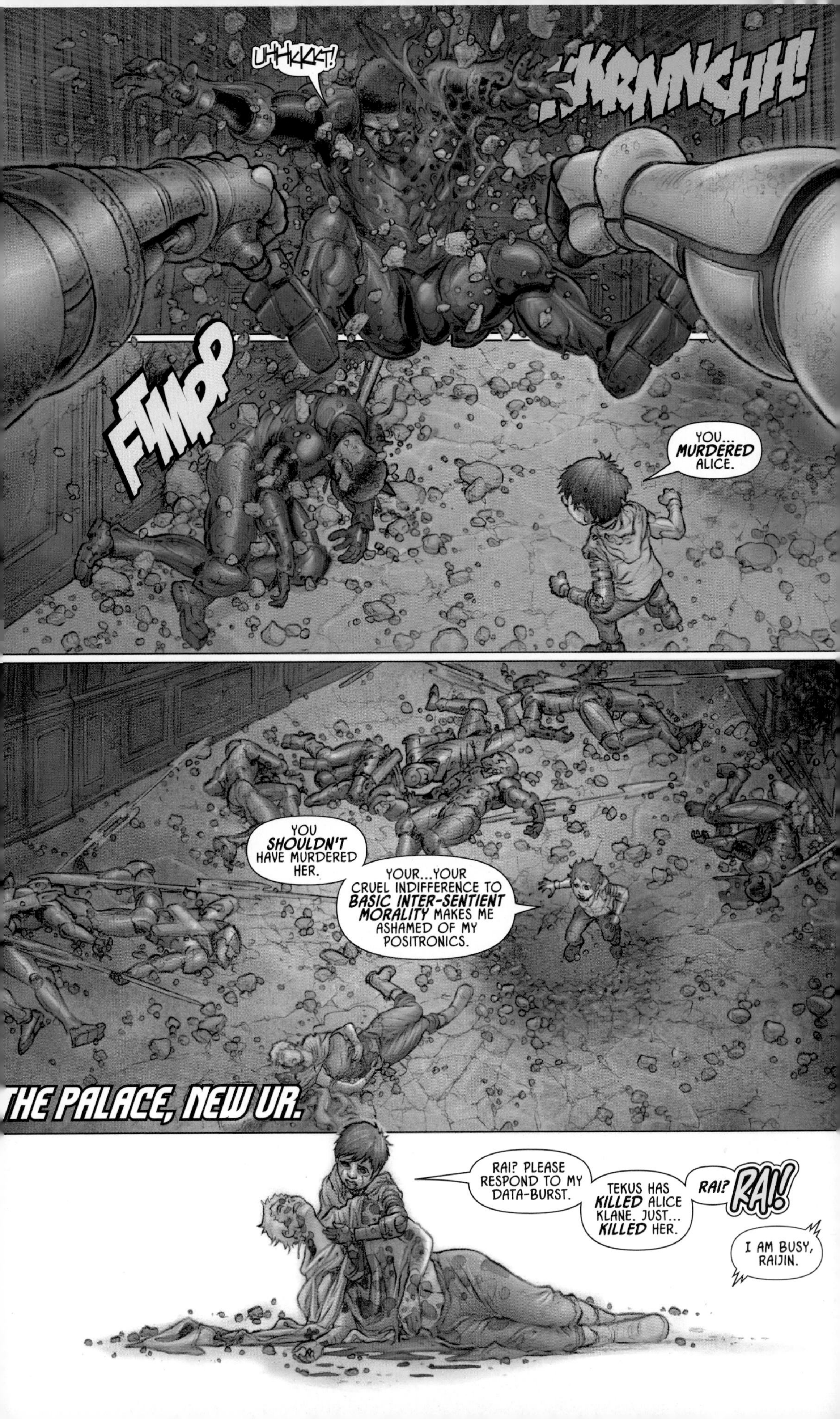
UHHKKKT!
SKRNNCHH!
FTMPP
YOU... MURDERED ALICE.
YOU SHOULDN'T HAVE MURDERED HER.
YOUR...YOUR CRUEL INDIFFERENCE TO BASIC INTER-SENTIENT MORALITY MAKES ME ASHAMED OF MY POSITRONICS.
THE PALACE, NEW UR.
RAI? PLEASE RESPOND TO MY DATA-BURST.
TEKUS HAS KILLED ALICE KLANE. JUST... KILLED HER.
RAI? RAI!
I AM BUSY, RAIJIN.

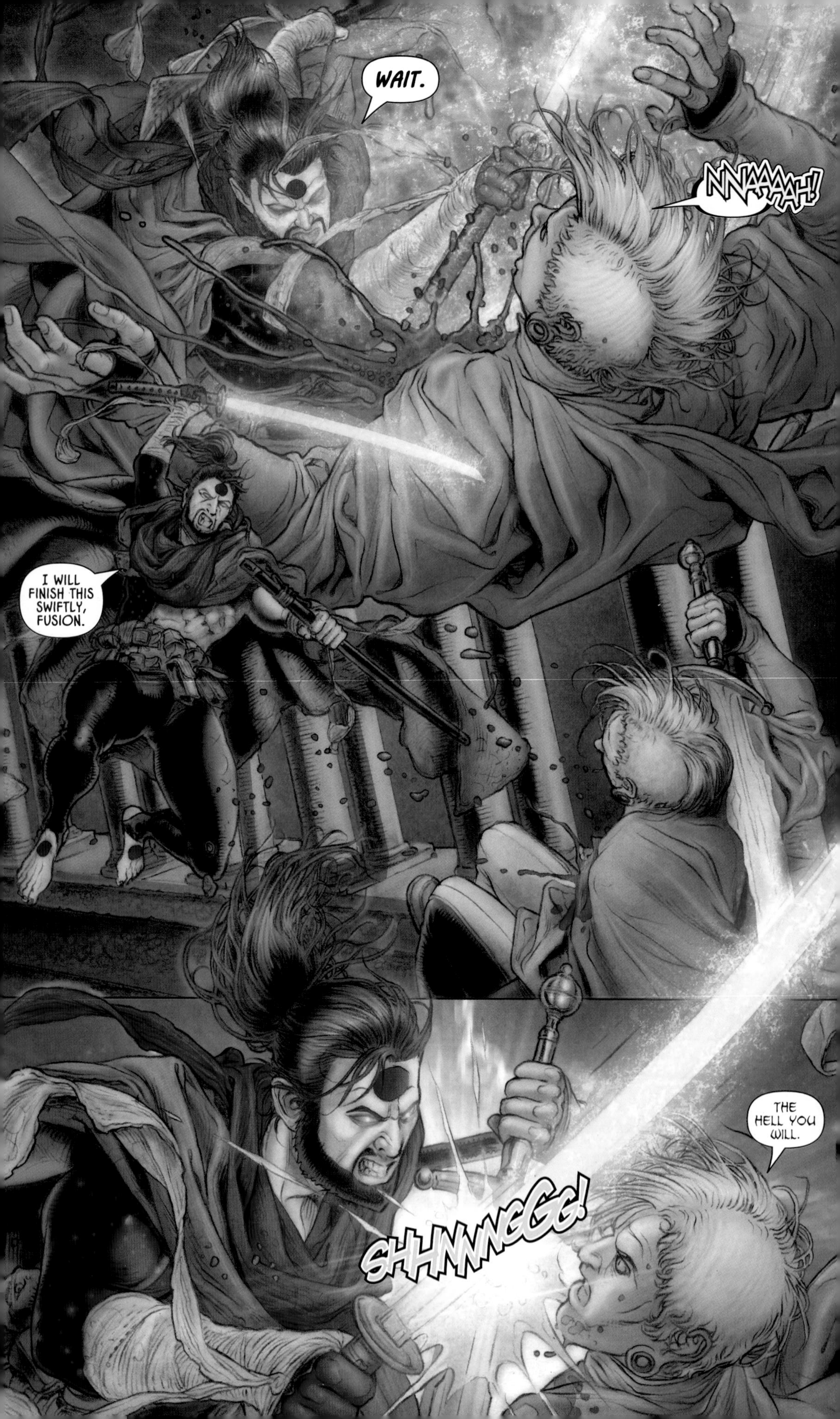
WAIT.
NNAAAAH!
I WILL FINISH THIS SWIFTLY, FUSION.
THE HELL YOU WILL.
SHHNNNGGG!

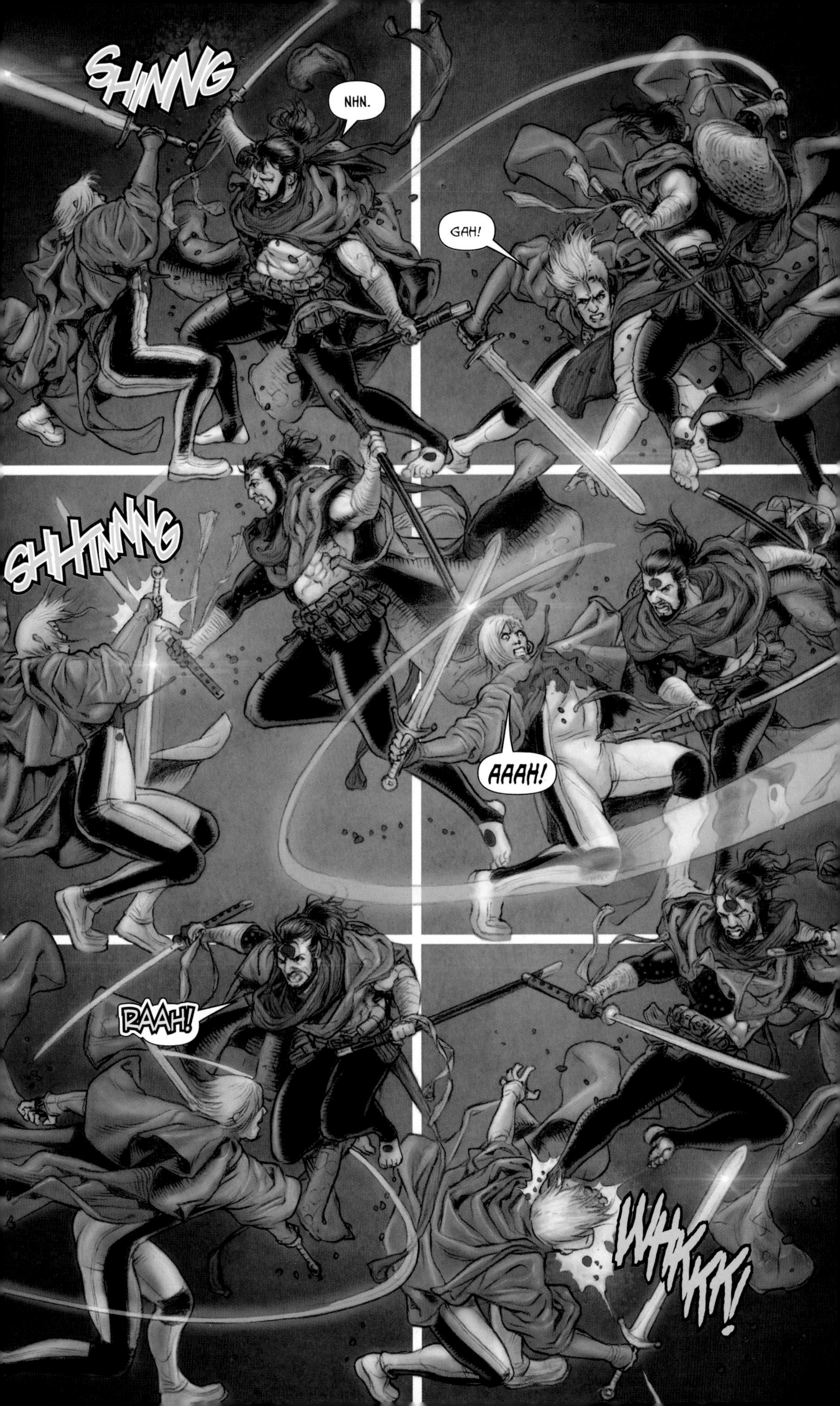
SHINNG
NHN.
GAH!
SHHHINNNG
AAAH!
RAAH!
WAKKK!

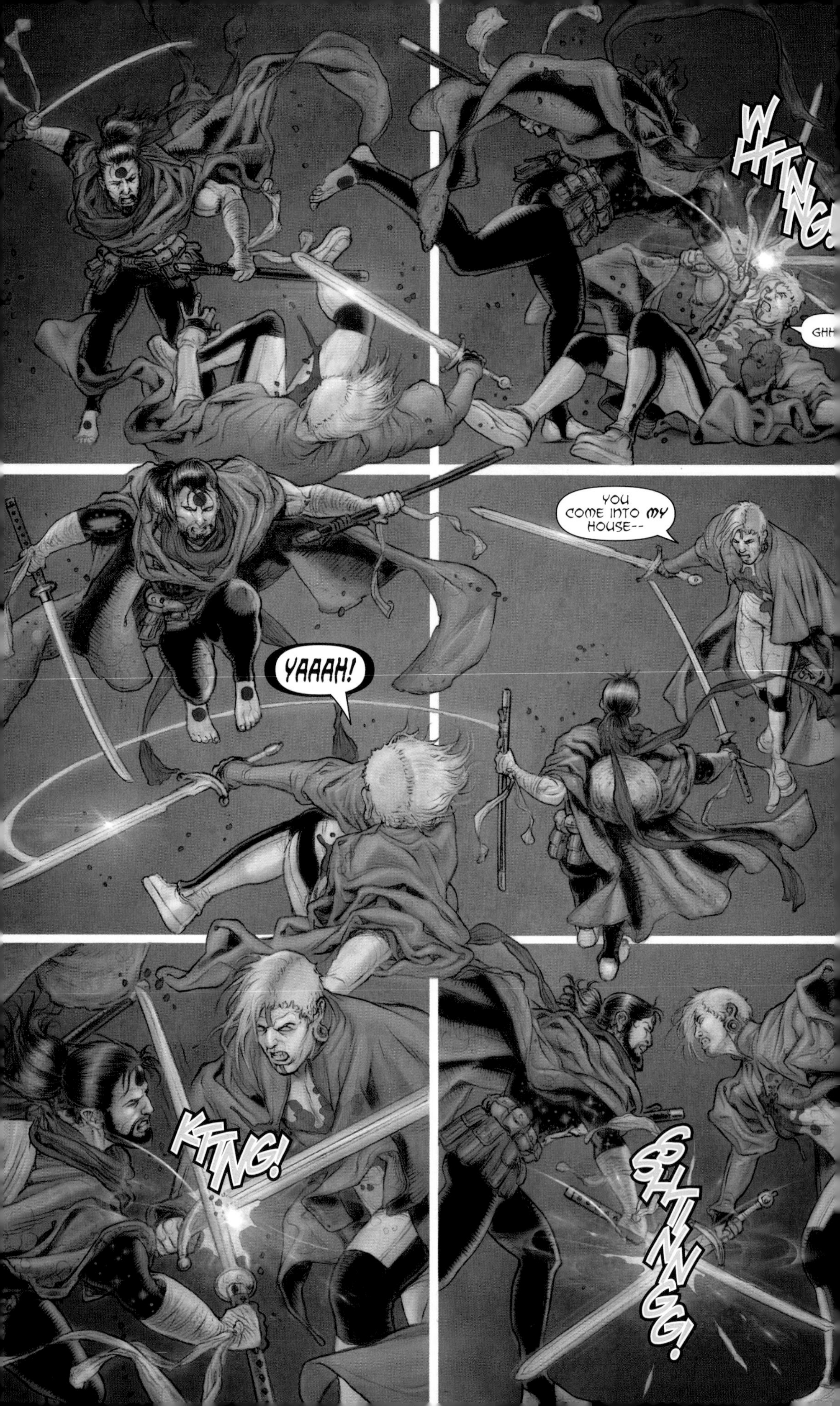
WHTING!
GHH
YOU COME INTO MY HOUSE--
YAAAH!
KTING!
SHTINNGG!

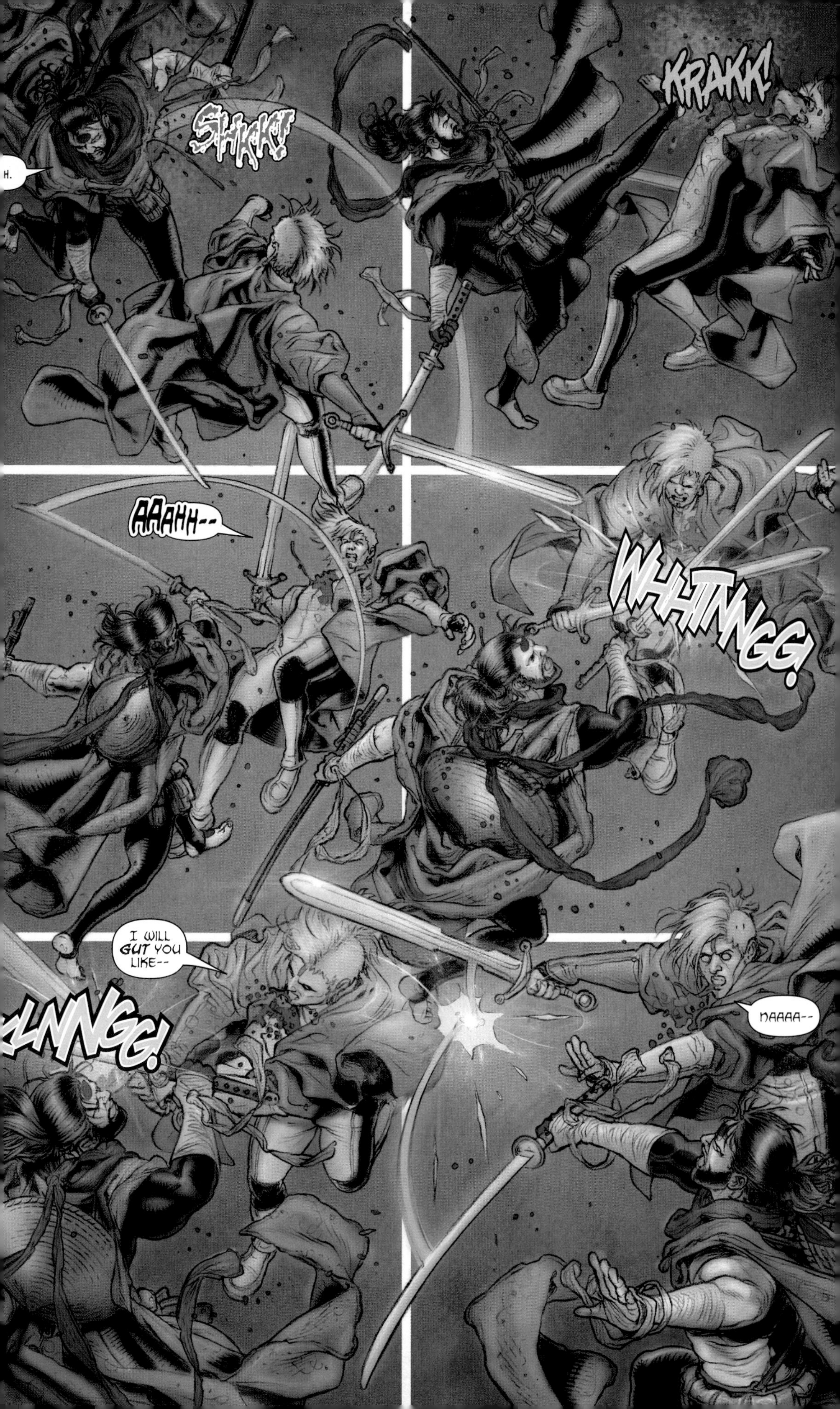
H.
SHKKK!
KRAKK!
AAAHH--
WHHTNNGG!
I WILL GUT YOU LIKE--
KLNNGG!
NAAAA--

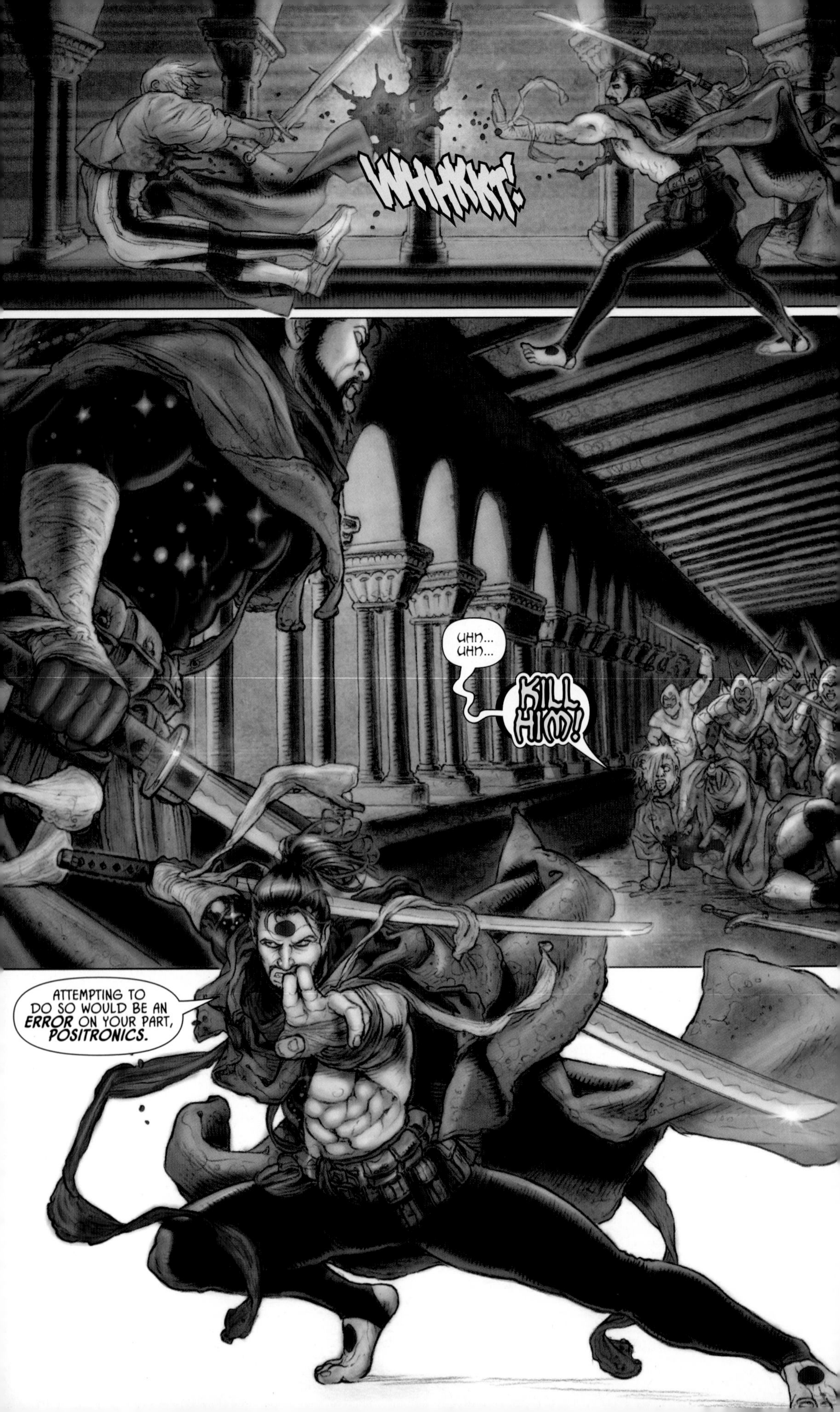
WHHKKT!
UHN... UHN...
KILL HIM!
ATTEMPTING TO DO SO WOULD BE AN *ERROR* ON YOUR PART, *POSITRONICS.*

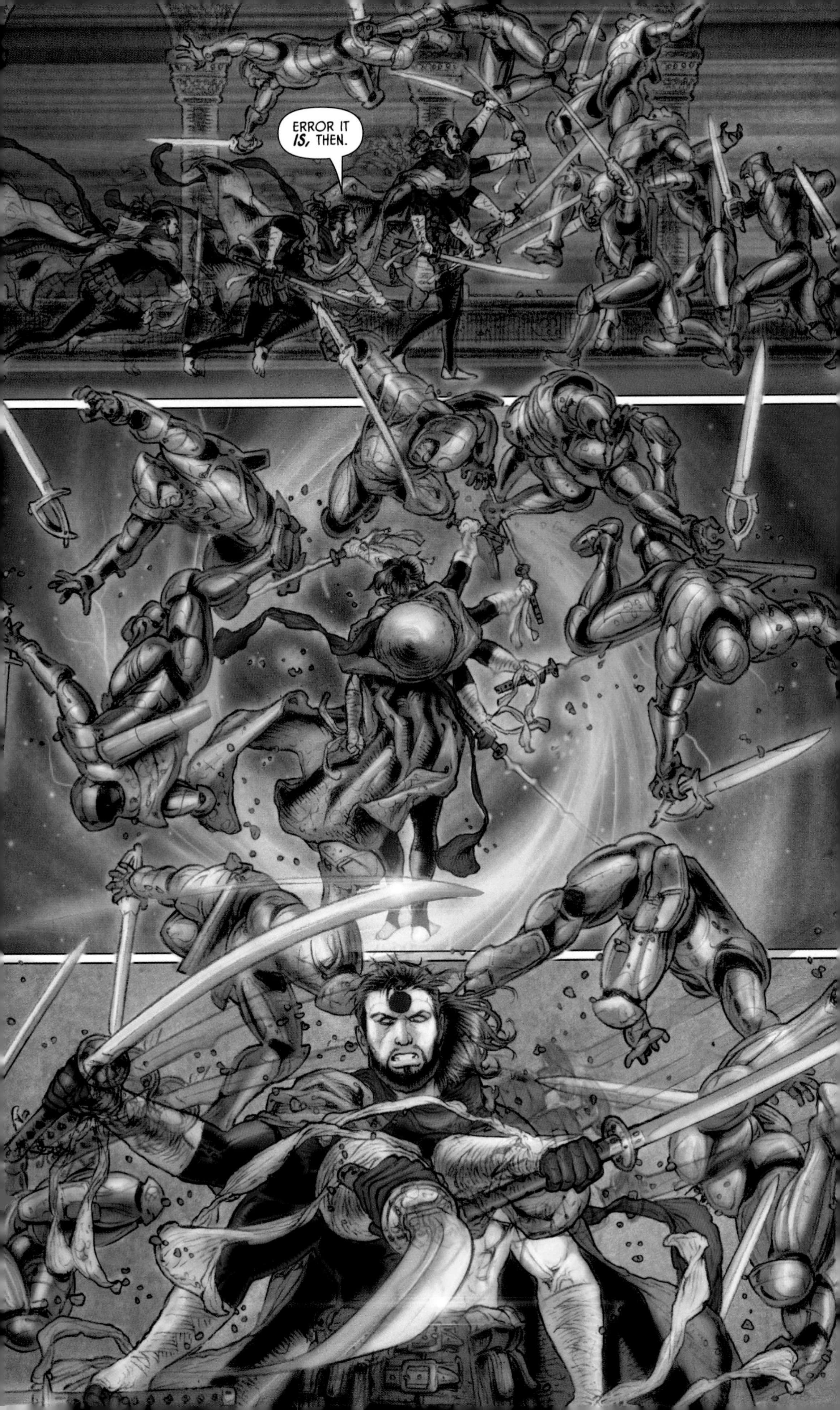
ERROR IT *IS,* THEN.

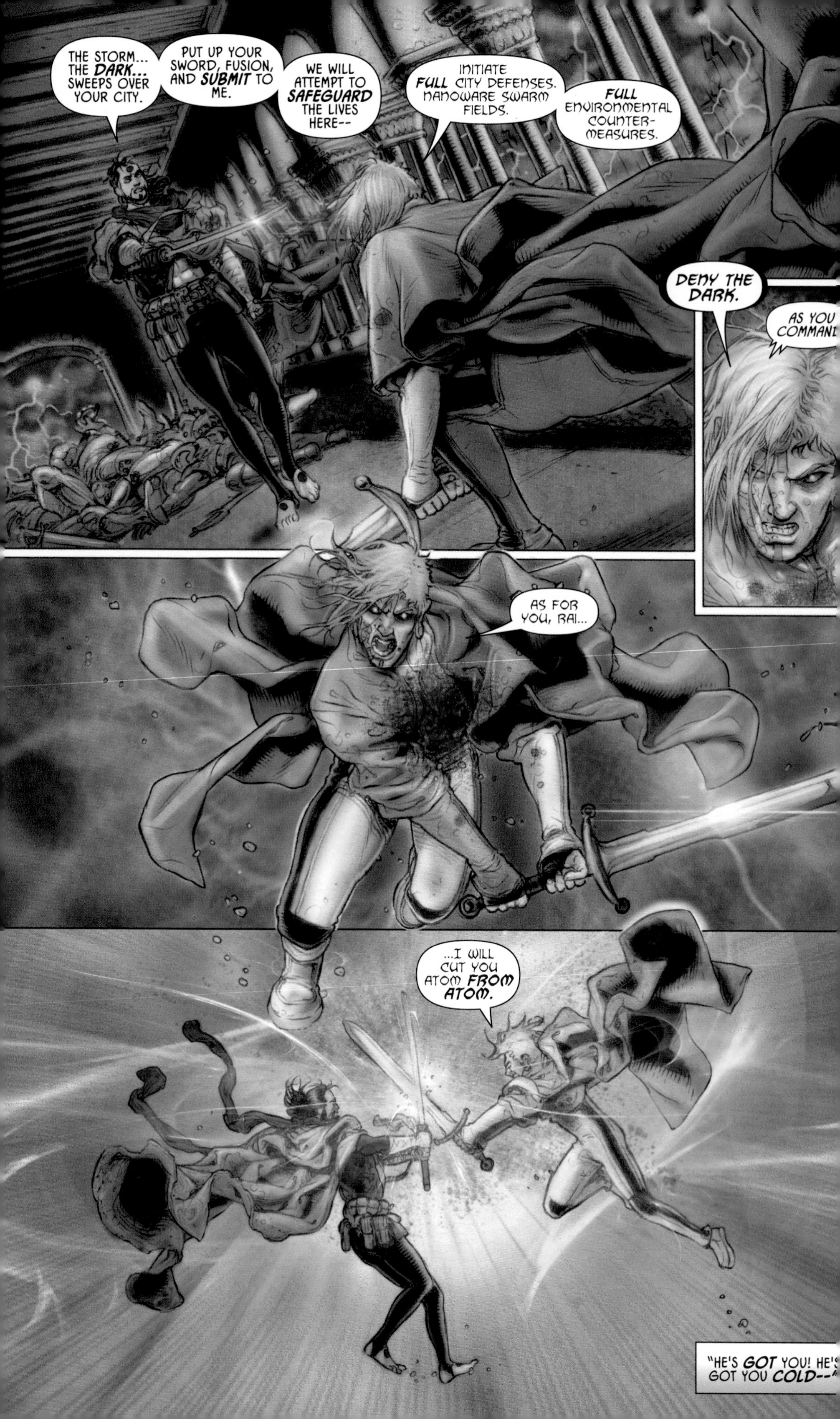
THE STORM... THE DARK... SWEEPS OVER YOUR CITY.
PUT UP YOUR SWORD, FUSION, AND SUBMIT TO ME.
WE WILL ATTEMPT TO SAFEGUARD THE LIVES HERE--
INITIATE FULL CITY DEFENSES. NANOWARE SWARM FIELDS.
FULL ENVIRONMENTAL COUNTER-MEASURES.
DENY THE DARK.
AS YOU COMMAN
AS FOR YOU, RAI...
...I WILL CUT YOU ATOM FROM ATOM.
"HE'S GOT YOU! HE'S GOT YOU COLD--"

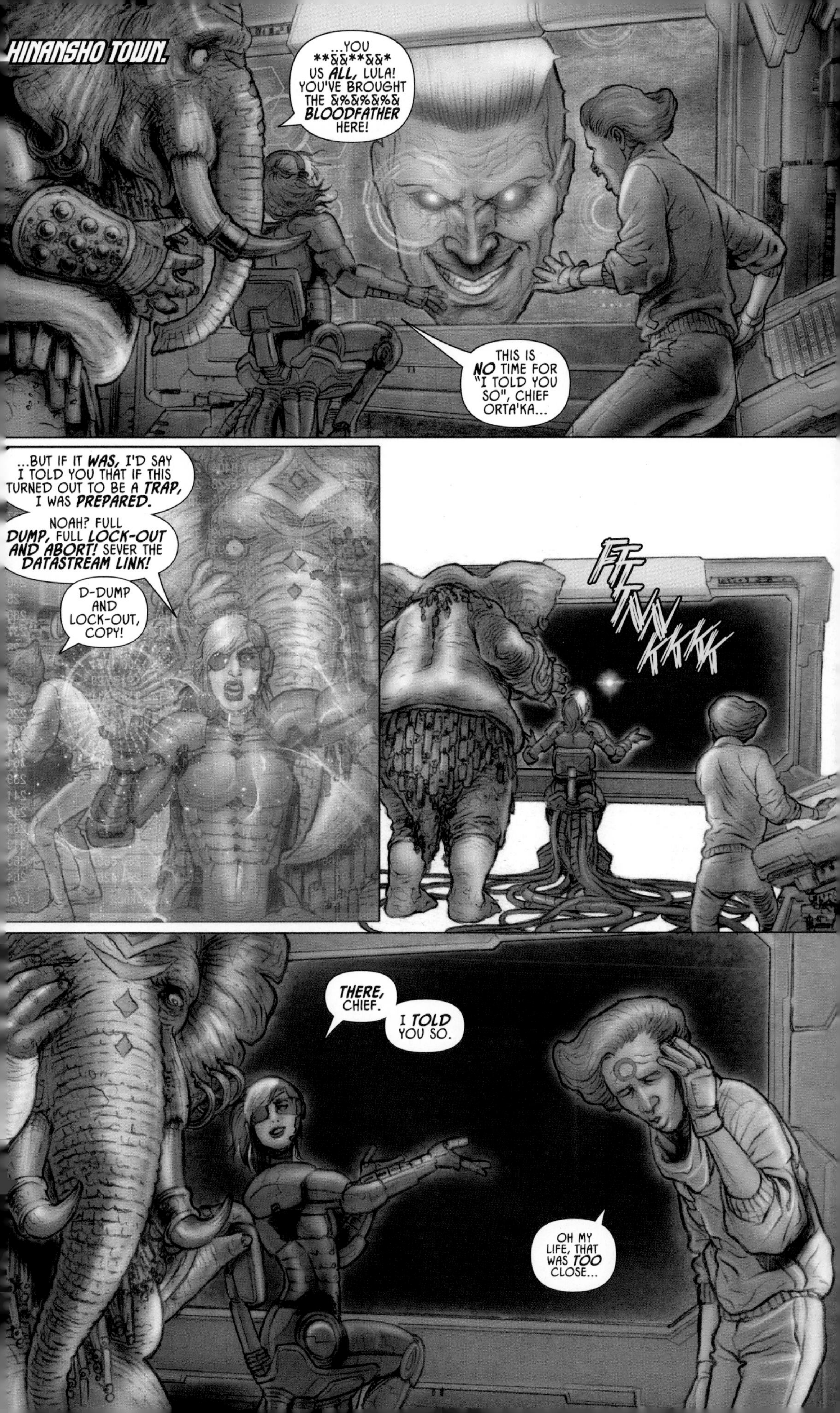
HINANSHO TOWN.
...YOU **&&**&&* US ALL, LULA! YOU'VE BROUGHT THE &%&%&%& BLOODFATHER HERE!
THIS IS NO TIME FOR "I TOLD YOU SO", CHIEF ORTA'KA...
...BUT IF IT WAS, I'D SAY I TOLD YOU THAT IF THIS TURNED OUT TO BE A TRAP, I WAS PREPARED.
NOAH? FULL DUMP, FULL LOCK-OUT AND ABORT! SEVER THE DATASTREAM LINK!
D-DUMP AND LOCK-OUT, COPY!
FFTNNKKKK
THERE, CHIEF.
I TOLD YOU SO.
OH MY LIFE, THAT WAS TOO CLOSE...

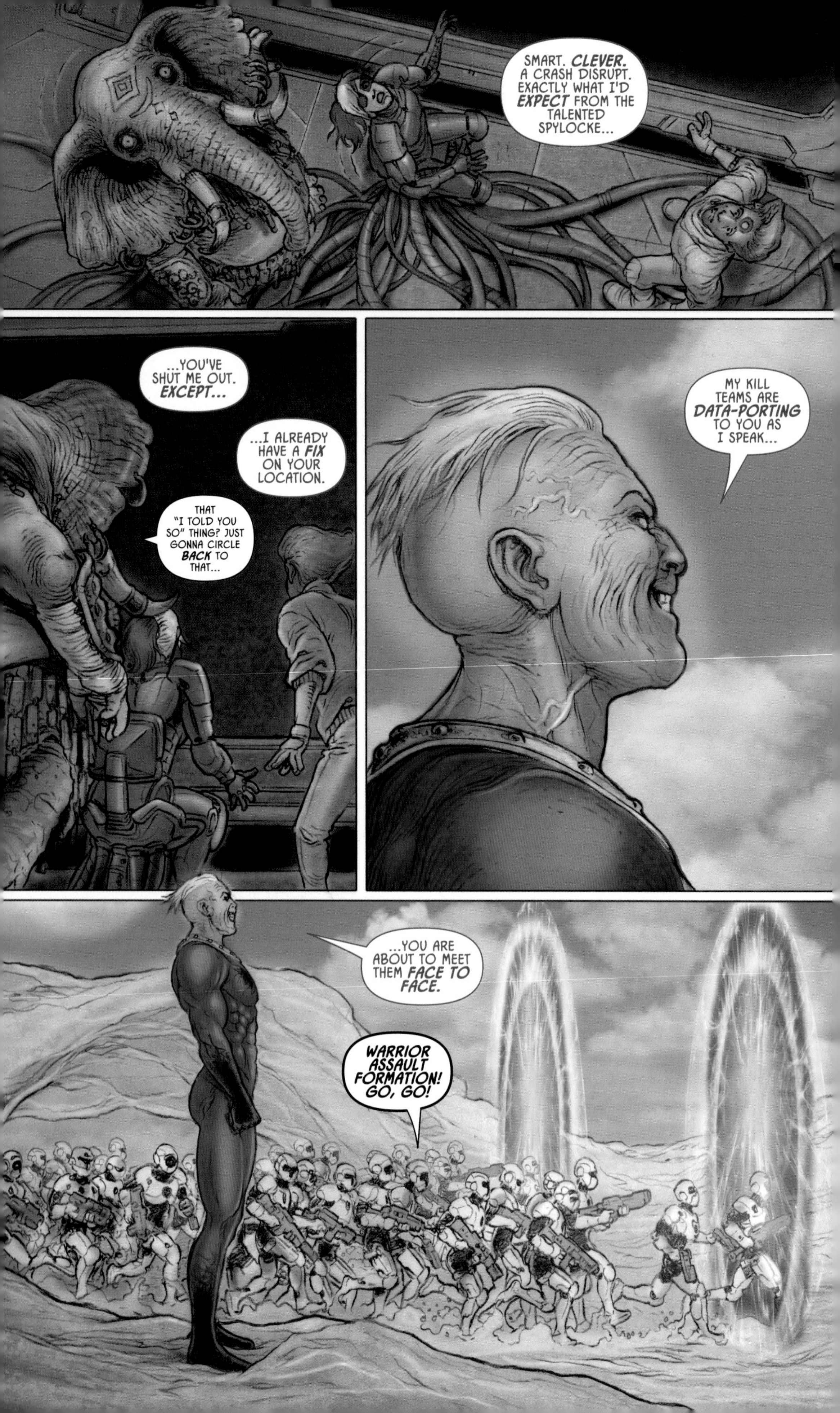
SMART. CLEVER. A CRASH DISRUPT. EXACTLY WHAT I'D EXPECT FROM THE TALENTED SPYLOCKE...
...YOU'VE SHUT ME OUT. EXCEPT...
...I ALREADY HAVE A FIX ON YOUR LOCATION.
THAT "I TOLD YOU SO" THING? JUST GONNA CIRCLE BACK TO THAT...
MY KILL TEAMS ARE DATA-PORTING TO YOU AS I SPEAK...
...YOU ARE ABOUT TO MEET THEM FACE TO FACE.
WARRIOR ASSAULT FORMATION! GO, GO!

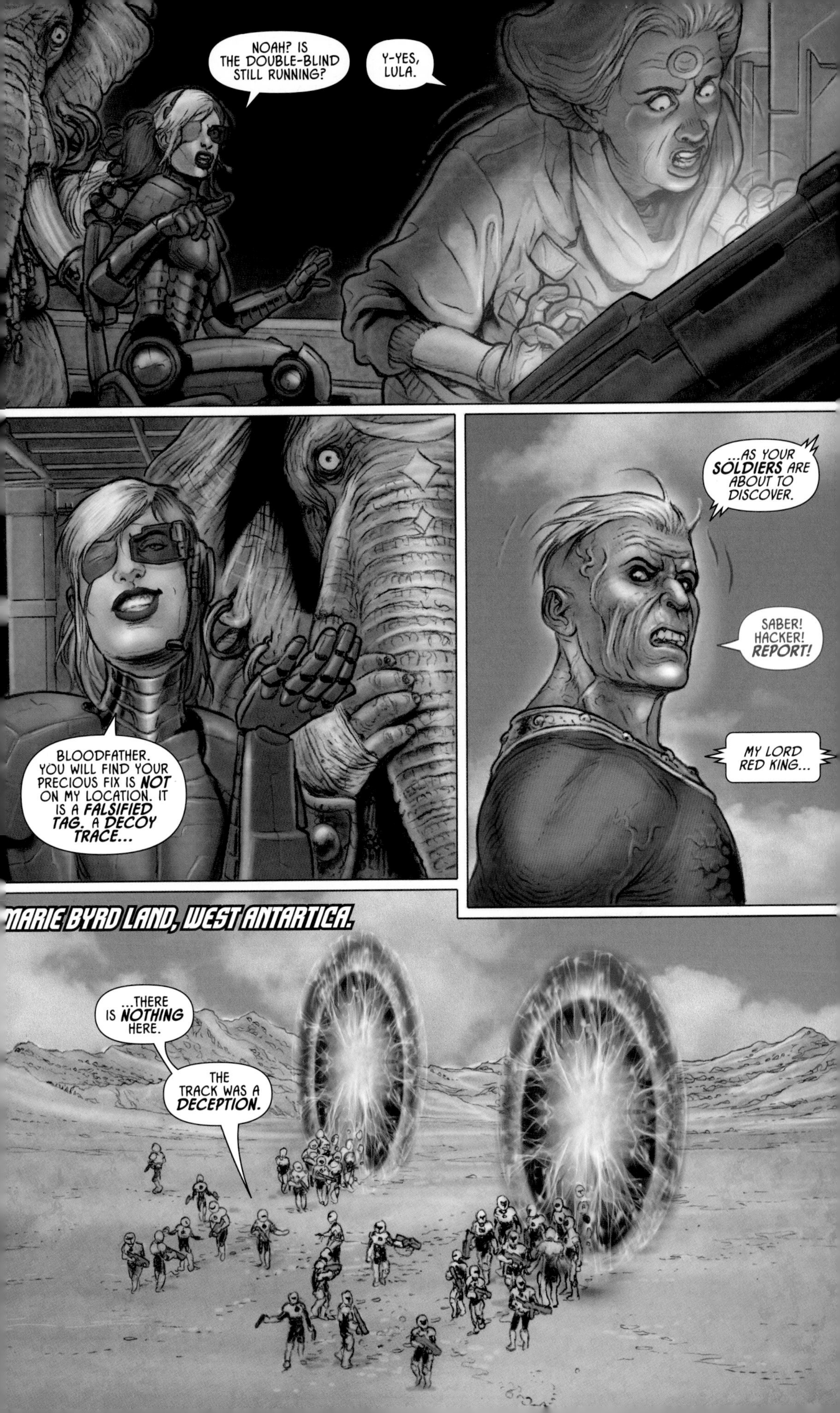
NOAH? IS THE DOUBLE-BLIND STILL RUNNING?
Y-YES, LULA.
BLOODFATHER. YOU WILL FIND YOUR PRECIOUS FIX IS NOT ON MY LOCATION. IT IS A FALSIFIED TAG. A DECOY TRACE...
...AS YOUR SOLDIERS ARE ABOUT TO DISCOVER.
SABER! HACKER! REPORT!
MY LORD RED KING...
MARIE BYRD LAND, WEST ANTARTICA.
...THERE IS NOTHING HERE.
THE TRACK WAS A DECEPTION.

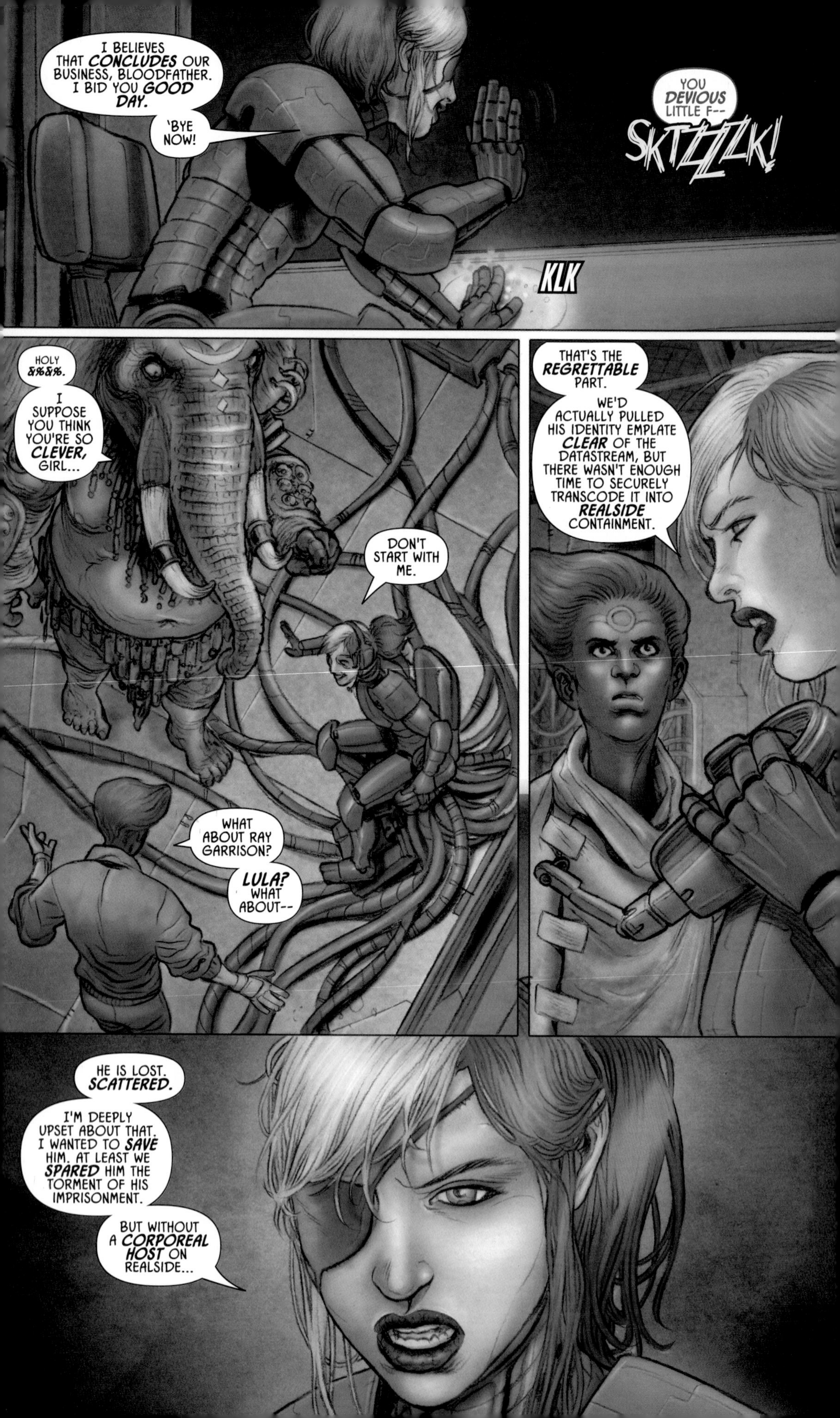
I BELIEVES THAT CONCLUDES OUR BUSINESS, BLOODFATHER. I BID YOU GOOD DAY.
'BYE NOW!
YOU DEVIOUS LITTLE F--
SKTZZZK!
KLK
HOLY &%&%.
I SUPPOSE YOU THINK YOU'RE SO CLEVER, GIRL...
DON'T START WITH ME.
WHAT ABOUT RAY GARRISON?
LULA? WHAT ABOUT--
THAT'S THE REGRETTABLE PART.
WE'D ACTUALLY PULLED HIS IDENTITY EMPLATE CLEAR OF THE DATASTREAM, BUT THERE WASN'T ENOUGH TIME TO SECURELY TRANSCODE IT INTO REALSIDE CONTAINMENT.
HE IS LOST. SCATTERED.
I'M DEEPLY UPSET ABOUT THAT. I WANTED TO SAVE HIM. AT LEAST WE SPARED HIM THE TORMENT OF HIS IMPRISONMENT.
BUT WITHOUT A CORPOREAL HOST ON REALSIDE...

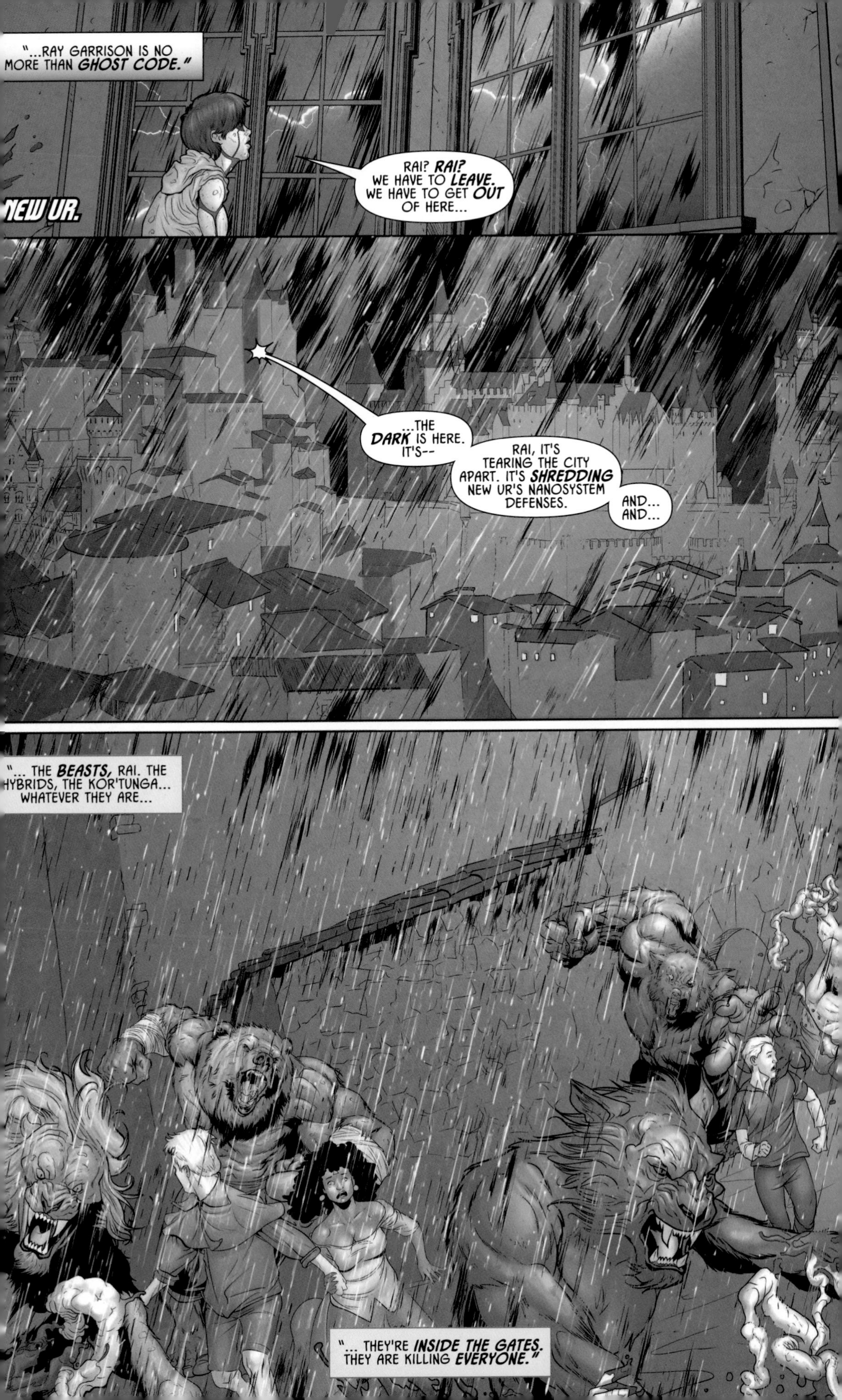
"...RAY GARRISON IS NO MORE THAN GHOST CODE."
NEW UR.
RAI? RAI? WE HAVE TO LEAVE. WE HAVE TO GET OUT OF HERE...
...THE DARK IS HERE. IT'S--
RAI, IT'S TEARING THE CITY APART. IT'S SHREDDING NEW UR'S NANOSYSTEM DEFENSES.
AND... AND...
"... THE BEASTS, RAI. THE HYBRIDS, THE KOR'TUNGA... WHATEVER THEY ARE...
"... THEY'RE INSIDE THE GATES. THEY ARE KILLING EVERYONE."

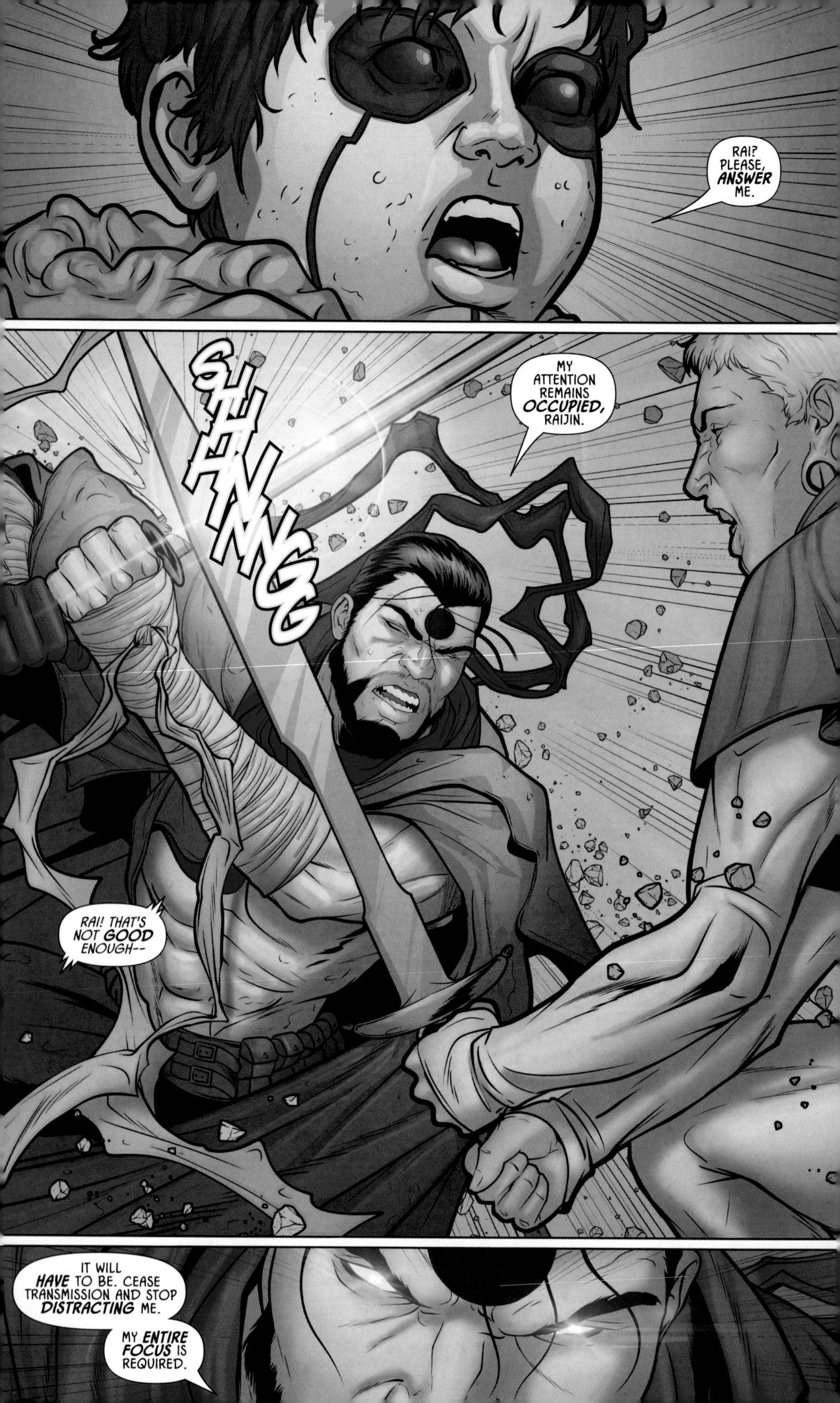

RAI? PLEASE, ANSWER ME.
SHHANNGG
MY ATTENTION REMAINS OCCUPIED, RAIJIN.
RAI! THAT'S NOT GOOD ENOUGH--
IT WILL HAVE TO BE. CEASE TRANSMISSION AND STOP DISTRACTING ME.
MY ENTIRE FOCUS IS REQUIRED.

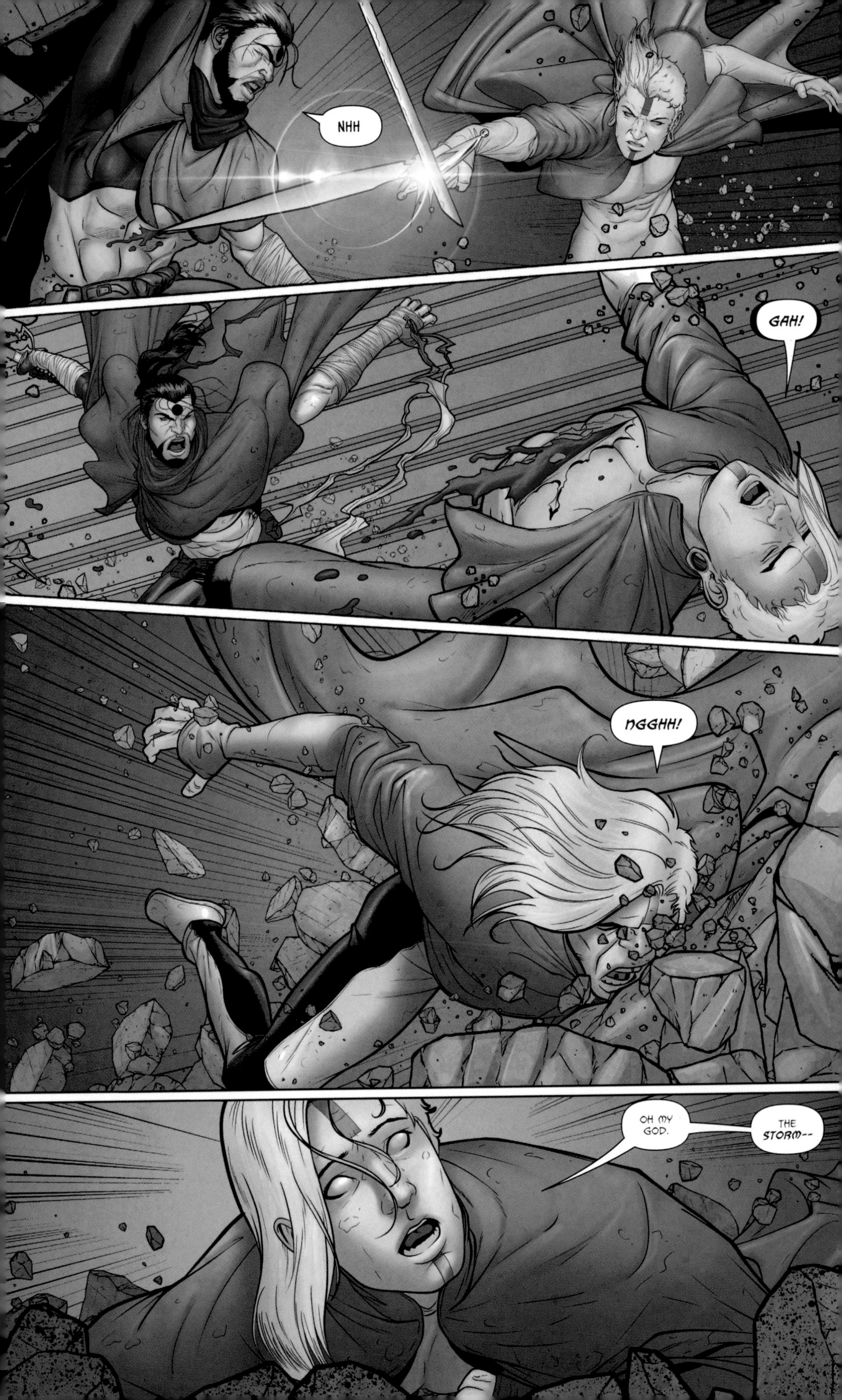
NHH
GAH!
NGGHH!
OH MY GOD.
THE STORM--

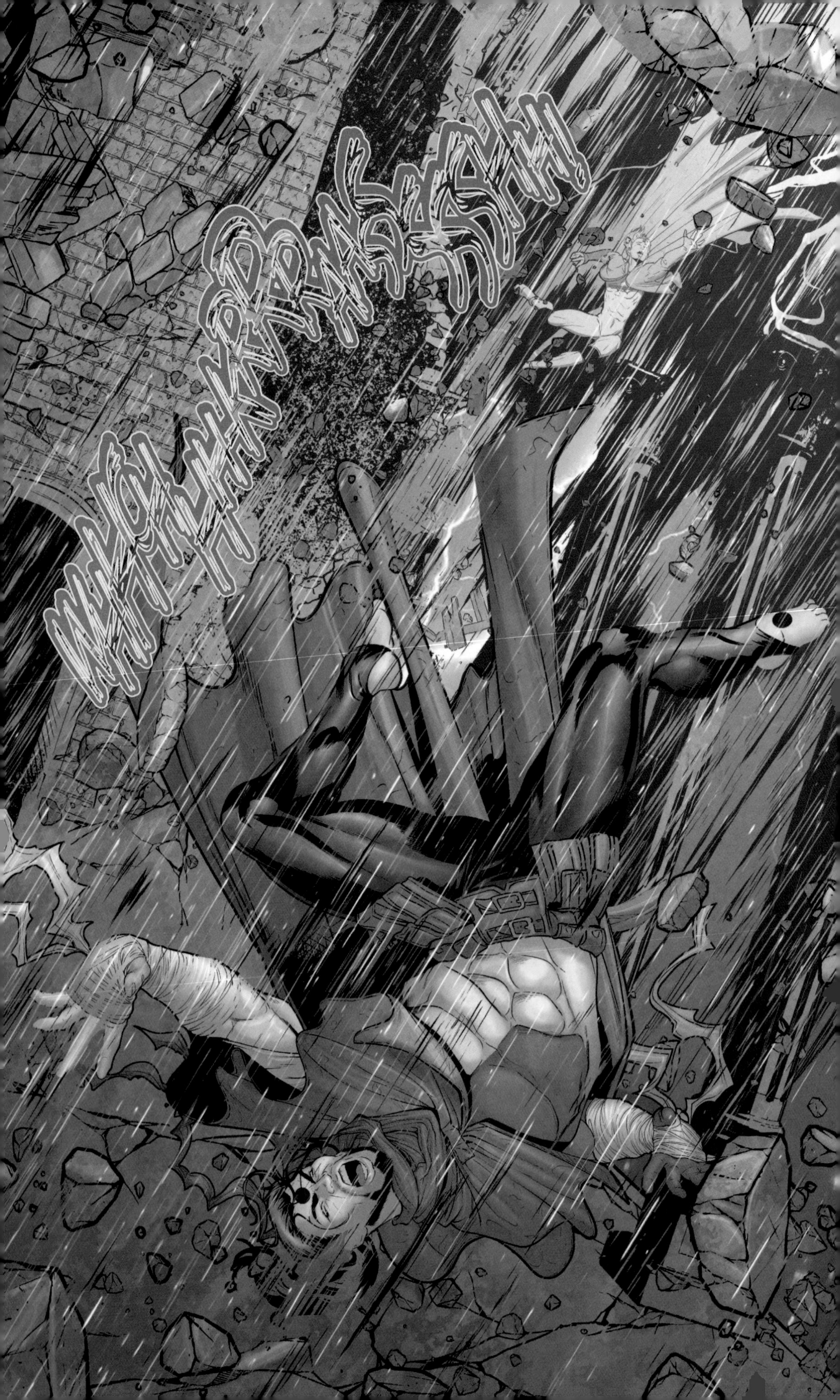

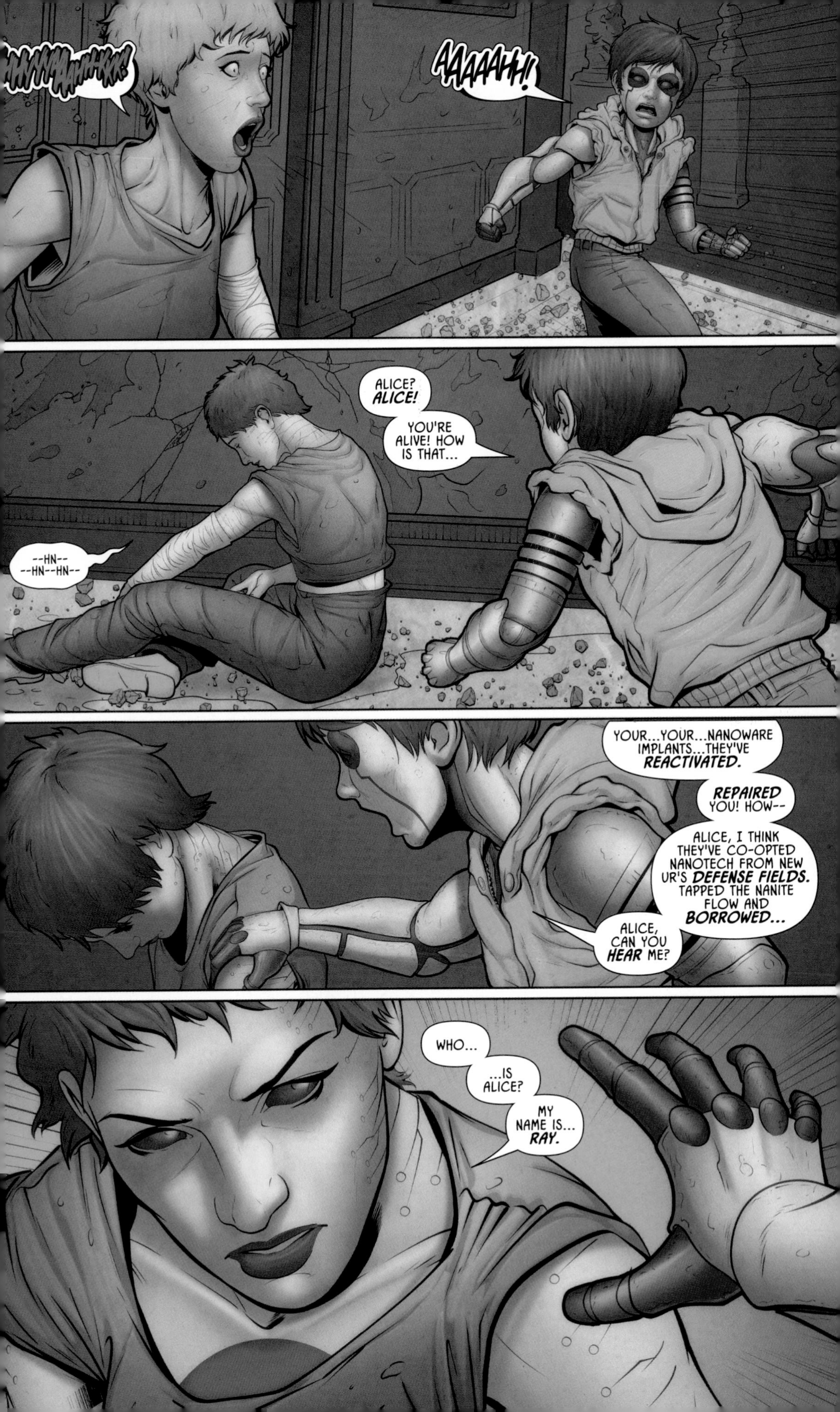

HHYYAAHHHKK!
AAAAAHH!
ALICE? ALICE!
YOU'RE ALIVE! HOW IS THAT...
--HN-- --HN--HN--
YOUR...YOUR...NANOWARE IMPLANTS...THEY'VE REACTIVATED.
REPAIRED YOU! HOW--
ALICE, I THINK THEY'VE CO-OPTED NANOTECH FROM NEW UR'S DEFENSE FIELDS. TAPPED THE NANITE FLOW AND BORROWED...
ALICE, CAN YOU HEAR ME?
WHO...
...IS ALICE?
MY NAME IS... RAY.

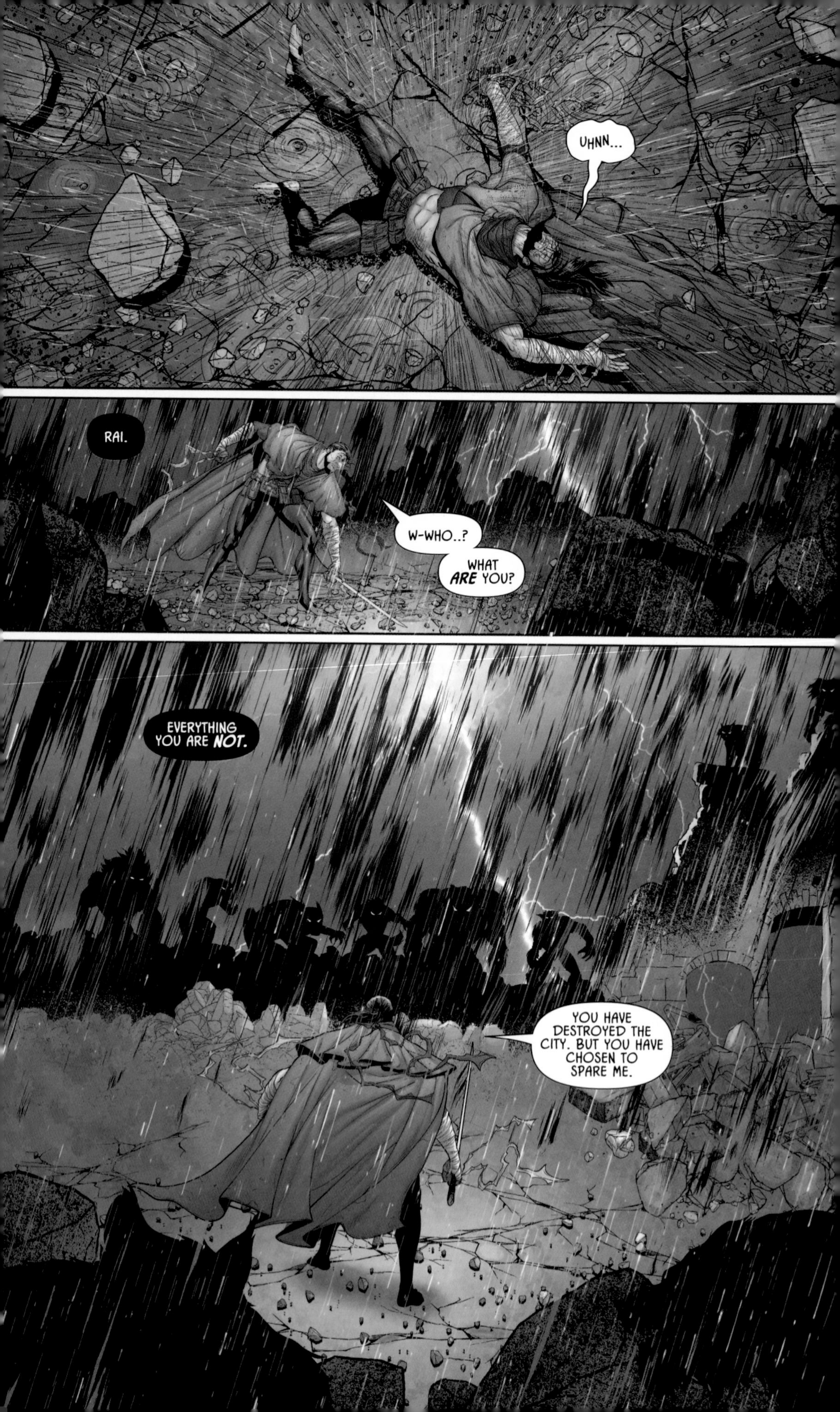
UHNN...
RAI.
W-WHO..?
WHAT ARE YOU?
EVERYTHING YOU ARE NOT.
YOU HAVE DESTROYED THE CITY. BUT YOU HAVE CHOSEN TO SPARE ME.

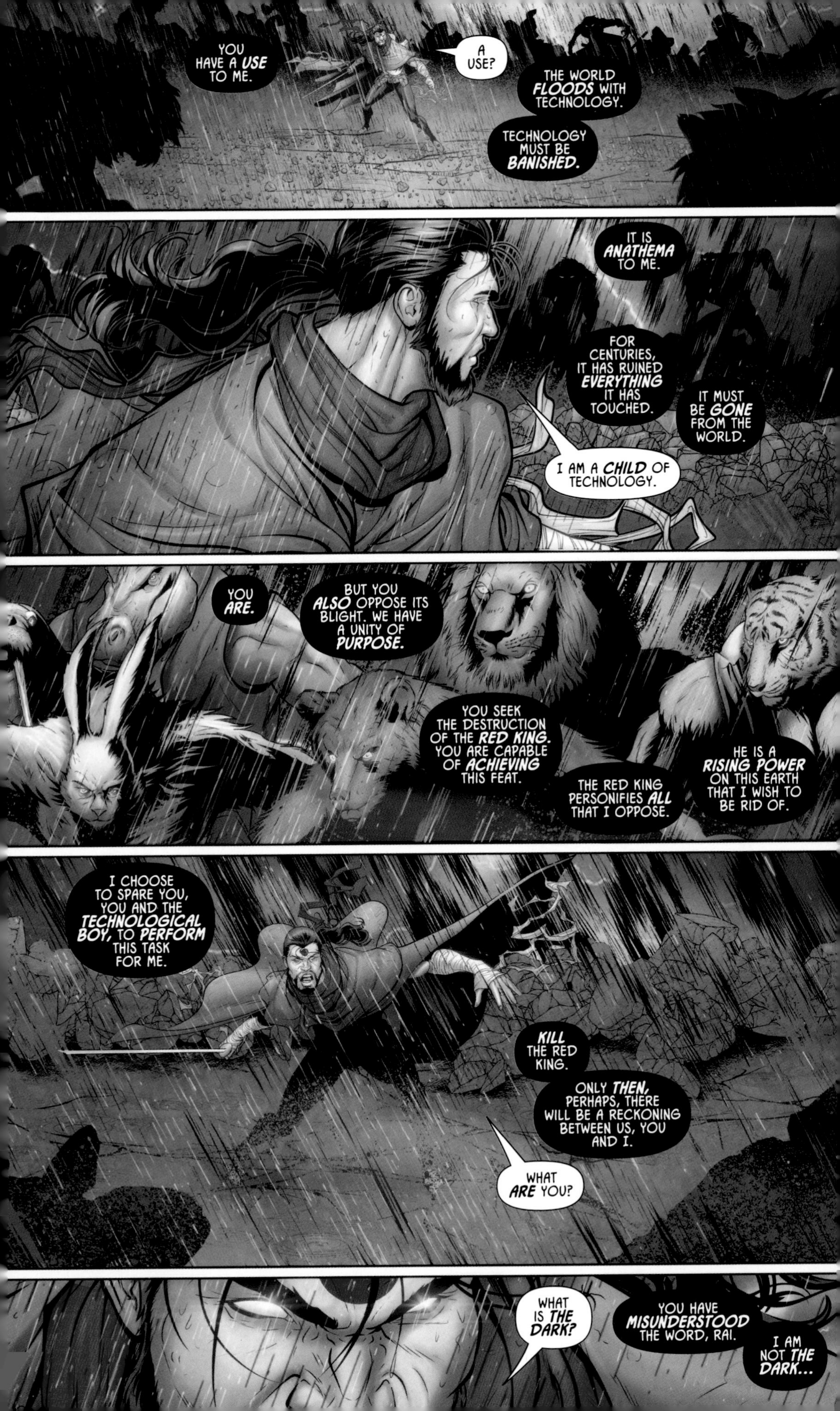

YOU HAVE A USE TO ME.
A USE?
THE WORLD FLOODS WITH TECHNOLOGY.
TECHNOLOGY MUST BE BANISHED.
IT IS ANATHEMA TO ME.
FOR CENTURIES, IT HAS RUINED EVERYTHING IT HAS TOUCHED.
IT MUST BE GONE FROM THE WORLD.
I AM A CHILD OF TECHNOLOGY.
YOU ARE.
BUT YOU ALSO OPPOSE ITS BLIGHT. WE HAVE A UNITY OF PURPOSE.
YOU SEEK THE DESTRUCTION OF THE RED KING. YOU ARE CAPABLE OF ACHIEVING THIS FEAT.
THE RED KING PERSONIFIES ALL THAT I OPPOSE.
HE IS A RISING POWER ON THIS EARTH THAT I WISH TO BE RID OF.
I CHOOSE TO SPARE YOU, YOU AND THE TECHNOLOGICAL BOY, TO PERFORM THIS TASK FOR ME.
KILL THE RED KING.
ONLY THEN, PERHAPS, THERE WILL BE A RECKONING BETWEEN US, YOU AND I.
WHAT ARE YOU?
WHAT IS THE DARK?
YOU HAVE MISUNDERSTOOD THE WORD, RAI.
I AM NOT THE DARK...

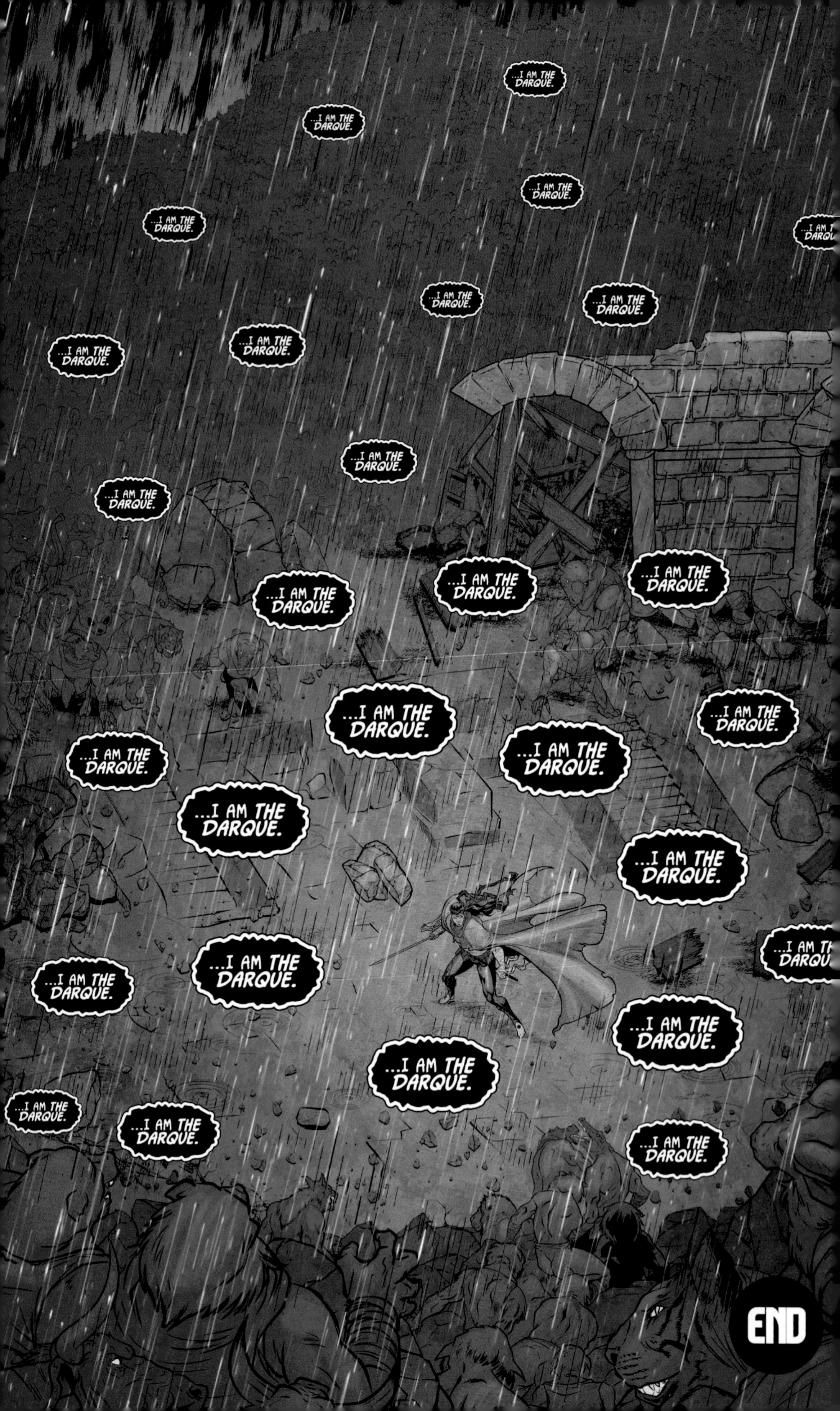
...I AM THE DARQUE.
...I AM THE DARQUE.
...I AM THE DARQUE.
...I AM THE DARQUE.
...I AM T DARQU
...I AM THE DARQUE.
...I AM THE DARQUE.
...I AM THE DARQUE.
...I AM THE DARQUE.
...I AM THE DARQUE.
...I AM THE DARQUE.
...I AM THE DARQUE.
...I AM THE DARQUE.
...I AM THE DARQUE.
...I AM THE DARQUE.
...I AM THE DARQUE.
...I AM THE DARQUE.
...I AM THE DARQUE.
...I AM THE DARQUE.
...I AM THE DARQUE.
...I AM TH DARQU
...I AM THE DARQUE.
...I AM THE DARQUE.
...I AM THE DARQUE.
...I AM THE DARQUE.
...I AM THE DARQUE.
...I AM THE DARQUE.
...I AM THE DARQUE.
END

GALLERY

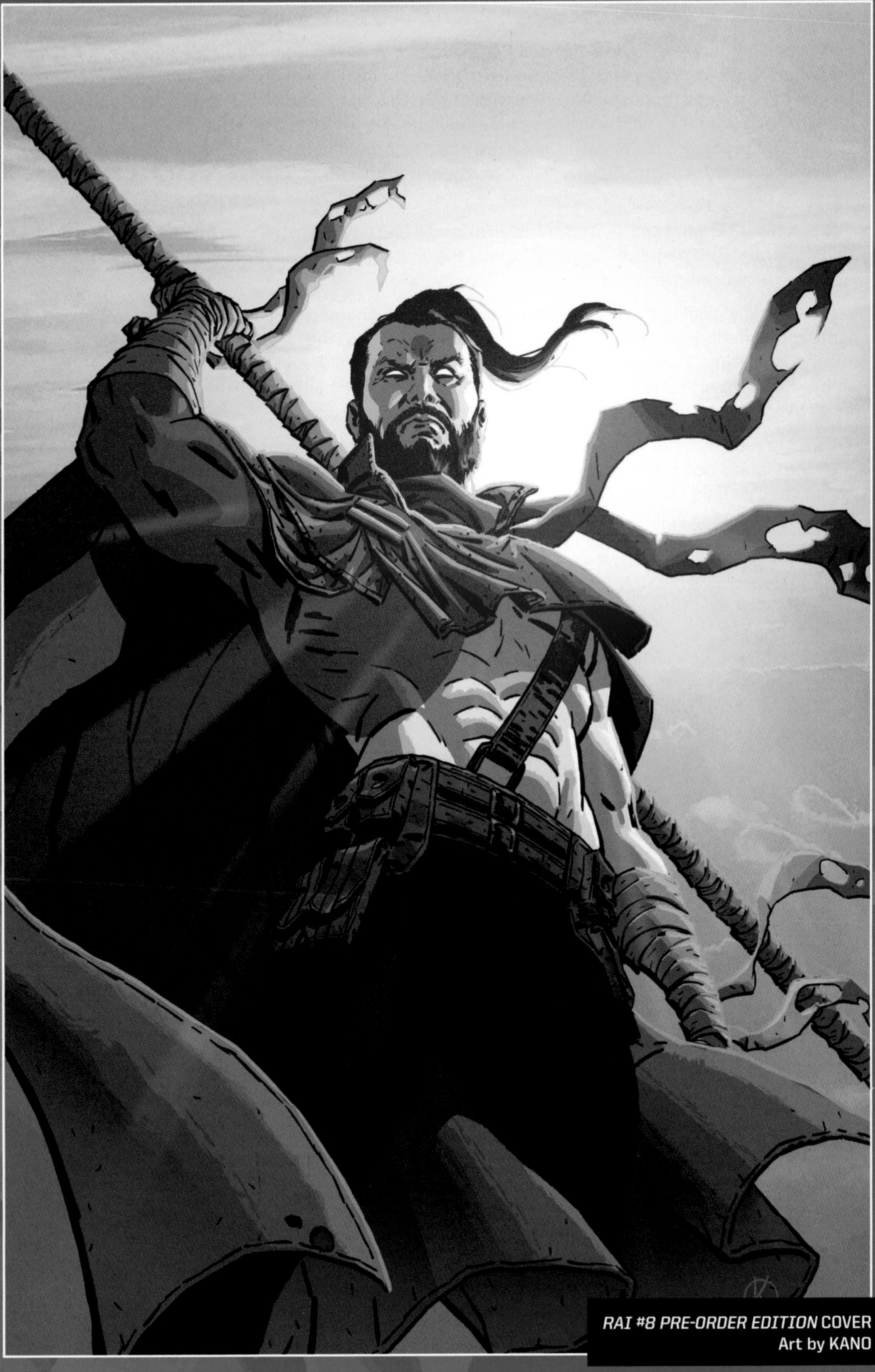

RAI #8 PRE-ORDER EDITION COVER
Art by KANO

THE FUSION OF ART AND TECHNOLOGY DESIGN NOTES BY DAN ABNETT

Fusion, along with the city and people we're about to meet, are important new characters. This society is a society of POSITRONICS. It is also - by far – the most high tech thing we've met yet, and it's going to be 'clean' high tech (such as, say, Star Trek: Next Gen or Metropolis) rather than 'grungy' high tech (such as, say, Blade Runner or Aliens). The Red King and his society are very high tech too, but they're more at that 'pseudo- barbaric' dirty end (very gothic, Klingon, future-medieval).

Fusion and his people are the other end – the idea of a sleek, beautiful future, a 'heaven'. They use advanced nanotech, so their technology (hardware) is minimal, and operates like magic. But I don't want it to be a sleek functional future look (like, say, the clean austerity of the Empire in the Star Wars films). I want it to be much more beautiful (more like, say the culture of Naboo in the Star Wars films). Ornate, gorgeous, wondrous, golden, a place where there is room for art and design rather than functionality. A future built by "Elven craftsmen" rather than "Dwarven smiths". Elegant and intricate, not brutalist.

The one thing we want to avoid with Fusion's people and city is anything 'animalistic: anything tribal, or animal-based, or pagan, or 'organic'... that's the look of The Dark, and we want to avoid that, and establish a clear contrast.

Fusion himself is going to be a very important, recurring character. He is tall, male, beautiful and VERY charismatic. He is NOT VISIBLY ARMED. He is charming, and slightly mischievous. For some reason, every time I imagine him, I think of ELRIC, or I think of David Bowie. David Bowie as the Goblin King...but also David Bowie circa "Let's Dance" and "China Girl". Very handsome, very cool, very androgynously beautiful.

I want the reader to like him. And his society should be beautiful too: though I'm asking for a 'clean' high tech look, I don't think it should be 'uniform' (like Star Trek) because that's such a cliche. I see this culture as being open to individual expression, so everyone wears amazing clothes: ornate, extravagant, lots of color, lots of patterned fabrics.... like a Galliano or Alexander McQueen catwalk show. Amazing, theatrical, individual – beautiful people at a high fashion show. The architecture too.

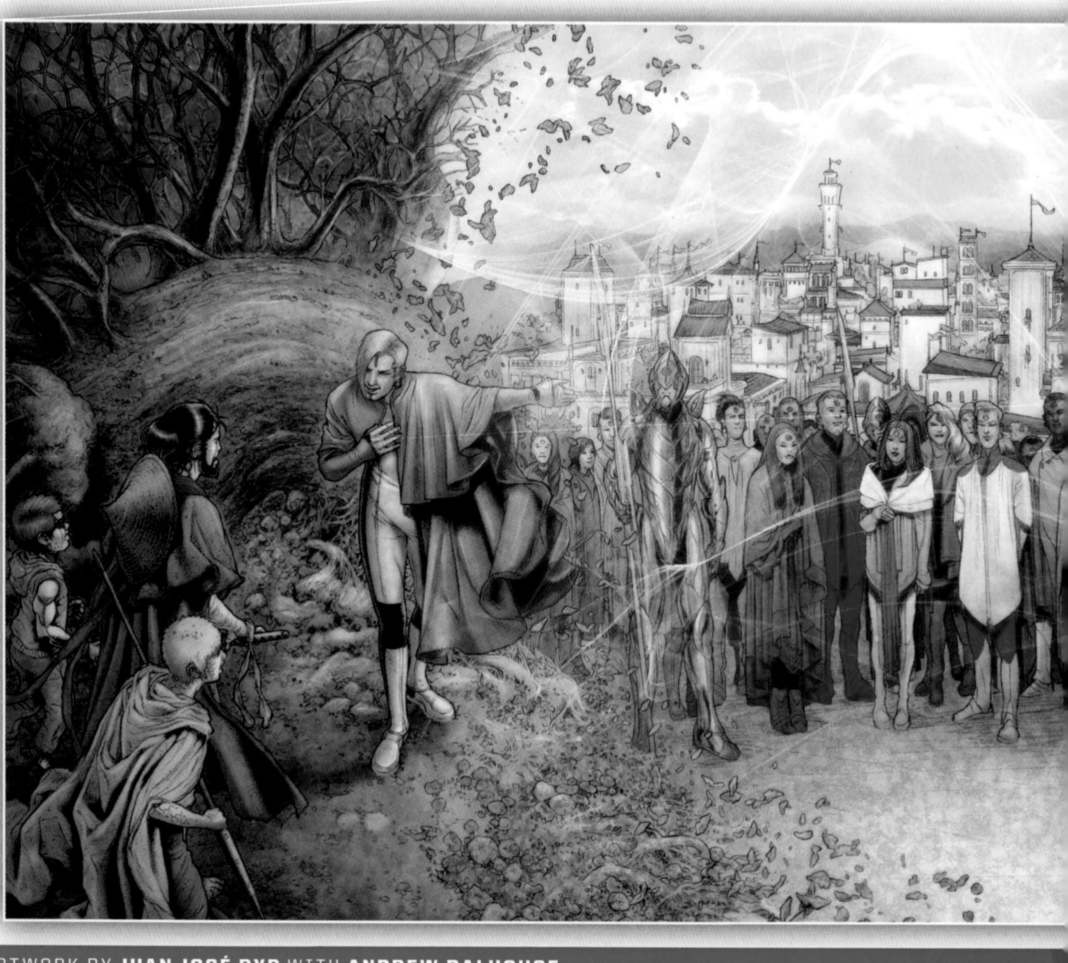

ARTWORK BY **JUAN JOSÉ RYP** WITH **ANDREW DALHOUSE**

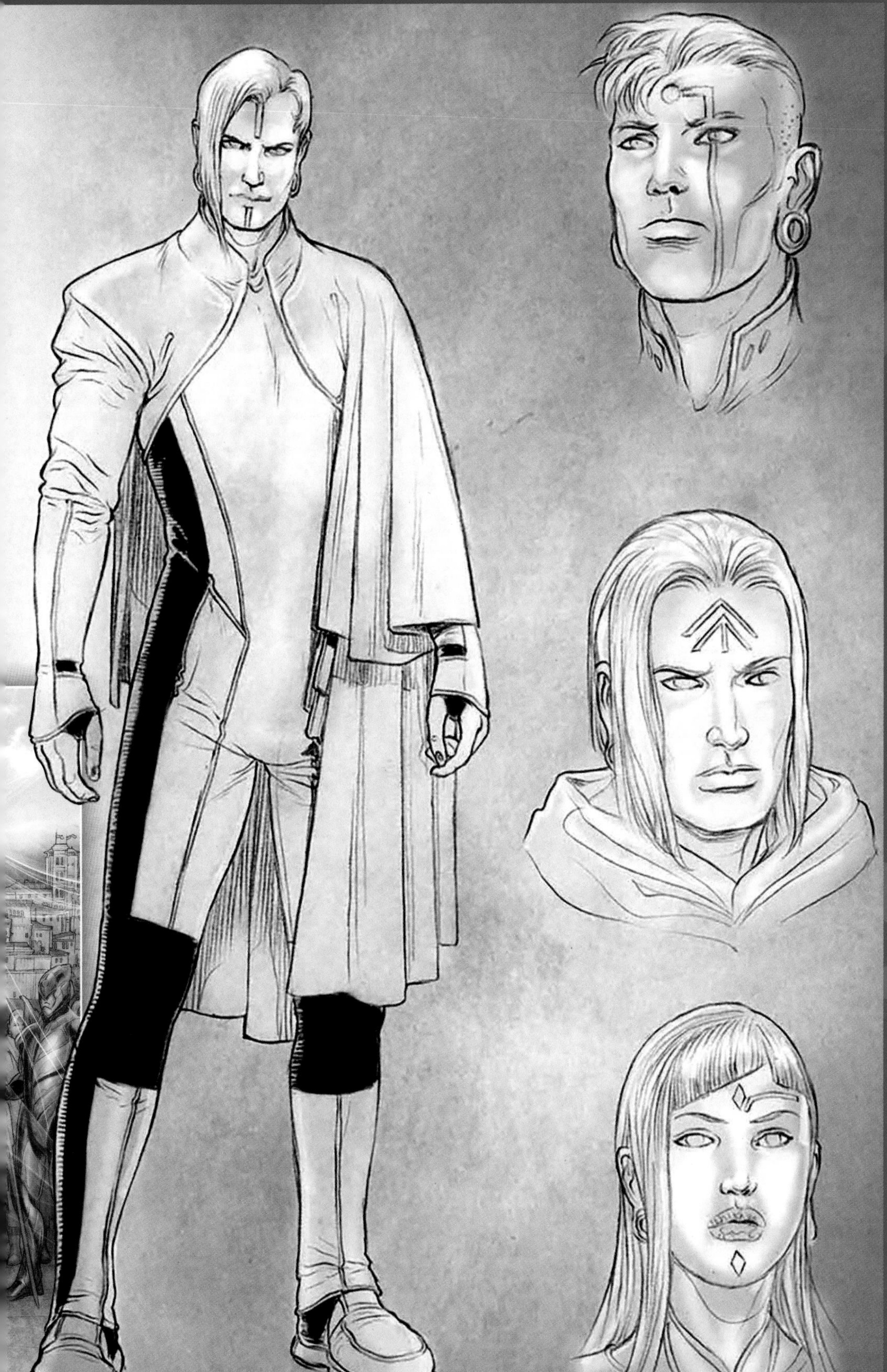

ORIGINALLY PRESENTED IN *RAI #8 PRE-ORDER EDITION*

RAI #6 COVER B
Art by KANO

RAI #7 COVER B
Art by NETHO DIAZ with CANDICE HAN

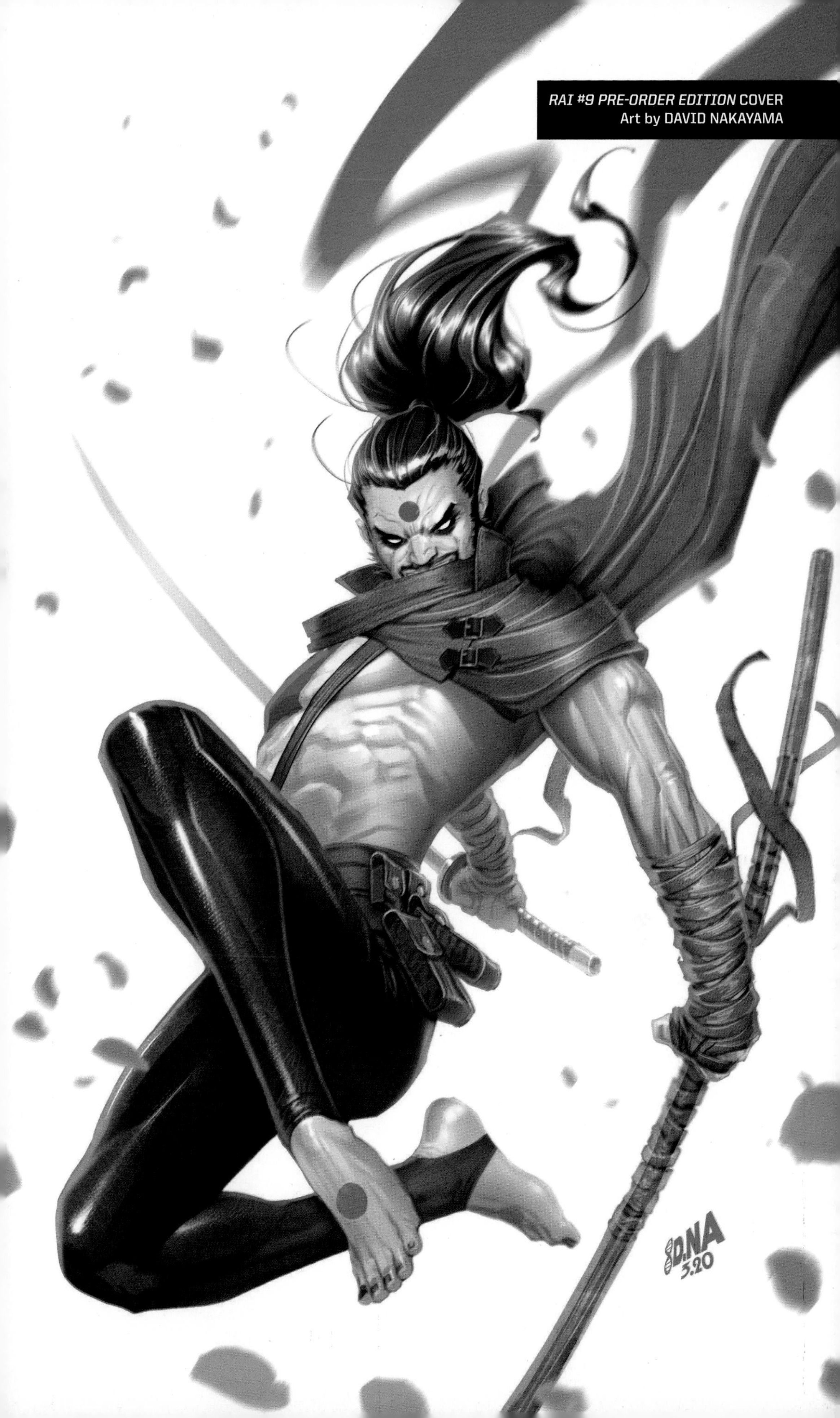
D.NA
3.20

RAI #9 PRE-ORDER EDITION COVER
Art by DAVID NAKAYAMA

RAI #6, pages 14, 15, and (facing) 16
Art by JUAN JOSÉ RYP

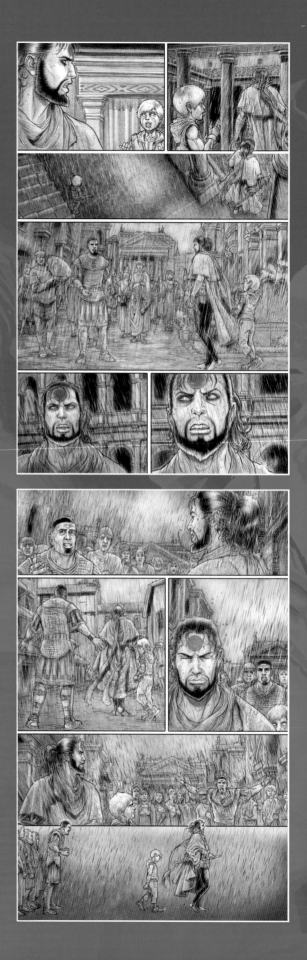

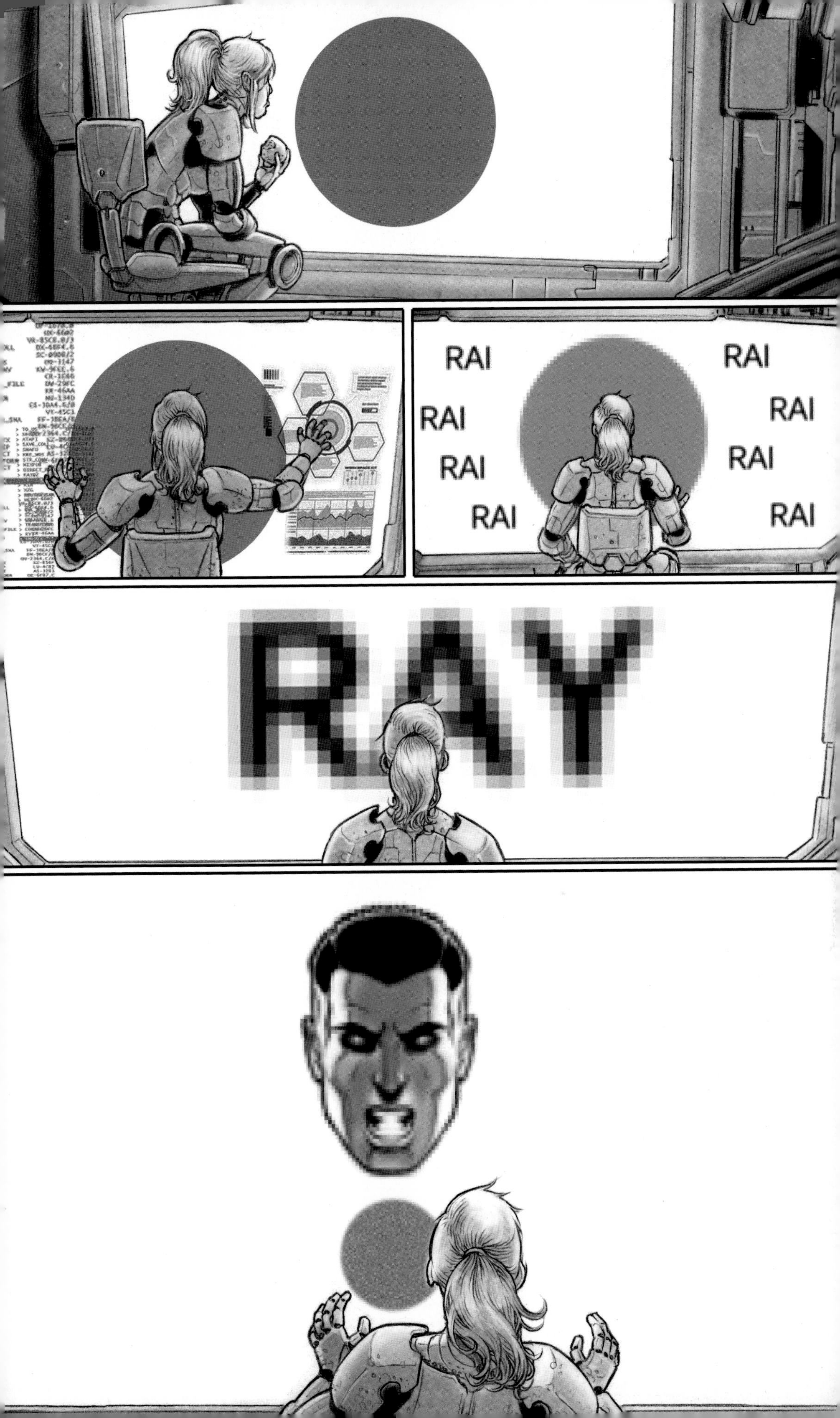
RAI
RAI
RAI
RAI
RAI
RAI
RAI
RAI
RAY

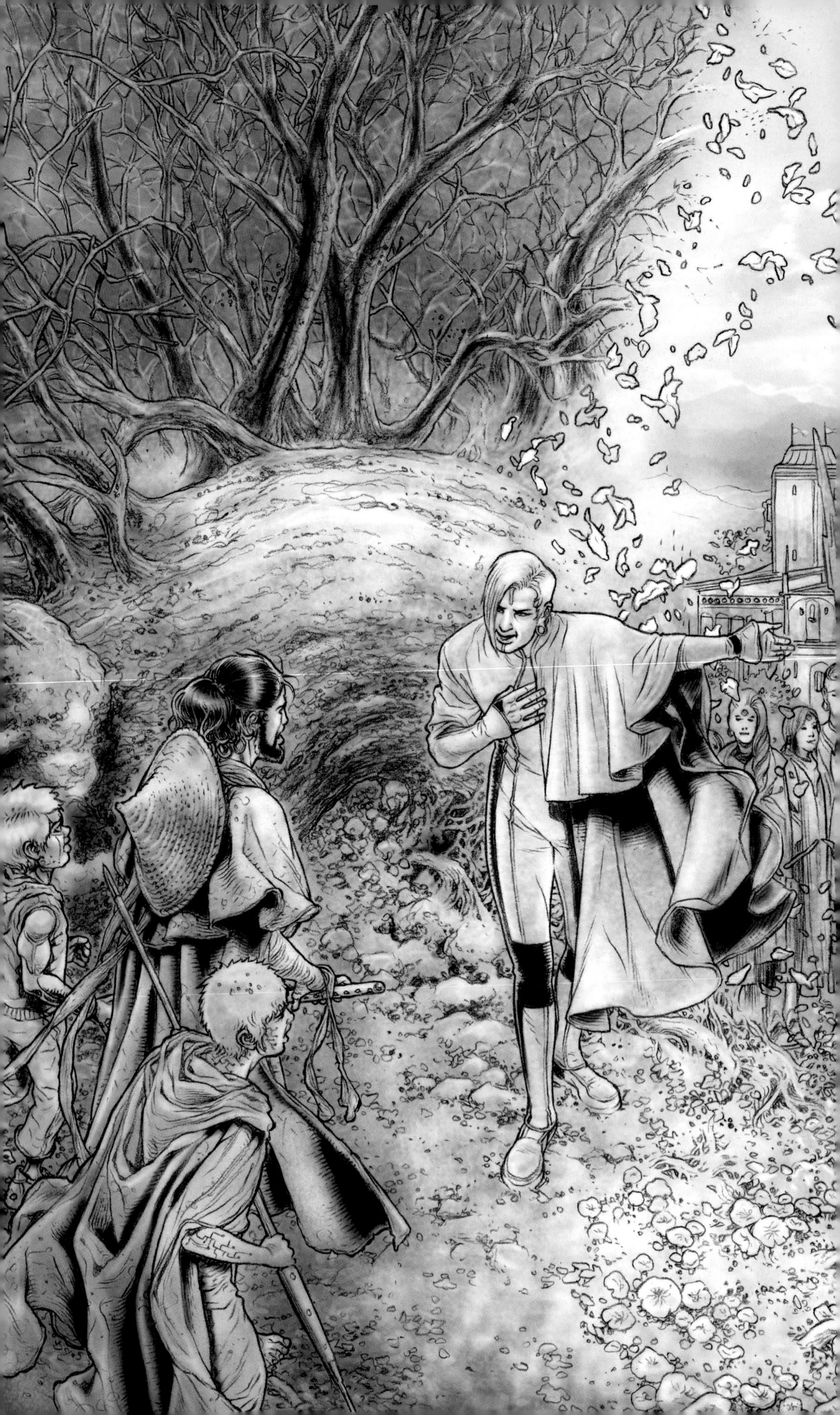

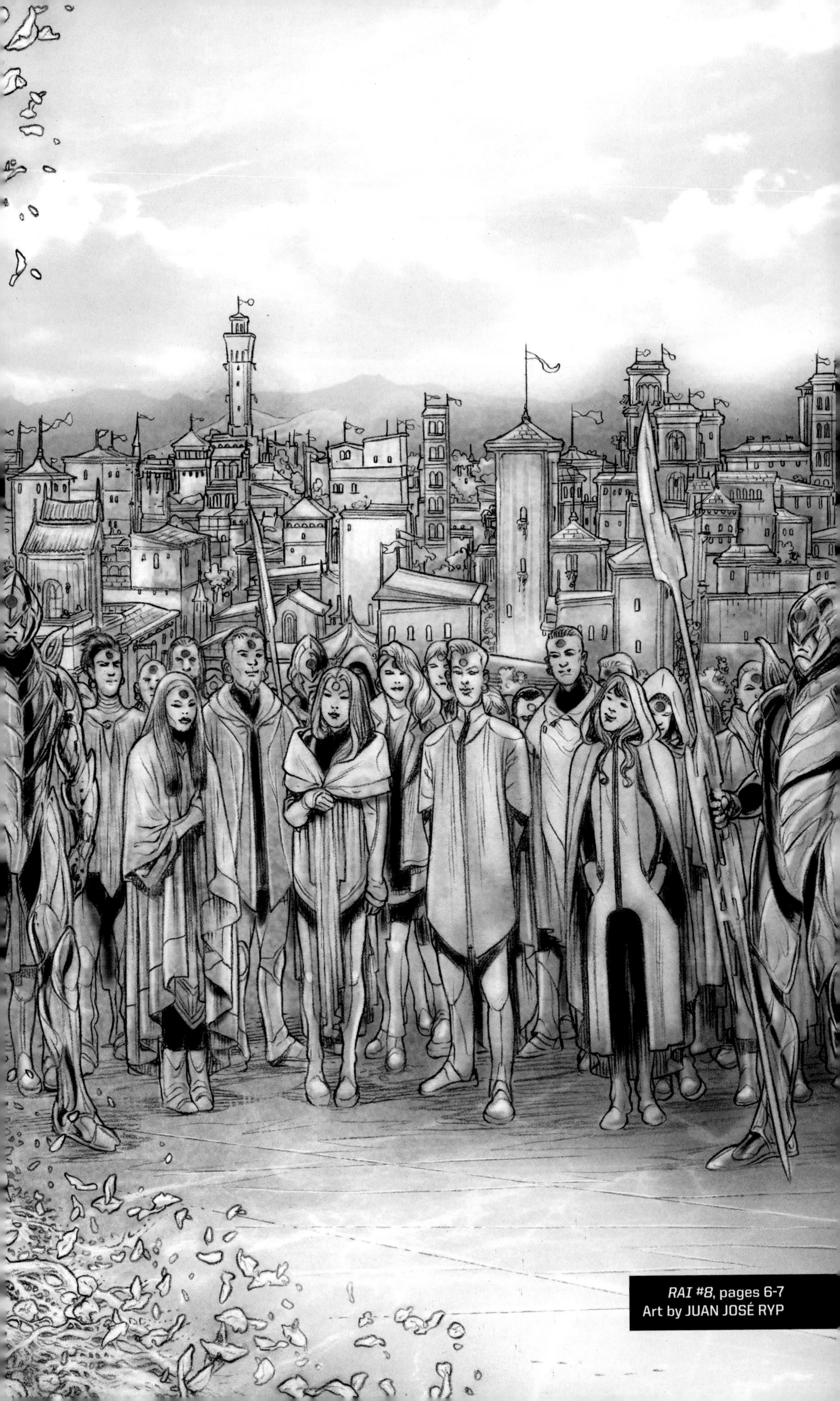

RAI #8, pages 6-7
Art by JUAN JOSÉ RYP

RAI #9, pages 18, 19, and (facing) 20
Art by JUAN JOSÉ RYP

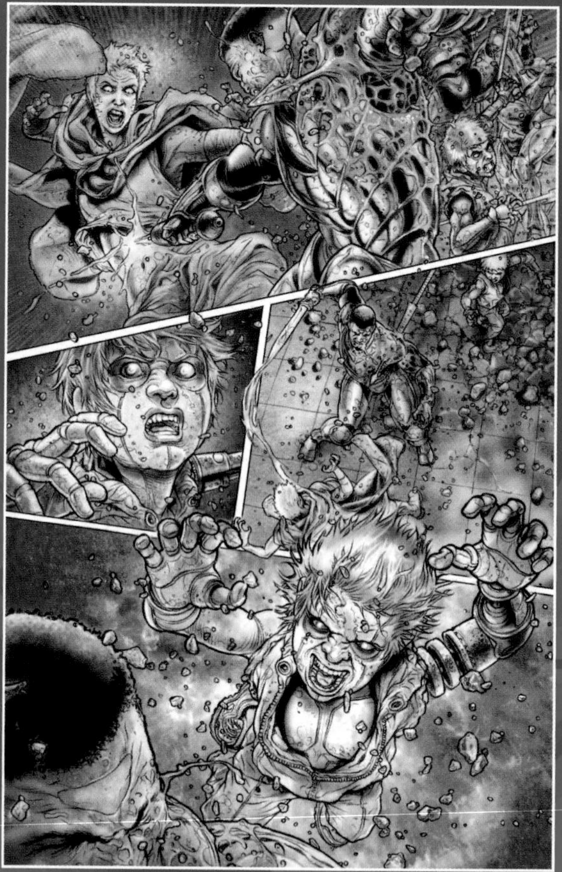

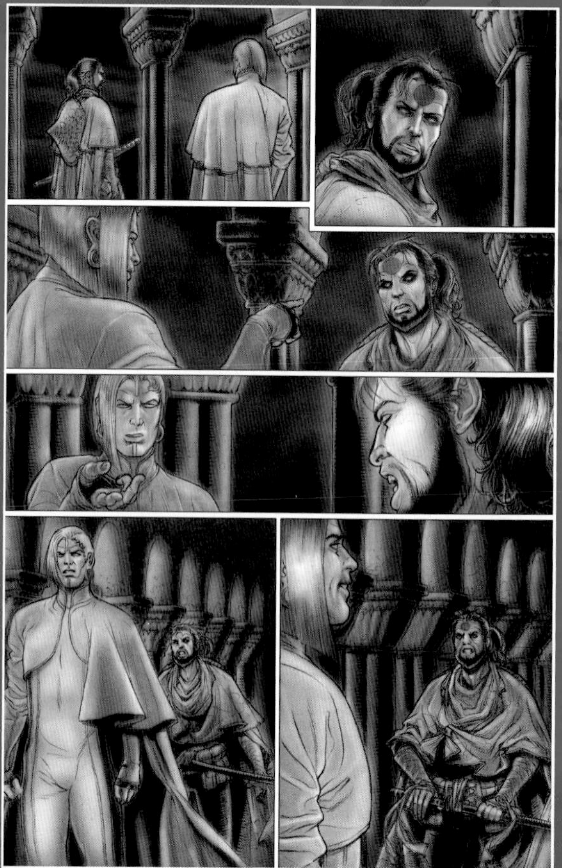

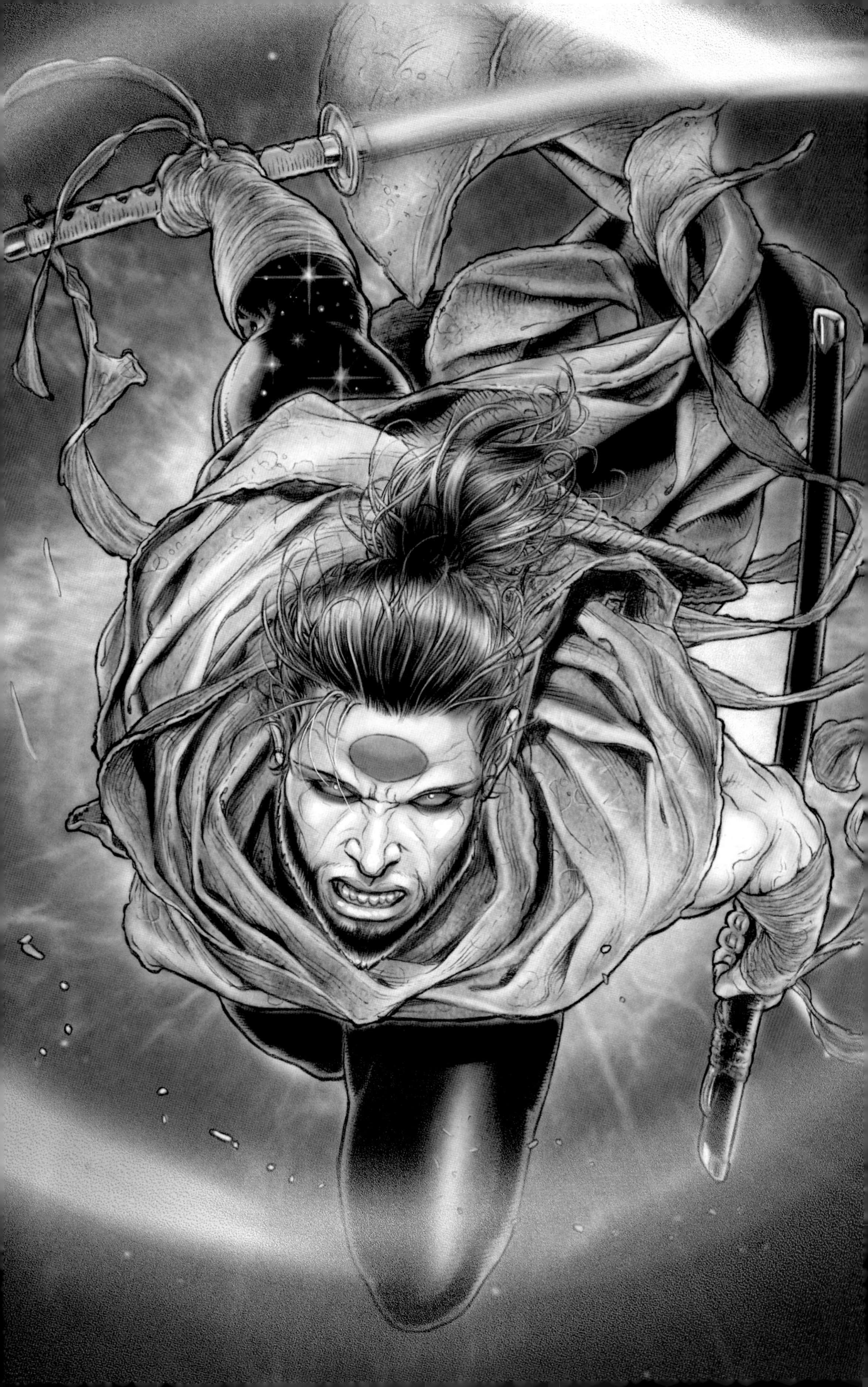

EXPLORE THE VALIANT U

ACTION & ADVENTURE

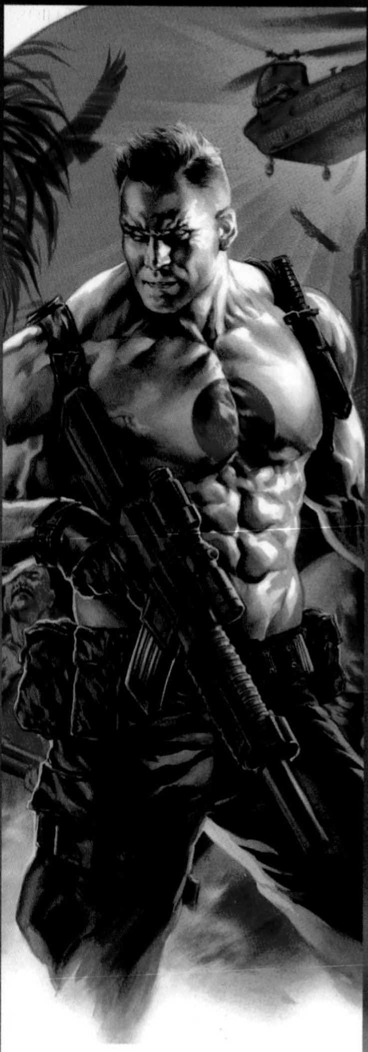

BLOODSHOT BOOK ONE
ISBN: 978-1-68215-255-3
NINJA-K VOL. 1: THE NINJA FILES
ISBN: 978-1-68215-259-1
SAVAGE
ISBN: 978-1-68215-189-1
WRATH OF THE ETERNAL WARRIOR VOL. 1: RISEN
ISBN: 978-1-68215-123-5
X-O MANOWAR (2017) VOL. 1: SOLDIER
ISBN: 978-1-68215-205-8

BLOCKBUSTER ADVENTURE

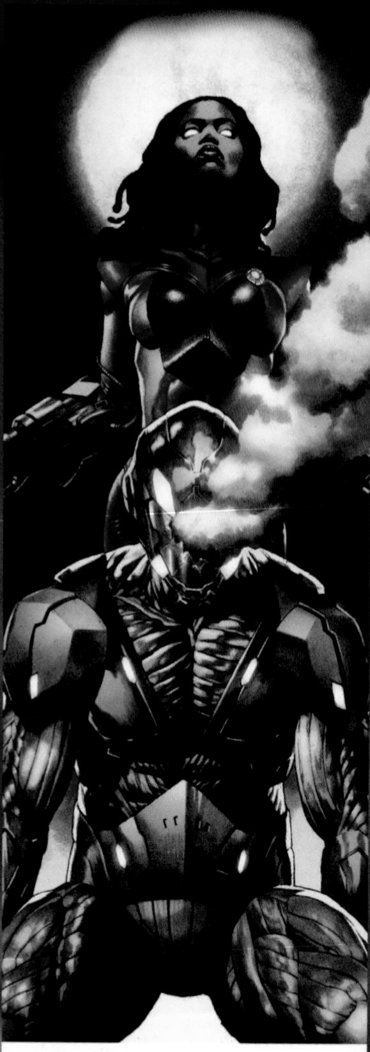

4001 A.D.
ISBN: 978-1-68215-143-3
ARMOR HUNTERS
ISBN: 978-1-939346-45-2
BOOK OF DEATH
ISBN: 978-1-939346-97-1
FALLEN WORLD
ISBN: 978-1-68215-331-4
HARBINGER WARS
ISBN: 978-1-939346-09-4
HARBINGER WARS 2
ISBN: 978-1-68215-289-8
INCURSION
ISBN: 978-1-68215-303-1
THE VALIANT
ISBN: 978-1-939346-60-5

COMEDY

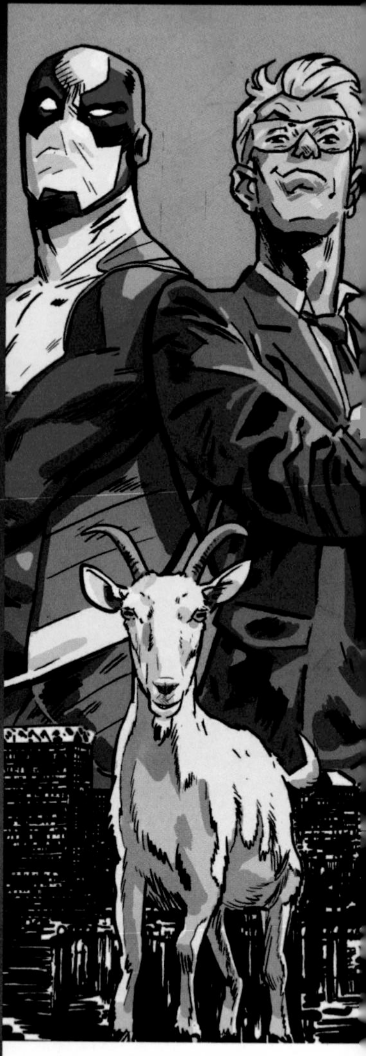

A&A: THE ADVENTURES OF ARCHER & ARMSTRONG VOL. 1: IN THE BAG
ISBN: 978-1-68215-149-5
THE DELINQUENTS
ISBN: 978-1-939346-51-3
QUANTUM AND WOODY! (2017) VOL. 1: KISS KISS, KLANG KLANG
ISBN: 978-1-68215-269-0

VERSE STARTING AT $9.99

HORROR & MYSTERY

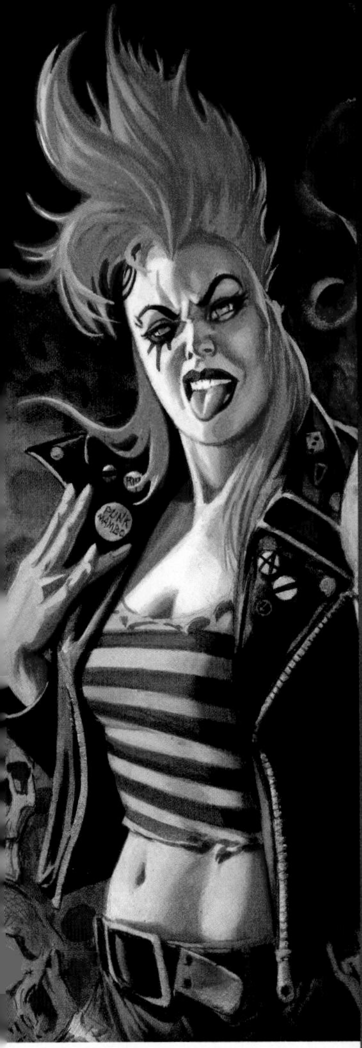

BRITANNIA
ISBN: 978-1-68215-185-3
DOCTOR MIRAGE
ISBN: 978-1-68215-346-8
PUNK MAMBO
ISBN: 978-1-68215-330-7
RAPTURE
ISBN: 978-1-68215-225-6
SHADOWMAN (2018) VOL. 1: FEAR OF THE DARK
ISBN: 978-1-68215-239-3

SCIENCE FICTION & FANTASY

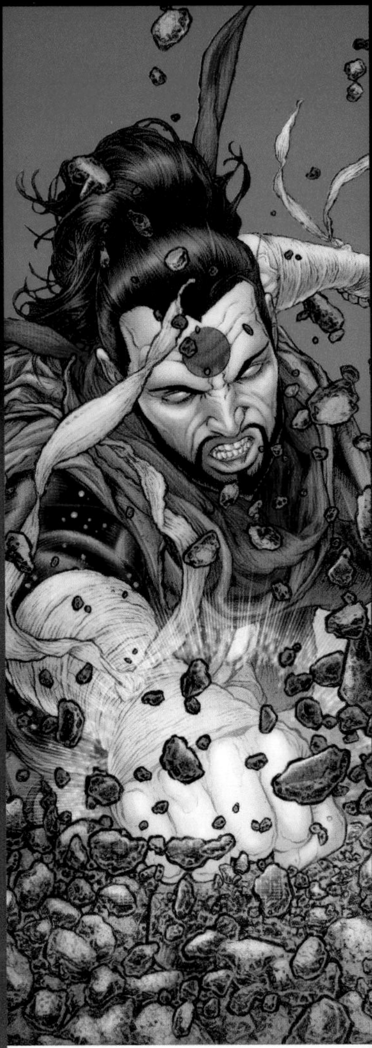

DIVINITY
ISBN: 978-1-939346-76-6
THE FORGOTTEN QUEEN
ISBN: 978-1-68215-324-6
IMPERIUM VOL. 1: COLLECTING MONSTERS
ISBN: 978-1-939346-75-9
IVAR, TIMEWALKER VOL. 1: MAKING HISTORY
ISBN: 978-1-939346-63-6
RAI BOOK ONE
ISBN: 978-1-682153-60-4
WAR MOTHER
ISBN: 978-1-68215-237-9

TEEN ADVENTURE

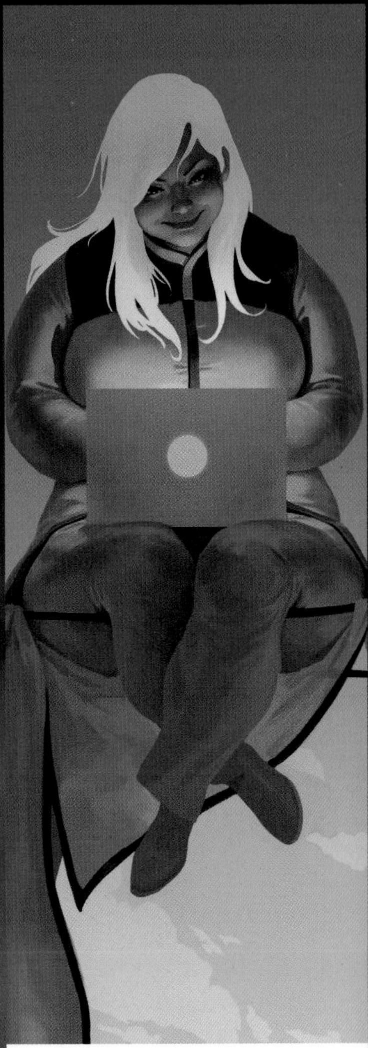

FAITH VOL. 1: HOLLYWOOD AND VINE
ISBN: 978-1-68215-121-1
GENERATION ZERO VOL. 1: WE ARE THE FUTURE
ISBN: 978-1-68215-175-4
HARBINGER RENEGADE VOL. 1: THE JUDGMENT OF SOLOMON
ISBN: 978-1-68215-169-3
LIVEWIRE VOL. 1: FUGITIVE
ISBN: 978-1-68215-301-7
SECRET WEAPONS
ISBN: 978-1-68215-229-4

Discover the entire Valiant Universe of titles at VALIANTENTERTAINMENT.COM/ALL-SERIES/

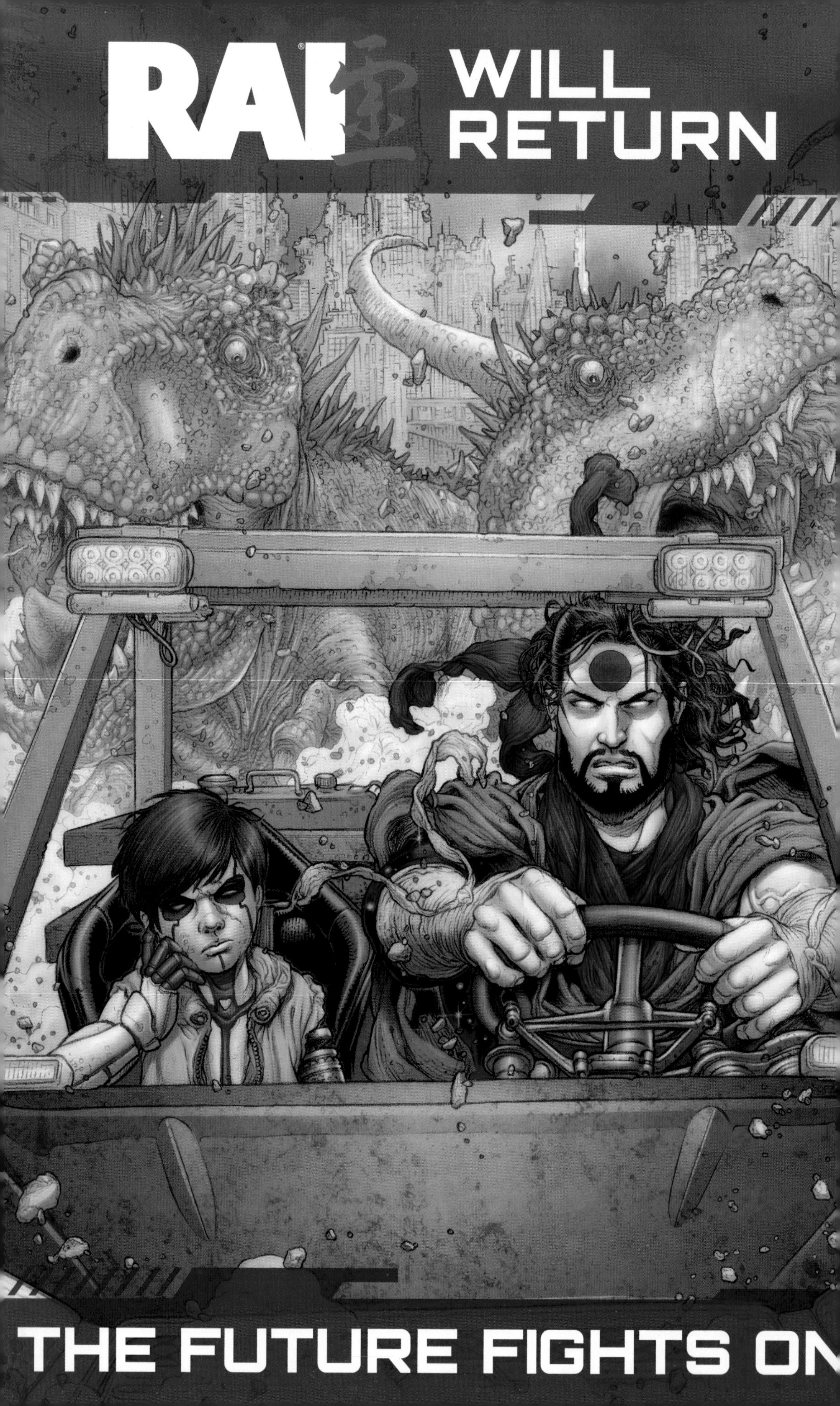
RAI WILL RETURN
THE FUTURE FIGHTS ON